Costume Construction

Costume Construction

Katherine Strand-Evans
Eastern Michigan University

WAVELAND
PRESS, INC.
Prospect Heights, Illinois

For information about this book, write or call:
   Waveland Press, Inc.
   P.O. Box 400
   Prospect Heights, Illinois 60070
   (847) 634-0081

For John Eliot
and Maja Kay Holkeboer

Contents

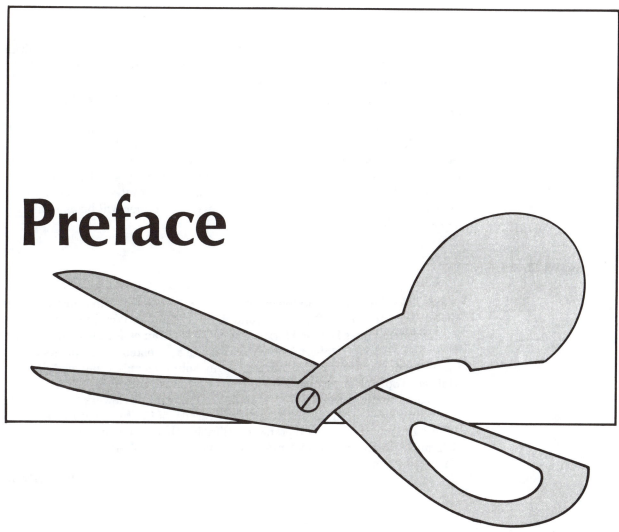

Preface

People who construct costumes for the theatre do much more than sew. It is useful to be able to sew, of course, but sewing constitutes only a portion of the job performed by costume techniques. Beyond sewing there is work for pattern makers, drapers, painters, dyers, sculptors, artists, milliners, and anyone who enjoys hand work. Some costumes and costume accessories involve no sewing whatsoever. This is why we speak of "building" rather than sewing costumes, and why creative people are always welcome workers in a costume shop whether or not they know how to sew. Costume construction combines a myriad of skills—creativity, insight, and initiative in the never ending quest to find more effective and less expensive ways of creating beautiful and appropriate theatre magic through costuming.

Having presented the case for nonsewers in a costume shop, let me now add that sewing is a most useful skill for a costume technician. If one is to work the full range of costuming jobs, sewing is certainly one of them. Those people who sew well by machine and by hand, and those who have an instinct for how to put two-dimensional flat shapes together to make a three-dimensional costume—whether it be a gown, a hat, or a shoe—are essential to the operation of a costume shop.

It is difficult to explain how to build a generic costume. There is no such thing. Each costume is unique, and costumers who have worked in the business for a number of years continue to change and perfect techniques. We work with an ever changing, constantly growing body of knowledge.

Costume construction in itself is an art form. Technicians create within the limitations imposed by budget, time, and design specifications. The execution of that design and the creativity and problem solving involved in its solution make work in the costume crafts a challenging and exciting creative and artistic endeavor.

These chapters are intended to expand and open the mind of students to the possibilities for individual development in the area of costume construction. The student will learn the basic procedures of sewing, drafting, draping, millinery, and so on, but these skills are only a starting point. Each individual will ultimately find his or her own path. This book is intended to open some doors, but where, and how far one goes beyond the door will be as individual as each of the readers.

ACKNOWLEDGMENTS

I would like to thank the following people who helped me either directly or indirectly with this book: Richard Strand, Dennis Zimmer, Wendy Barber, David W. Fathauer, James Berton Harris. Thom Coates, Janice I. Lines, Jim Siterlet, Timothy L. Blacker, Robert Holkeboer, Maja Kay Holkeboer, John Holkeboer, Clara Hoedema, Madeleine Huggins, Lynn Tobin, Dennis Beagen, Adonis El Mohtar, Tod Barker, Edith Leavis Bookstein, and Dick Schwarze.

And, finally, I would like to thank the following reviewers for their comments and suggestions: John Brandt, University of California at Los Angeles; James Berton Harris, University of Illinois, Urbana-Champaign; Kevin L. Seligman, Northern Illinois University; and Zelma H. Weisfeld, University of Michigan, Ann Arbor.

Katherine Strand-Evans

Getting Started

1

THE COSTUME SHOP

Costume shops vary in size, location, and efficiency. One element they have in common is that none seems to be quite big enough. In spite of this, careful arrangement of storage and equipment can improve the efficiency of any costume construction space.

Costume construction can be roughly divided into sewing, laundry, and craft functions. It is a good idea to separate the areas for each type of work. Whether this can be done in three separate rooms or simply by dividing a single space, the areas, equipment, and tools are best kept apart.

The Sewing Area

Pattern development, cutting, sewing, and pressing are processes that are so interconnected that it is important to have the equipment and supplies for these jobs located near each other. In the sewing area should be a large table for pattern development and cutting. Sewing machines and their tables, irons and ironing boards or ironing tables, and fitting forms complete the list of essential equipment located in this area. Shelves and cabinets to hold supplies and tools relating to sewing, pressing, cutting, and patterning should be conveniently located by the equipment or table they relate to. Bulletin boards are useful for hanging designer renderings, patterns, and various instructional and work charts.

1

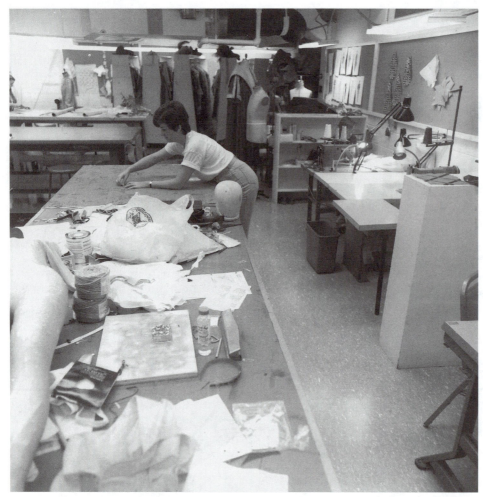

Figure 1.1 Main work area of the costume shop, Krannert Center for the Performing Arts, University of Illinois (David W. Fathaeur).

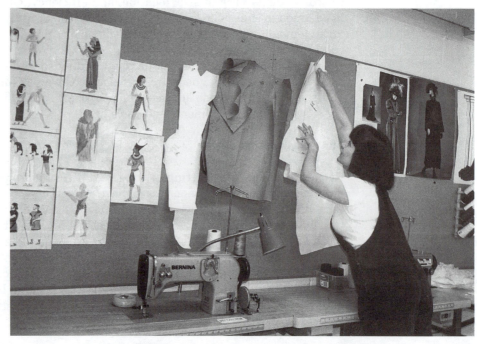

Figure 1.2 Costume shop bulletin board.

The Fitting Area

It is desirable to have a secluded fitting space in the costume shop. If shop space is confined, a dressing room or lavatory will serve. In the fitting room there should be space enough for the person doing the fitting, the actor, and, if possible, a third person to take notes. A full-length mirror is desirable for the actor and costumers as well.

The Laundry Area

It is desirable to have a washing machine and dryer in the costume shop. In the laundry area will be a washer, dryer, and laundry sink. Cabinets or shelves to store detergent, bleach, fabric softener, and other laundry items should be located in this area. A drying rack or portable clothesline is very useful in this area.

The Dye Area

Fabric dyeing may be handled in the laundry area or in a separate dye and fabric manipulation space. Wherever the dyeing is done, the area should be separated from the cutting and sewing area. The area should be well-ventilated, and anyone working with the dyes should take care to read specific instructions and cautions for each type of dye.

Materials stored in this area include dyes, measuring cups and spoons, and rubber gloves. Some shops use a separate dye vat or soup kettle for dyeing. It is useful to have a hand-operated or motor-driven wringer in the dye area. A hot plate and kettle may be used for dyeing small amounts of fabric or trim.

The Craft Area

A well-ventilated separate room or confined area of the costume shop should be designated for the various craft procedures needed in creating special costumes and costume accessories.

Figure 1.3 Craft area of the costume shop, Krannert Center for the Performing Arts, University of Illinois (David W. Fathaeur).

Such materials as paints, hardware, leather, glues, and jewelry parts might be found in this area. Many of the substances used in this area are toxic or flammable, so adequate ventilation and careful reading of instructions are essential. Of course, this area should be separated from other areas of the shop.

SEWING EQUIPMENT

Sewing Machines

Although subtle differences exist among the makes and models of sewing machines, once a person is able to use a basic model it is easy to adapt to others. For costume construction domestic straight and zig-zag sewing machines are most useful. Industrial sewing machines are used for heavy-duty and rapid sewing. It is good to learn to use both domestic and industrial sewing machines.

Domestic Sewing Machines. Although options vary and greatly affect the price of domestic sewing machines, the most useful capabilities for costume construction are zig-zag, hem stitching, buttonhole making, and a free arm. Additional features, such as capabilities for decorative stitches, stretch stitches, and monogramming, are usually not necessary for costume work. Often, simpler machines require less maintenance, so it is probably best not to invest in features that will not be used.

All sewing machines operate on the same principle of a precisely timed movement of needle and shuttle hook, which manipulates two threads (one from the spool and one from the bobbin) into an interlocking pattern, or stitch. Tension on both threads is maintained by the threading pattern through guides and tension discs on the spool thread, and by the bobbin case for the bobbin thread. The presser foot and feed move the fabric into position for each stitch. For zig-zag stitching the needle must move from side to side. These features are common to all domestic straight and zig-zag sewing machines.

Industrial Sewing Machines. Heavy-duty construction and speed are two of the major reasons that most costume shops use industrial sewing machines. They are built primarily for factories which demand their hard and constant

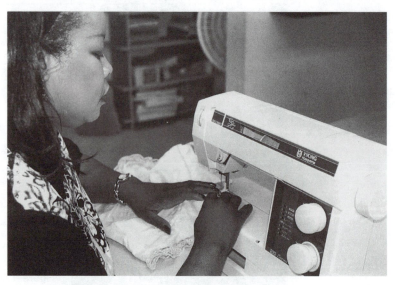

Figure 1.4 Domestic sewing machine.

Figure 1.5 Industrial sewing machine.

use. Often they are built to perform a single function very quickly, and usually they require far less maintenance than do domestic sewing machines. The basic structure and operation of industrial machines is similar to that of domestic sewing machines. They are simply built to last longer, and to operate more dependably and much faster. Specialized stitching is often not available on these machines, though some of the newer models have zig-zag and decorative stitch options. The user must take care to keep fingers away from the very powerful needle. It is a good idea to have finger guards installed on industrial sewing machines.

An industrial sewing machine usually comes with its own motor and table, which take up a bit more room than domestic models, and is not at all portable. Industrial sewing machines use bobbins and needles that differ from those of domestic sewing machines.

Sergers. Sergers, or overlock machines, create a flexible overcasting stitch to finish the raw edges of a cut piece of fabric. Like sewing machines, sergers differ in their threading scheme; some are extremely complicated and involve several spools or cones of thread and special threading wires to feed the thread into the intricate machine interior.

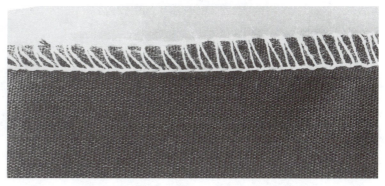

Figure 1.6 Serging or overcasting stitch.

Figure 1.7 Industrial serger.

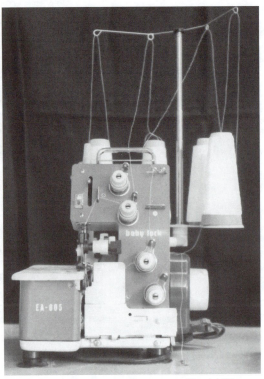

Figure 1.8 Domestic serger (David W. Fathaeur).

Figure 1.9 Blind hemmer.

Sergers come in domestic and industrial models. The industrial sergers are dependable and fast but often complicated to thread and to maintain. The lightweight domestic sergers are easy to use and adequate for most costuming needs.

Blindstitch Machines.   The blindstitch machine is used to create nearly invisible hems much more quickly than the domestic sewing machine blind hems or a hand hem. The stitch created is a chain stitch, which makes removal of the hem even easier than the rapid hemming itself.

Tables

Cutting Tables.   A cutting table should be at least 4' wide by 6' long. It is useful to have a surface to pin into. A muslin- or paper-covered cork or fiberboard top makes a good cutting table surface. The ideal height of the table depends on the person doing the cutting. Most people are comfortable cutting at about waist level. A good standard height for a cutting table is 40" off the floor. If many different people are using the same table for cutting, naturally a compromise height must be reached.

Work Tables.   Other tables and chairs of various sizes may be used for hand sewing and craft work. The surface of a craft table should be smooth and able to withstand the effects of the glues, paints, and solvents being used.

Sewing Machine Tables.   Many machines come with their own table which is adjusted to a comfortable machine sewing height. Other tables can accommodate sewing machines to save space in the shop as long as there is space in front of and to the left of the machine to place the garment being assembled. Sewing machine tables must be sturdy to withstand the vibration of the machine in operation.

Figure 1.10 Cutting table.

Pressing Equipment

Irons.   Domestic and industrial steam irons are both used in costume shops. The industrial steam iron, however, has many features not available in any domestic model. Most importantly, industrial steam irons involve greater steam pressure, which is produced by a manual or automatic pump and a water source.

Ironing Boards and Tables.   It is useful to have a portable ironing board as well as a heavy-duty, sturdy ironing table that will not collapse when bumped into, and that can accommodate large pieces of fabric for pressing.

Steamers.   Steamers project steam to ease wrinkles from fabric, to soften and remold hats, and to enliven crushed and delicate trimmings. They often serve when the heat, weight, or position of a steam iron will not. Steamers come in table models, hand-held versions, and floor units.

Figure 1.11   Industrial iron.

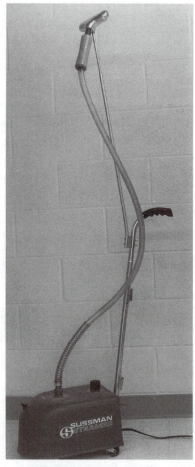

Figure 1.12   Steamer.

Figure 1.13 Soup kettle used for fabric dyeing (David W. Fathaeur).

Laundry Equipment

Washing Machines. Washing machines may be used for prewashing fabric, dyeing, and cleaning costumes. Heavy-duty and large-capacity machines are most useful.

Dryers. Dryers, like washers, should be heavy-duty. A dryer that allows drying at different temperatures is useful.

Dye Vats. Some costumers use commercial dye vats or soup kettles rather than laundry tubs and hot plates, or the washing machine, to do extensive dyeing. These machines produce higher heat and steam pressure to more successfully set dyes into the fabric. Dye vats operate off a steam line or electricity.

TOOLS

Measuring and Drafting Tools

Measuring devices are used in costume construction to measure the dimensions of the body and to create and adapt patterns for specific costumes. Most measuring tools are marked in both inches and centimeters.

Measuring Tapes. Measuring tapes are made in plastic, fiberglass, cloth, metal, and paper. The best measuring tapes are those that will not stretch or tear (metal, plastic, or fiberglass). They are 60 inches in length and used to take body measurements. Most measuring tapes have markings on both sides. It is important not to flip the tape while taking measurements and read the marking off the back of the tape.

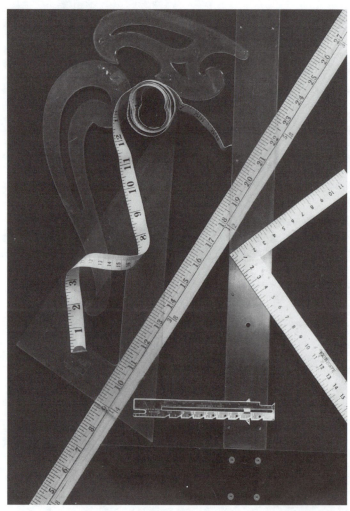

Figure 1.14 Measuring and drafting tools: curves, angles, rulers, and gauges.

Yardstick or Meterstick. Yardsticks and metersticks are made of wood or metal. They are useful in taking some body measurements, especially those from the floor. They are used in creating patterns by drafting and in enlarging patterns. For pattern making, metal rules are better since they are far more accurate than the wooden ones.

Rulers. Clear rulers in 6″ and 12″ sizes are useful tools in both pattern making and costume construction. They are especially useful for marking hem allowances, determining the placement of buttons and buttonholes, and figuring out the location of trim on a costume.

Skirt Marker. A skirt marker is a ruler on a tripod and is used to mark hem lengths at a specific adjustable distance from the floor. Hem markers have a metal pin guide that clamps and holds the fabric of the garment in place while the marking pin is inserted.

Sewing Gauge. A sewing gauge is a 6″ ruler with a sliding marker that may be set and held constant at a specific measurement. Sewing gauges, like clear plastic rulers, are particularly useful in hem marking and button placement.

T-Square and Right Angles. T-squares and right angles are used in pattern drafting and flat pattern manipulation. They are useful in locating and checking cross grains and determining essential right angles in patterns. Transparent ruled T-squares are most useful in costume and pattern making.

French Curve.   French curves are used to create necklines, armholes, and other curved pattern lines. Transparent ruled curves are the most useful.

Marking Tools

Tailor's Chalk.   Tailor's chalk may be purchased in several forms: wedge, sharpenable pencil, or refillable pencil. The wedge may be either chalk or wax based. The wax pencils and wedges are easier to see but more difficult to remove from the fabric. All tailor's chalk comes in a variety of colors, including red, yellow, blue, black, and white.

Tracing Wheels.   Tracing wheels are used to transfer pattern markings accurately onto fabric. The tracing wheel may have a serrated edge or, for difficult to mark fabrics, a smooth edge.

Tracing Paper.   Dressmaker's tracing paper comes in a variety of colors, including white, red, yellow, navy blue, and orange. It is used with tracing wheels to transfer markings from a pattern to fabric. The markings left by tracing paper usually wash or dry clean out of the finished garment, but in any case markings are usually made only on the inside of the costume.

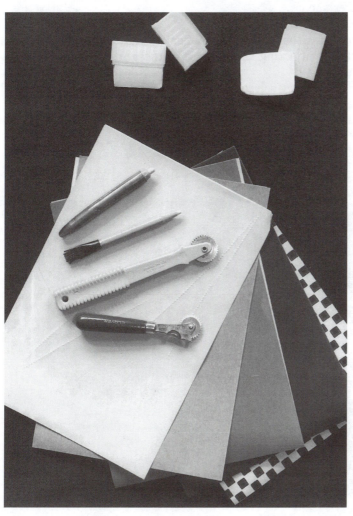

Figure 1.15 Marking tools: tailors chalk, tracing wheels and tracing paper.

Cutting Tools

Dressmaker Shears.   Shears come in lengths from six to twelve inches. They are made for right-handed and left-handed users. The best dressmaker shears are designed with a bent handle for easy pattern cutting on a table. The blades of the shears are held with a screw or rivet. A screw allows the shears to be adjusted when sharpened. All shears must be sharpened from time to time if they are used frequently. Shears stay sharp longer if they are used only for fabric cutting. Synthetic fabrics dull the blades faster than natural fabrics.

Pinking Shears.   Pinking shears may be purchased in lengths from 5 1/2 " to 10 ". They are used to create a zig-zag ravel-resistant edge to the cut fabric. They are useful in finishing seams and raw edges or cutting slashes (pinks) into period costumes.

Sewing Scissors.   Sewing scissors are five or six inches long. They have one blunt point and one sharp point and are used to clip and trim seams.

Embroidery Scissors.   Embroidery scissors are small scissors particularly useful for clipping buttonholes and doing delicate cutting. The scissors have two very sharp blades.

Paper Scissors.   Paper scissors are for cutting paper patterns in order to spare the dressmaker shears.

Leather Scissors.   Leather scissors are a heavy-duty tool that easily cuts through leather without affecting the balance of the scissor blades.

Craft Scissors.   When any scissors can no longer be effectively sharpened or balanced for fine fabric cutting, they may become craft scissors, which are used to cut plastics, cardboards, glued felts, and vinyls and anything else the costume shop may need to have cut.

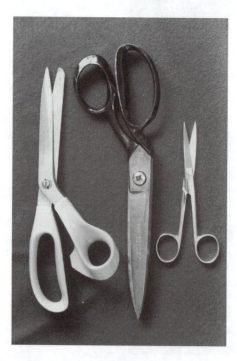

Figure 1.16   Scissors.

Seam Rippers.   Seam rippers are used for opening up basted or stitched seams. A seam ripper has a point for picking out threads and a sharp curved blade for cutting.

Pressing Tools

Tailor's Ham.   This is a very firm rounded cushion which is covered on one side with wool which holds steam for pressing tailored garments, and on the other with cotton. It is used for pressing shaped areas of a garment such as curved seams and bust darts.

Seam Roll.   Like the tailor's ham, the seam roll is a firm cushion covered in wool on one side and cotton on the other. The seam roll is a narrow cylinder which may be inserted into narrow areas such as sleeves or pants legs.

Sleeve Board.   A sleeve board is like a small ironing board. Like the seam roll it is used for pressing very narrow areas like sleeves and the legs of trousers.

Tailor's Board.   The tailor's board is especially useful in pressing shaped areas of a garment such as curves, points, and facing seams. It is made of wood and is composed of a number of curves, points, and angles.

Needle Board.   This is a surface used for pressing pile fabrics such as velvet, velour, and corduroy. It is made of canvas and numerous steel wires, which keep the pile from being crushed during ironing.

Fitting Equipment

Fitting Forms.   Fitting forms come in male and female shapes in a number of different sizes. Some forms are adjustable. Typical fitting forms consist of only the torso, but pants forms and full body forms that include arms and legs may be purchased as well. Fitting forms are used in pattern draping and fitting.

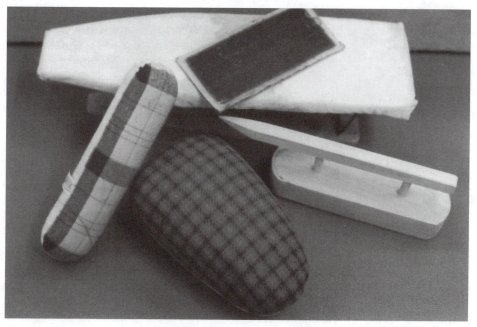

Figure 1.17 Pressing tools.

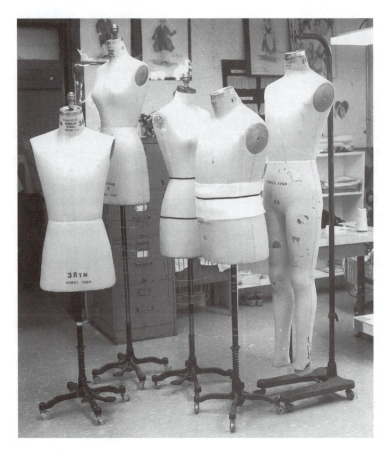

Figure 1.18 Fitting forms (David W. Fathaeur).

SEWING SUPPLIES

Notions

Thread. The thread used in costume construction usually does not have to match the fabric color as closely as thread used for street wear. Some costume shops use only black, gray, and white thread and select on the basis of color value rather than hue. In most cases thread color will not be seen by the audience anyway.

Most costume work may be accomplished with a high-grade, cotton-coated polyester, size 50 thread. This thread may be used in domestic and industrial sewing machines (though a heavier weight thread is sometimes used with the industrial machines). It is also appropriate for most handwork.

A lighter-weight (size 60) thread is usually used in sergers and blind-hemmers. These and other industrial machines are set up to use thread wound onto a cone rather than a spool. Cones of thread come in 2000 and 6000 yard sizes, while spools usually hold no more than 500 yards of thread.

Heavy-duty threads may be used for sewing buttons, large hooks and eyes, hardware, and jewelry items onto costumes.

Pins. Straight pins (silk pins) are used for pinning patterns to fabric and fitting costumes to a form or to a human body. They are also used to hold the pieces of the costume together in preparation for sewing. Long needles with glass heads are easier to use than the smaller steel-headed pins. Some sewing machines will sew right over a pin inserted perpendicular to the seam, but it is possible to break or bend needles and pins this way.

T-pins are larger pins with a pronounced head which will not disappear in pile fabrics or loose knits. T-pins are useful for a number of craft projects to hold pieces in place.

Safety pins are used to insert elastic or cording into casings. Small safety pins may be used to secure small items to a costume and for quick repairs. Safety pins may be used as brooch backings or necklace clasps. Some costumers prefer to use safety pins for fittings since they are more secure and won't accidentally fall out when a costume is being removed. Costumers have uses for all sizes of safety pins.

Hand Needles. Needles come in a variety of sizes; for costuming it is a good idea to have an assortment. General hand-sewing needles include sharps, which are of medium length and weight with a round eye; betweens, which are short needles capable of taking fine stitches in thick fabric; and milliner's needles, which are longer and useful for millinery work as well as hand basting. Needles with longer eyes will accommodate thicker threads. Needles with ballpoints are useful for knit fabrics. Heavy-duty sewing may require glover's needles, which will penetrate leather, vinyl, and plastic, or sailmaker's needles, which can be used with canvas and heavy leather. Curved needles are useful when sewing nonflexible materials such as celastic or buckram.

Figure 1.19 Thread.

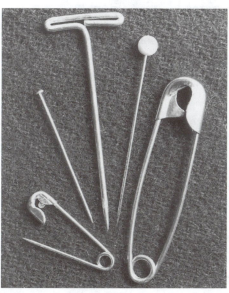

Figure 1.20 Pins.

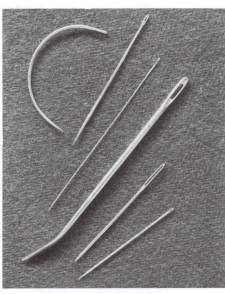

Figure 1.21 Needles.

Figure 1.22 Thimbles.

Figure 1.23 Pin cushions and needle threader.

Thimbles. Thimbles protect the middle finger during hand sewing. They are made of metal, plastic, and leather. They come in a range of sizes to fit any finger.

Bodkins and Loop Turners. Bodkins and loop turners are used for turning bias tubing. Bodkins may be used also to insert elastic or cording through a casing.

Beeswax and Needle Threaders. Needle threaders and beeswax are both used to make threading the needle easier. Beeswax is used also to strengthen thread for hand sewing. The thread is run across the wax, thus making it easier to insert into the opening of the needle and less likely to knot or tangle during sewing.

Pin Cushions. Pin cushions provide easy access and handy storage for straight pins and needles. Some pin cushions can be worn like bracelets for convenience. Often an emery pack, designed to clean pins and needles, is attached to the pin cushion pretending to be a strawberry.

Fasteners and Closures

Hook and Eye Tape. Hook and eye tape is a series of hooks and eyes embedded into two strips of fabric for easy insertion into costumes. Hook and eye tape is manufactured in black and white but the white tape may be dyed to any other color.

Zippers. Zippers come in a wide variety of colors and lengths. They may be made of metal or plastic with a chain or coil construction. Metal zippers are far more durable than the plastic ones, and are therefore preferable for costume use. Although zippers are the most common closure for street wear, they have limited use in costuming since they were not widely used until the 1940s, and a zipper placket in a period costume may seem anachronistic to members of the audience.

Velcro. This type of fastener is composed of two strips of tape, one with a looped nap, and the other with a hooked nap. When the two tapes are pressed against each other, they grip until they are pulled apart. Velcro may be purchased in sew-on, iron-on, or stick-on varieties.

Buttons. Buttons are manufactured from an enormous range of materials, from bone to wood to plastic to leather. Size and color vary with materials. Buttons are created in two basic styles: shank and sew-through. Shank buttons are solid on top with a loop or shank underneath to accommodate thick fabrics by holding the button head away from the garment. Sew-through buttons usually have two or four holes to accommodate thread.

Snaps. Snaps are a two-part fastener consisting of a ball and socket. Snaps are manufactured in silver and black colors, though decorative fabric-covered snaps are also available. Pronged attachment snaps are available in decorative metal and plastic colors and patterns. Snap tape, like hook and eye tape, comes with snaps attached to cotton tape for easy installation into garments. Since snap closures are not as secure as hooks and eyes, snap tape is usually not used for fitted costumes.

Hooks and Eyes. Hooks and eyes are manufactured in black and nickel finish. The eyes are shaped in bars or loops, depending on the specific use. Larger hooks and eyes may be shaped flatter to suit waistbands, or covered with cord for coats and heavy fabrics.

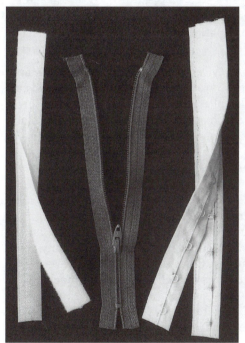 

Figure 1.24 Fasteners: velcro, zipper, and hook and eye tape.

Figure 1.25 Buttons.

Figure 1.26 Snap.

Figure 1.27 Hooks and eyes.

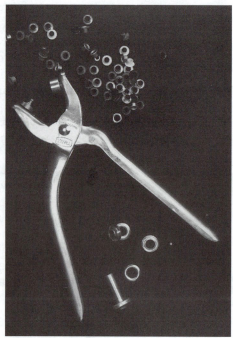

Figure 1.28 Eyelets and eyelet setter.

Figure 1.29 Grommet and setter.

Grommets and Eyelets. Grommets and eyelets are round metal reinforcements for holes that are made in belts and laced closures. Eyelets are applied with special eyelet pliers. Grommets are manufactured in two pieces and require a hammer and metal mold to secure them in place. Eyelets come in several colors, while grommets are normally aluminum- or brass-colored.

Elastics and Tapes

Elastic. Elastics are either braided or woven rubber and cotton (or synthetic) bands. Braided elastics provide a tighter grip; woven elastics, which do not diminish in width when stretched, are softer and may be stitched directly into a costume. Elastics are manufactured in many colors, but black and white are the most common. Cord elastic comes in several thicknesses, some so fine that it may be used as thread in a sewing machine.

Bias Tape. Bias tapes, which come in all colors, are bias strips of fabric with pre-folded edges. Bias tape is useful for binding edges and making facings or casings because of its ability to adapt to a curve. Bias tape comes pre-folded or unfolded in narrow and wide widths.

Seam Binding. Seam binding is a straight lace or rayon tape used to finish raw edges and hems. It may also be used for reinforcing seams.

Twill Tape. Twill tape is a sturdy, light tape used to strengthen and stay seams. It is available in a range of colors and widths and may be used functionally or decoratively, as for ties, bands, or drawstrings.

Grosgrain Ribbon. Grosgrain ribbon is used as a binding or decoration for costumes and hats. It may be pressed into a curve for a curved pattern, or folded to form angles. It may be used as a lacing or belting, and to stay a seam as well.

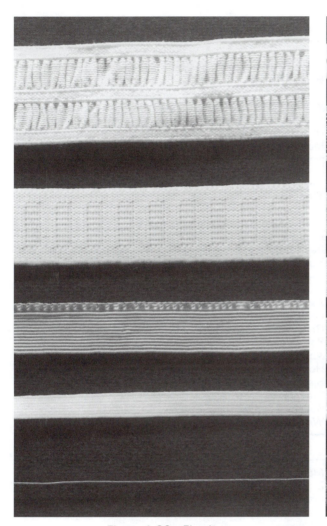

Figure 1.30   Elastic.

Figure 1.31   Tapes: bias tape, seam tapes, twill tape, grosgrain, cording, and fusible webbing.

Cotton Cord.   Cotton cord in a number of thicknesses may be covered to create a decorative cording for seams in costumes. Cotton cord may be dyed and used uncovered as trim or cord belts. It is also glued onto jewelry, crowns, and armor to form edging and decorations.

Belting.   Belting is a cardboard-like stiffener used to structure belts. It may be used to reinforce areas of stress in corsets and to provide a backing for grommets.

Fusible Tapes.   Press-on tape in various colors may be used for quick repairs and costume labels. Fusing webs are used to bond two sections of fabric together for appliqué and quick hemming.

STOCK COSTUME SHOP SUPPLIES

A costume shop which is properly stocked and equipped will make the construction process easier. The following is a list of equipment, tools, and supplies used for both sewn and nonsewn costumes. Specific uses of these materials are described in later chapters.

Stock Sewing Supplies

Equipment

Sewing machines
Work tables
Irons
Ironing board (table)
Steamers
Washing machine
Dryer
Dye vat

Tools

Measuring tapes
Yardsticks
Skirt marker
Sewing gauge
Hem gauge
T-square (right angle)
French curve
Tailor's chalk
Tracing wheels
Tracing paper
Scissors (dressmaker, pinking, sewing, paper)
Seam rippers
Tailor's hams and roll
Sleeve board
Tailor's board
Needle board
Fitting forms

Supplies

Thread
Pins (straight, safety pins in several sizes)
Hand needles
Thimbles
Sewing machine needles
Needle threaders
Hook-and-eye tape
Zippers
Velcro
Buttons
Snaps
Hooks and eyes
Elastic
Bias tape
Seam binding
Twill tape
Grosgrain ribbon
Cotton cord
Belting
Fusible tapes
Brown paper
Pencils, markers
Spray starch
Spot remover

Stock Craft Items

Equipment

Sinks
Tables
Washer
Wringer
Hot plate
Industrial sewing machine

Tools

X-acto knife
Craft knife
Pliers (needle nose, round nose)
Heavy shears
Paint brushes
Hammer
Files
Screwdrivers
Awl
Leather punch
Grommeter
Pop riveter
Airbrush
Hot-melt glue gun
Sponges
Brayers
Rollers
Wood-cutting tools

Supplies

Masking tape
Duct tape
Plastic tape
Metal tape
Cardboard
Sandpaper
Millinery wire
Piano wire
Découpage medium
Bronzing powders
Glitter
Sequins
Jewelry findings
Acrylic paints
Markers
Dyes
Enamel spray paint
Glues (flexible white glue, white glue, rubber cement, hot glue, Barge contact cement)
Celastic
Dip 'n' Drape (or Drape and Shape)
Buckram
Felt
Leather
Plaster
Moulage
Alginate
Dental stone
Petroleum jelly
Plaster bandages
Plastic clay
Push pins

EXERCISES

1. Analyze your own costume construction space for efficiency and safety.
2. Determine which stock items are used frequently enough to make it advantageous to purchase them in bulk. Compare the prices of single items and items purchased in quantity at your fabric store or through a supply catalog.

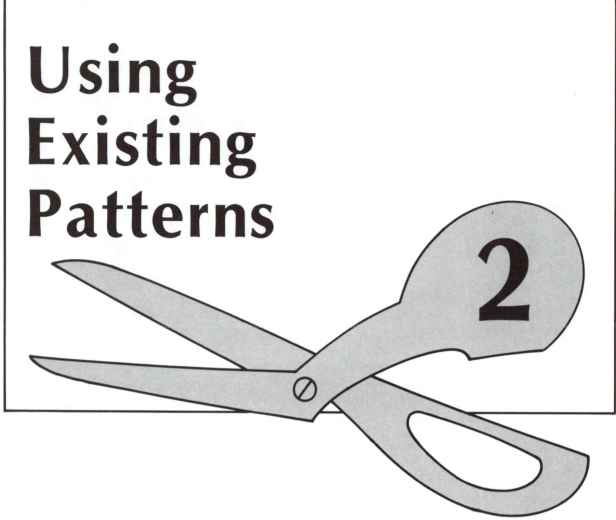

Using Existing Patterns

2

Whether you are using commercial patterns or creating your own, accurate measurements are important. Different systems of measurements are used in different shops. It is important that all people measuring for the same production take measurements in the same way. Because many of the patterns used for theatre productions are created from an actor's measurements, the typical measurement chart is very complete. With a bit of practice two people (one to measure and one to record) can complete a set of measurements on an actor very rapidly.

Figure 2–1 illustrates a typical measurement chart. Since many measurements are taken to or from the waist it is useful to tie a tape around the waist so you are always measuring from the same location. Other focal points on the body are indicated by the underlying bone structure and will be specifically and individually explained.

Some actors are sensitive about their bodies and it is therefore a good idea to take measurements in an efficient, professional manner. Obviously it is not a good idea to comment on anything unusual about the actor's body (size, proportion, or asymmetry) when taking measurements. If an actor promises to lose weight before the production, explain that you still need the present measurements to begin with and that it will be easy to alter the costume later when the weight loss occurs.

Some of the blanks on a measurement chart can be filled in by the actor. Name, production, character, and telephone number are certainly matters the actor knows of better than anyone. Most people also know their own height,

MEASUREMENT CHART

Name _____ Phone _____

Play _____ Role _____

Height _____ Suit/Dress _____ Glove _____

Weight _____ Shirt _____ Shoe/Width _____

Hat _____ Trousers(w) _____ (i) _____

a. Neck _____ t. Waist to floor (f) _____ (b) _____

b. Chest/Bust _____ u. Waist to knee (f) _____ (b) _____

c. Ribcage _____ v. Neck to floor (f) _____ (b) _____

d. Waist _____ w. Length of hip _____

e. Hips _____ x. Inseam _____

f. Neck to waist (f) _____ (b) _____ y. Outseam _____

g. Across shoulders (f) ___ (b) ___ z. Girth _____

h. Width of front _____ (b) ___ A. Crotch _____

i. Height of dart _____ B. Complete crotch _____

j. Shoulder _____ C. Thigh _____

k. Armscye _____ D. Calf _____

l. Underarm to waist _____ E. Above knee _____

m. Bust span _____ F. Below knee _____

n. Head around _____ G. Ankle _____

o. Arm (out to elbow) _____ (to wrist) _____

p. Arm (in to wrist) _____

q. Bicep _____

r. Elbow _____

s. Wrist _____ Date _____

Figure 2.1 Measurement chart.

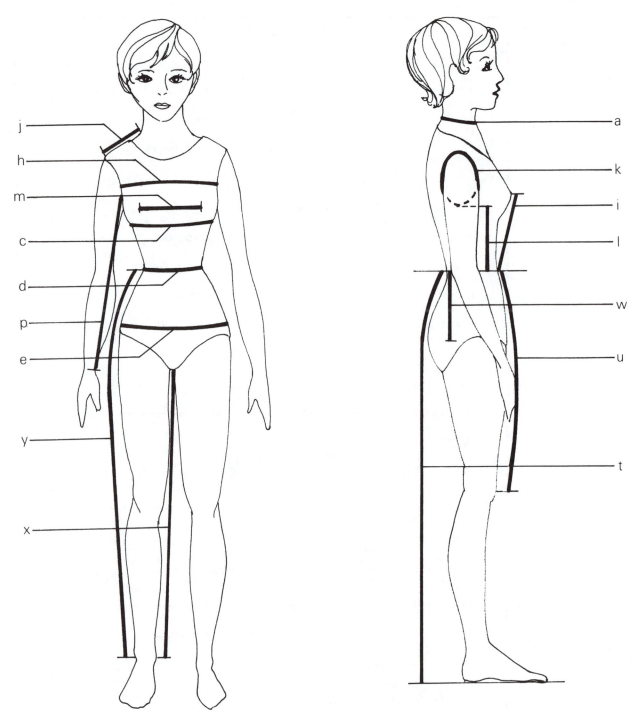

Figure 2.2 The location of measurements on the male and female body.

weight, shoe size, dress or suit size, and shirt size. Some people even know glove and hat size. Any of these sizes may be determined, if unknown, with the shop measurement devices.

Height and weight may be verified with measuring tape and scale, but it is usually not necessary to check these items even if you have some question about the answers the actor has given. People sometimes err in these estimates on the side of what they would like to be. Certainly it is not worth creating

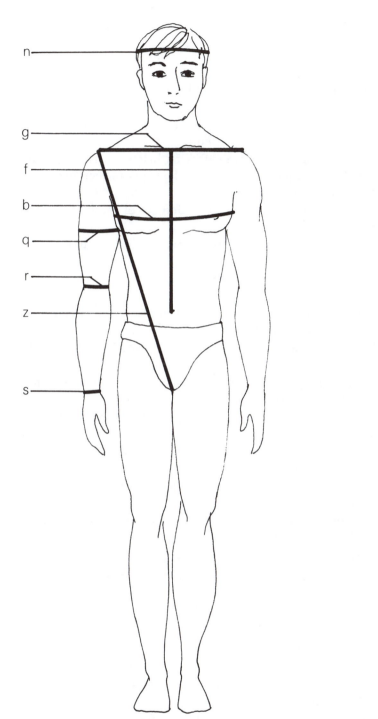
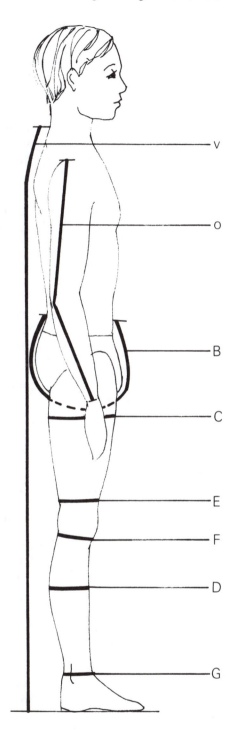

Figure 2.2 continued

ill feeling by asking an actor to step on a scale to prove that he or she gave the correct weight. The combination of other measurements will likely be sufficient for pattern development.

Figure 2–2 illustrates the approximate location of the measurements indicated on the measurement chart. A description of each follows. (Letters on the figures and in the following list correspond to the letters in the measurement chart, Figure 2–1.)

Specific Measurements

a. **Neck**—The circumference of the base of the neck.

b. **Chest/Bust**—The circumference of the fullest part of the chest. The body should be relaxed and the tape held loosely and parallel to the floor.

c. **Ribcage**—The circumference of the torso directly below the bust on women or the pectoral muscles on men.

d. **Waist**—The waist is above the hipbones and below the rib cage. In men it is usually directly over the navel. The waist measurement is a snug but not tight measurement.

e. **Hips**—The hip measurement is the circumference of the fullest part of the hips.

f. **Neck to waist (front)**—The measurement from the hollow in the collar bone to the waist.

   Neck to waist (back)—The measurement from the top of the backbone to the waist.

g. **Across shoulders**—The distance from the end of one shoulder bone to the other. It is taken in the front and back.

h. **Width of front**—The measurement across the chest from the point where the arms join the body.

   Width of back—The measurement across the back from the point where the arms join the body.

i. **Height of dart**—The measurement from the base of the neck to the fullest part of the bust or chest.

j. **Shoulder**—The distance from the base of the neck at the side to the end of the shoulder bone.

k. **Armscye (or armhole)**—The measurement around the arm and over the shoulder where the arm joins the body.

l. **Underarm to waist**—The distance from under the arm to the waist.

m. **Bust span**—The distance from bust point to bust point.

n. **Head around**—The circumference of the head.

o. **Arm (out to elbow)**—The distance from the shoulder bone to the elbow.

   Arm (out to wrist)—The distance from the shoulder bone to the wrist with a slightly bent elbow.

p. **Arm (in to wrist)**—The measurement from the point where the arm joins the body to the wrist.

q. **Bicep**—The measurement around the flexed bicep.

r. **Elbow**—The measurement around the bent elbow.

s. **Wrist**—The circumference over the wristbone.

t. **Waist to floor**—The distance, front and back, from the waist to the floor.

u. **Waist to knee**—The distance, front and back, from the waist to the middle of the knee.

v. **Neck to floor**—The distance, front and back, from the neck to the floor. Measurement is taken from the same location on the neck as neck-to-waist.

w. **Length of hip**—The distance from the waist to the fullest part of the hip.

x. **Inseam**—The measurement from crotch to ankle bone.

y. **Outseam**—The measurement on the side from waist to anklebone.

z. **Girth**—The distance from one shoulder through the legs and back to the shoulder.

A. **Crotch**—When the person is seated on a hard flat surface, this is the distance from the waist to the surface.

B. **Complete crotch**—The distance from the centerfront waist through the legs to the centerback waist.

C. **Thigh**—The circumference of the largest part of the thigh.

D. **Calf**—The circumference of the largest part of the calf.

E. **Above knee**—The circumference directly above the knee.

F. **Below knee**—The circumference directly below the knee.

G. **Ankle**—The circumference of the ankle over the ankle bone.

Shoe—Shoe size should include width. Make a tracing of the stockinged foot on the back of the measurement chart.

Hat—Divide the head circumference by 3.14. A hat size represents the diameter of the head.

Dress—Refer to standard size charts.

Suit—This corresponds roughly to chest measurements and height. Refer to standard size charts.

Shirt—Men's shirts are measured by neck and sleeve length. The neck measurement is taken at the base of the neck. The sleeve measurement is taken from the center back neck at the top vertebra, over the shoulder and to the wrist.

Trousers—Men's trousers are measured by waist and inseam.

Glove—Measure around the hand and over the knuckles.

SOURCES FOR PATTERNS

Nearly every home sewer is familiar with commercial packaged patterns which come in specific sizes for standard body types. Theatre costumers must rely on a wider range of sources for patterns to most effectively recreate a costume from a costume rendering. No source should be rejected automatically. To rely only on commercial patterns, for example, or draping, or drafting, or period pattern books, would seriously limit the ease with which the final costume could be created.

Commercial patterns have a value in that most people are familiar with them and accustomed to the processes and systems developed by the pattern companies. Creating your own patterns requires changes in some of these systems. For example, patterns created from period sources or by drafting are developed without seam allowance. Many books of historical garments are exact recreations of museum pieces; thus, the size corresponds to the size of the garment in the museum, and in all probability that will not be the size of the actor who will wear the costume you are making. In spite of the differences in procedures, creating and adapting patterns is an essential skill for effective costuming. Let's look at the variety of sources for costume patterns.

Commercial Patterns

Again, most home sewers are familiar with the standard commercial pattern companies—McCall's, Simplicity, Butterick, and Vogue. Most people learn to sew using this type of pattern. Although most theatre costuming does not rely on commercial patterns, there are times when these patterns may be used either in part or totally for a specific costume. Adaptations of standard garments from commercial patterns are common, and basic items are frequently easier to acquire by using commercial rather than developed patterns.

Charts for standard commercial size specifications are listed on each envelope and in the back of the catalogs for each company. These pattern specifications overlap, so that a size 12 Misses pattern from one company will be fitted to the same measurements as a size 12 Misses pattern from another company. Just as there is some variation in store-bought clothing, there is variation in the sizing of patterns. The fact that these patterns are created for a number of different body types as well as a standardized set of measurements is a plus for the commercial pattern. Although no two bodies are alike, and almost no one fits perfectly into a standard size, the number of options presented by the commercial pattern allows the constructionist more options than any other pre-illustrated flat pattern. Anyone who has used commercial patterns will have a good idea of which size pattern best fits their body.

Commercial patterns are especially useful in modern-dress productions. It is quite easy to find, in collections of commercial patterns, styles that can be easily adapted to any modern costume design.

One of the most frequently used commercial patterns is the fitted basic garment known as a shell or sloper. These fitted shells come in all women's sizes. This garment is selected in the size closest to matching the actor's measurements and then is carefully fitted for even more accuracy. The sloper can then be altered through flat-pattern manipulation (see chapter 6) to take on almost any form. Although slopers may be developed directly from a person's measurements (see chapter 3) or draped directly on an individual (see chapter 5), sometimes the fastest and easiest solution is to start with a commercial sloper and handle variations through the fitting process.

Other commercial patterns occasionally used by costumers are the historic garments found in the specialty sections of pattern books. These patterns are simplifications of historical garments designed as costumes for adults and children. They therefore fit modern, noncorseted bodies. They are generally modified to fit current taste. The "Past Patterns" company has reproduced patterns for a limited collection of historical garments that are taken directly from old patterns.

A few animal costume and fantasy patterns, usually included with the historic garments in the back of pattern books, can provide the bases for theatre costumes as well.

Commercial patterns may be redesigned and adapted in the creation of modern-dress costumes, of course. A sleeve from one garment often will fit well into another pattern, and so on.

Commercial patterns are easy for many costumers to deal with primarily because they are accustomed to sewing by this method: sizes are already indicated, yardages are computed, instructions are carefully laid out. The transition from commercial pattern to self-made patterns is frightening for some people, but the freedom available to the costumer when all options are open makes this challenge worthwhile. (If you have ever considered the "roadmap" presented to the sewer from a German pattern magazine, you will surely recognize how much commercial patternmakers in this country have pampered home sewers, and at the same time stifled the learning process, by doing so much of the thinking and planning.)

A standard measurement chart for commercial patterns follows. First determine body type, then find the measurements that correspond to the measurements of the person for whom you are building the costume. Note that

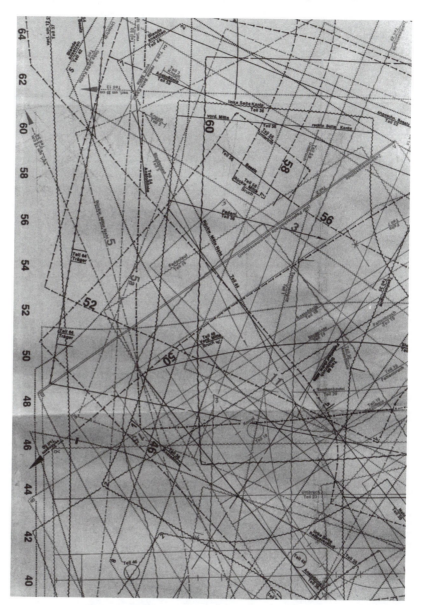

Figure 2.3 German fashion magazine patterns.

the patterns include quite a lot of ease, and if you want a snug-fitting garment, you may wish to start with a smaller size, or expect to take in the garment during the fitting.

Commercial Pattern System. Commercial patterns are easy to use. They include the addition of a standard 5/8″ seam allowance, lines for sewing and darts, arrows indicating the straight of grain, notches and circles for matching, and indications of zipper and button placement.

These patterns are clearly labeled with the name of the pattern piece, the size of the pattern, and the pattern code number. Each piece indicates how many pieces of the pattern are to be cut, and where ease, pleats, gathers, tucks, or pockets are to be placed. In addition, information on pattern altering is included.

A set of explicit instructions accompanies each commercial pattern. These instructions suggest a layout for the pattern for a variety of fabric widths, and a procedure to follow in assembling the garment. Also included are sewing hints to make the construction process easier and the final result more attractive.

Figure 2.4 Women's standard measurement chart.

MISSES'

Size	6	8	10	12	14	16	18	20
Bust	30½	31½	32½	34	36	38	40	42
Waist	23	24	25	26½	28	30	32	34
Hip	32½	33½	34½	36	38	40	42	44
Back waist length	15½	15¾	16	16¼	16½	16¾	17	17¼

MISS PETITE

Size	6mp	8mp	10mp	12mp	14mp	16mp
Bust	30½	31½	32½	34	36	38
Waist	23½	24½	25½	27	28½	30½
Hip	32½	33½	34½	36	38	40
Back waist length	14½	14¾	15	15¼	15½	15¾

JUNIOR

Size	5	7	9	11	13	15
Bust	30	31	32	33½	35	37
Waist	22½	23½	24½	25½	27	29
Hip	32	33	34	35½	37	39
Back waist length	15	15¼	15½	15¾	16	16¼

JUNIOR PETITE

Size	3JP	5JP	7JP	9JP	11JP	13JP
Bust	30½	31	32	33	34	35
Waist	22½	23	24	25	26	27
Hip	31½	32	33	34	35	36
Back waist length	14	14¼	14½	14¾	15	15¼

YOUNG JUNIOR/TEEN

Size	5/6	7/8	9/10	11/12	13/14	15/16
Bust	28	29	30½	32	33½	35
Waist	22	23	24	25	26	27
Hip	31	32	33½	35	36½	38
Back waist length	13½	14	14½	15	15⅜	15¾

HALF-SIZE

Size	10½	12½	14½	16½	18½	20½	22½	24½
Bust	33	35	37	39	41	43	45	47
Waist	27	29	31	33	35	37½	40	42½
Hip	35	37	39	41	43	45½	48	50½
Back waist length	15	15¼	15½	15¾	15⅞	16	16⅛	16¼

WOMEN'S

Size	38	40	42	44	46	48	50
Bust	42	44	46	48	50	52	54
Waist	35	37	39	41½	44	46½	49
Hip	44	46	48	50	52	54	56
Back waist length	17¼	17⅜	17½	17⅝	17¾	17⅞	18

Figure 2.5 Men's standard measurement chart.

Size	34	36	38	40	42	44	46	48
Chest	34	36	38	40	42	44	46	48
Waist	28	30	32	34	36	39	42	44
Hip (seat)	35	37	39	41	43	45	47	49
Neckband	14	14½	15	15½	16	16½	17	17½
Shirt sleeve	32	32	33	33	34	34	35	35

The American commercial pattern is very helpful, but reliance on these patterns is sometimes detrimental to the costumer, since all other types of patterns begin to seem very mysterious.

Patterns are not mysterious. They are logically drawn and arranged shapes which, when cut in cloth and assembled, create a garment. Commercial patterns should be only one of many sources to consider when developing patterns for a production.

Book Patterns

A valuable source for theatre costumers are costume books, which are devoted to or contain sections of actual patterns drawn to scale (see bibliography of pattern book sources).

Patterns found in historic costume books are either reproductions of patterns taken directly from actual garments in museum collections or modifications of period patterns sized to fit modern bodies. Naturally, altering the pattern and fitting the actor are extremely important if you are culling from this source.

Some of these books include information about laying out patterns and historic construction details. Patterns presented in this way invariably must be enlarged to fit today's actors. Typical size for patterns in books is 1/8 scale. These patterns must be enlarged eight times. Some books use an inconsistent scale for pattern reproduction. In these cases a bar indicating length is included somewhere on the page and is used in the same way a mile indicator is used on a roadmap. Other books have their own systems of indicating how much the pattern is to be enlarged. You can be certain that whatever book you decide to use will explain the scale either in the introduction or along with the pattern section.

It is sometimes tempting to enlarge a pattern to fit a specific actor, rather than sticking to the scale indicated in a book. This is especially true when using patterns taken from specific garments, since these patterns are most likely to be too small even when enlarged to full scale. I would suggest, however, that you enlarge the pattern pieces exactly as drawn in the book first, and do alterations on the patterns later. If you enlarge to fit only one measurement, you are likely to throw off other measurements for that actor. Human beings are larger today than they were one hundred years ago, but we are not merely telescoped versions of 19th century people. We have grown taller, for example, but not all proportions have blossomed in the same degree. Our standard shapes have varied as have our specific measurements.

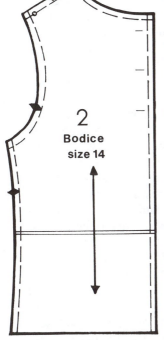

Figure 2.6 Typical commercial pattern piece.

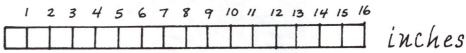

Figure 2.7 Bar enlargement indicator.

Enlarging Patterns from a Book. There are three common methods of enlarging patterns from a book. You should select the method most appropriate to the pattern book. A book that has a varying scale, for example, is easier to enlarge by means of an opaque projector or by the grid and triangle methods than by the radial projection method. With a consistent 1/8″ equals 1″ scale, the radial projection method is often the easiest.

Opaque projector. Using an opaque projector is often the fastest method to enlarge any pattern. Several pattern pieces will be enlarged at once and the technician has only to trace around the outline projected on the wall. It is important that the scale be maintained accurately throughout this process. Scale on the projected object may be checked by measuring a portion of the pattern in the book, then verifying that the projected image of that same portion of the pattern is eight times the size of the book pattern (if the scale is 1/8″ equals 1″). If the scale of a pattern is indicated by a bar measure, simply position the opaque projector so that the bar scale is brought up to the indicated size.

Grid and triangle enlargement. The grid and triangle enlargement methods are similar, and most familiar to many home sewers. This is the method most frequently indicated in craft and sewing magazines for enlargement of patterns. It is especially useful if your book has illustrated patterns on a grid. If not, you may trace the pattern to be enlarged, then draw an appropriate-sized grid on top of the pattern. (A 1/8″ grid is used if you are enlarging a pattern eight times.) Then draw a 1″ grid on pattern paper with the same number and configuration of squares as the one on the original pattern. Transfer the lines of the original pattern to the new grid by following the line from square to square.

The triangle method is similar to the grid method, but easier to manage if the original pattern has not been illustrated on a grid. First draw a box around the original pattern. Draw a box eight times as large (or as the scale indicates) on the pattern paper. Divide the original pattern box into sections by first connecting corners of the box, then dividing it further by drawing horizontal and vertical lines through the center cross. Continue to divide the box in this fash-

Figure 2.8 Opaque projector.

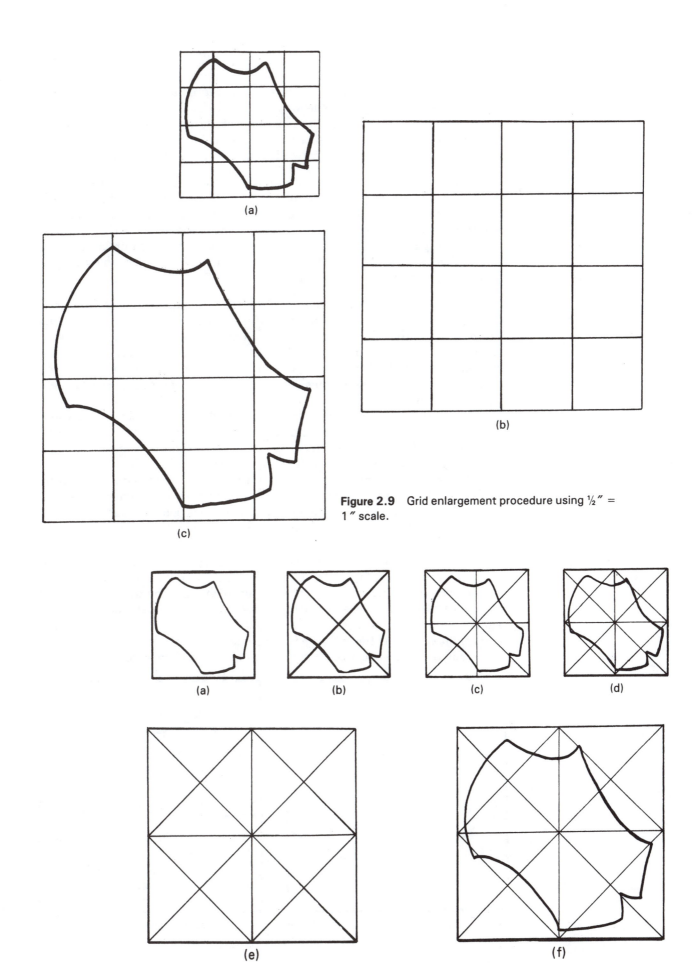

Figure 2.9 Grid enlargement procedure using ½″ = 1″ scale.

Figure 2.10 Triangle enlargement procedure using ½″ = 1″ scale.

ion as many times as are needed to accurately reproduce the original. Divide the larger box in exactly the same way; then transfer the pattern as you would with the grid method. This system is easier because it does not require measuring each section of the grid. After accurately enlarging the box the proper amount, the subdivisions are drawn by simply connecting points.

Radial projection. This method is very quick if the scale you are working with is standard. Trace the pattern from the book, then adhere it to the lower left corner of the pattern paper. Extend lines from a lower left point through all key points on the original pattern. Mark on the extended lines the length of the original pattern line times the appropriate amount based on the specific scale. If the scale is 1/2″ equals 1″, you would multiply each length by 2. Connect the points on the new pattern.

Adapting Book Patterns to Fit a Specific Body. Book patterns, as mentioned before, come in standard and limited modern sizes, or, in the case of patterns taken directly from an existing garment, a specific, unique, and likely much smaller set of measurements. To use these patterns for today's actor is a challenge. Naturally, fitting the garment becomes most important, but even before the fitting process, changes may be made in the pattern to greatly help the cutter and fitter.

The body measurements most likely to be different are the chest, waist, across shoulders, width of front and back, and neck to waist. The neckline and armscye will change more subtly. Below the waist the major measurements of hip, waist, and inseam are likely to be different.

The important issue in pattern adaptation is that you have enough fabric to work with once the garment gets to the fitting stage. To create a perfect flat pattern from a book and a set of measurements is possible, but would take a great deal of time, and it is probably easier to make the final adjustments in the fitting stage.

The first measurement to check on an upper-body garment is the neck-to-waist measurement for the front and back. If this is not correct, make a mark on the pattern to correct it. The next thing to check is the waist. Divide the waist measurement and distribute the correction between seamlines and darts. Do the same with the chest, across shoulders, width-of-front measurements, and height of dart. If the armscye is too small in the fitting, it is an easy matter to clip away the excess. If the armscye seems too large, you may cut the

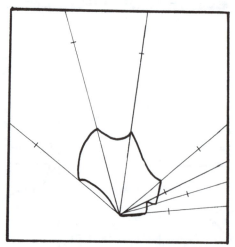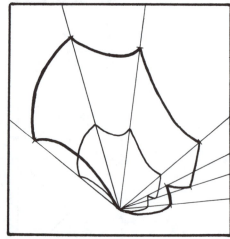

Figure 2.11 Radial projection enlargement procedure using ½″ = 1″ scale.

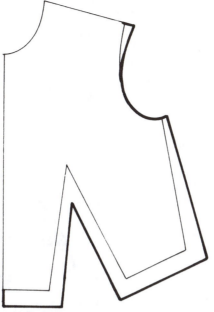

Figure 2.12 Pattern alteration process.

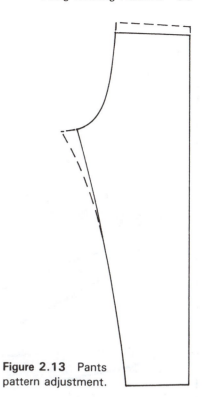

Figure 2.13 Pants pattern adjustment.

pattern with extra seam allowance along the curve, which will effectively diminish the armhole and allow you to re-mark it during the fitting. Like the armscye, the neckline may need to be clipped and adjusted on the body. By now your pattern should be adapted to the point that it may be used for a first fitting. If the actor is substantially different from the pattern size, it is a good idea to test the pattern first in muslin before cutting the final fabric. If time and budget permit, it is always a good idea to create a muslin mock-up of any pattern you are unfamiliar with.

For sleeve patterns check the length, the bicep, wrist, and placement of the elbow. For skirts, the waist, hip, and length of skirt should be checked against the pattern. Pants are trickier to fit because of the crotch seam. If there is not enough fabric length for the crotch, extend the length at the waist and inner thigh. Waist, hip, crotch, thigh, and inseam are adjusted in the same manner as upper-body garments.

EXERCISES

1. Working with a partner, measure and fill in a measurement chart for each person.
2. From the standard commercial measurement chart and your own set of measurements, determine which pattern size you would use.
3. Enlarge a book pattern by the following methods:
   (a) Opaque projector
   (b) Grid
   (c) Triangle
   (d) Radial projection
4. Compare the patterns enlarged in Exercise 3. Are they the same? Which method is the most accurate?
5. Adapt a commercial sloper pattern to your specific measurements.

Fabric

3

It is essential that costumers have an understanding of fabric composition and qualities in order to select and use fabric effectively on stage. It is probably more important to understand how a fabric will move and drape than to know about the specific fiber content of a piece of fabric, but the more one can learn about fabric the easier will be the decisions about which fabric to select.

Fabrics may be classified by fiber content (what the fabric is made of), construction (how the fabric is structured), and finish (how the fabric is treated). It is important to understand the options in these classifications in order to determine how a fabric will be maintained. Will it be machine washable? Will it fall apart after a year? Can it be dyed or bleached? How will it react to paints or markers? But it is equally important to look at, feel, and move a piece of fabric in order to determine if the drape and weight will be appropriate for the movement and flow of the intended costume.

FIBERS

The basic component of fabric is fiber. Individual fabric qualities may be altered by the structure of yarn, the construction of the fabric, and the finish imposed on the fabric, but at the core of any fabric is the fiber. This gives the fabric its unique characteristics, which in part determine its capabilities.

Fibers may be divided into natural and synthetic. All historic garments up until the first half of the twentieth century were composed of natural-fiber

Figure 3-1 Characteristics of natural fibers

Fiber	Fabrics	Characteristics	Maintenance
Cotton	muslin, corduroy denim, terry, velveteen	strong, absorbent, dyes well, shrinks and wrinkles unless treated	washable
Flax	linen	strong, absorbent, dyes poorly, may wrinkle, shrink, and stretch unless treated	dry-clean
Jute	burlap	weak, poor color fastness, brittle, stiff, wrinkles, has strong odor	washable
Ramie	grasscloth, blends with other fibers	strong, absorbent, resists rotting and mildew, dyes well, wrinkles	washable
Silk	brocades, satin, chiffon, crepe	strong, absorbent, dyes well, wrinkle-resistant	dry-clean or hand wash
Wool	crepe, flannel, felt, gabardine	weak, very absorbent, dyes well, wrinkle-resistant, may shrink unless treated	dry-clean, sometimes washable

fabrics. In this century hundreds of pure synthetic and synthetic/natural-blend fabrics have been developed. Some of these have unique qualities and some attempt to imitate and improve on natural-fiber fabrics.

Natural Fibers

Natural fibers, as the name implies, come from naturally growing things. The most commonly used natural fabrics are cotton, which is created from the soft fiber surrounding the seeds of the cotton plant; wool, which comes from the fleece of sheep; linen, which is made from the fibers of the flax plant; and silk, which comes from the silkworm cocoon.

Natural fibers may be used in the creation of a wide variety of beautiful and comfortable-to-wear fabrics. Many people prefer any natural-fiber fabric to any synthetic because of the subtle irregularities in natural fibers and their absorbency and adaptability to weather changes. Figure 3-1 describes the qualities of natural fibers.

Natural fibers are typically spun into yarns before fabric can be woven or knitted.

Synthetic Fibers

Synthetic fibers may be used to create fabrics that very closely resemble natural-fiber fabrics. Unlike most natural fabrics, synthetic fabrics tend to be wrinkle-resistant, so pressing chores are minimized. On the other hand, most synthetic fabrics are less responsive to weather changes and are neither as warm under cold conditions nor as cool in warm situations.

Names of synthetic fibers may be confusing because chemical companies often register an individual trademark for a chemical fiber that closely resembles the composition of a number of other fibers. Figure 3-2 describes characteristics of synthetic fabrics.

Figure 3–2 Characteristics of synthetic fibers

Fiber	Fabrics	Characteristics	Maintenance
Acetate	lining taffeta, lace, tricot	weak, dyes well, mildew, stretch, and shrink resistant, imitates silk	dry-clean or hand wash
Acrylic	fake fur, knits, fleece, blends with wool, cotton, rayon	strong, poor absorbency, wrinkle resistant, dyes well, pills, resists mildew, imitates wool	washable
Metallic	brocades, lace, lamé	weak, nonabsorbent, dyes poorly, may tarnish unless treated with plastic coating	wash or dry-clean
Modacrylic	fake fur	strong, poor absorbency, wrinkle resistant, heat sensitive, flame resistant	wash in cool or dry-clean dry without heat
Nylon	satin, tricot, chiffon, knits	strong, poor absorbency, resists wrinkling and mildew, elastic	washable
Polyester	double knits, lining, cotton/poly blends	strong, poor absorbency, static electricity, may be heat set, resists wrinkling and mildew	washable
Rayon	rayon blends	weak, absorbent, dyes well, wrinkles, shrinks, stretches unless treated	dry-clean or wash
Spandex	stretch fabric blends, swimwear	strong, nonabsorbent, elastic	washable
Triacetate	Arnel	weak, dyes well, resists wrinkling and shrinking, may be heat set	washable

Fiber Blends

To derive benefits of both synthetic and natural fibers, many fabric manufacturers have combined fibers to create fabrics that exhibit qualities of both parent fibers. Because of the confusing array of fiber possibilities in fabrics today, the specific content of fibers is generally listed on the end of any bolt of fabric constructed within the last few years.

YARNS

Before a fabric may be constructed by either weaving or knitting, the fiber being used must be manipulated into continuous strands called yarns. There are two types of yarn, spun yarn and filament yarn.

Fabrics identified as being constructed from "combed" cotton or "worsted" wool are generally more refined and more durable, since these terms refer to a longer length of fiber used in the spinning of the yarn. Silk fiber is created by the silkworm in a continuous strand called a filament. Shorter sections of silk may be twisted together to create a rougher "spun silk" yarn.

Synthetic fibers all begin as chemical solutions, which are extruded into a chemical bath or air chamber. These filaments harden and then may be texturized or spun to alter the smooth, slippery quality of the fiber.

Spun Yarns

Spun yarns are created by twisting together short fibers (natural or synthetic or both) until they grip onto each other and form a continuous length. The spinning process varies according to the fibers used and the amount of twist on the yarn. In general a hard twist will result in a smoother, more durable yarn and a fabric with a very regular finish. Variations on spun yarns can be used to create novelty fabrics.

Ply yarns are comprised of two or more single yarns twisted together. Sometimes these individual yarns vary in thickness, twist, or color, providing interesting textures and patterns to the resulting fabric.

Filament Yarns

Filaments are long single strands of fiber that is characteristically smooth and fine. Silk and most synthetic fibers begin as filaments.

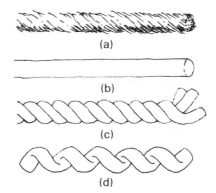

(a)

(b)

(c)

(d)

Figure 3–3 Yarn variety: a. spun, b. filament, c. ply, and d. crimped

Monofilament yarns are those made from a single strand of the filament. Multifilament yarns are created when two or more filaments are twisted together. Multifilament yarns are generally stronger.

Texturizing is a process of melting and heat-setting a crimp or coil into a filament to produce stretch yarn, which is useful in woven stretch fabrics.

WOVEN FABRICS

The majority of fabrics used in costume construction are woven fabrics. Woven fabrics are created by the interlacing of yarns perpendicular to each other. Lengthwise yarns are called warp yarns. These provide the base or structure into which the filler (the crosswise yarn or the weft yarn) is inserted. Variations in the weave can occur by rearranging the pattern in which the warp and weft intersect.

Basic Weaves

Plain weave. This is the simplest of the weave constructions. It is formed by allowing the weft yarn to alternately pass over and under the warp yarns. Variations occur in the weight of the yarns used, differing colors

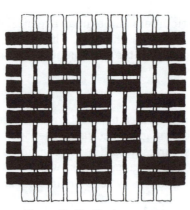

Figure 3-4 Plain weave

Figure 3-5 Basket weave

Figure 3-6 Twill weave

for warp and weft, and the compactness of the weave structure. Most printed fabrics are composed of a plain weave.

Basket weave. This is a variation of the plain weave in which two or more weft yarns laid side by side pass under and over the same number of warp yarns to form a looser and often softer textured fabric. Oxford cloth and hopsacking are examples of basket weave fabrics.

Twill weave. This is a system where the weft yarn passes over and under at least two, but no more than four warp yarns, and on each successive line moves one step to the right or left to form a diagonal ridge. Denim, gabardine, and serge are examples of twill weaves.

Herringbone weave. This is a variation of the twill weave in which the diagonal ridge switches direction to form a zig-zag pattern.

Rib weave. This is a variation of the plain weave where fine and coarse yarns are alternated, forming a ridged or corded effect. Faille, grosgrain, broadcloth, and taffeta are examples of rib weave.

Satin weave. This is achieved when the warp yarn passes over four to eight weft yarns in a staggered pattern exposing lengths of unbroken warp yarns on the surface of the fabric to reflect and create a sheen. Satin and cotton sateen are constructed with variations on a satin weave.

Pile weave. This is created by adding an additional filler yarn or warp yarn into a plain or twill weave fabric and drawing the new yarn into loops on the fabric surface. Terry cloth is an example of a pile weave fabric in which the loops are left uncut. Corduroy, velvet, and fake fur are examples of pile fabrics in which the loops have been sheared.

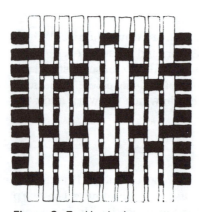

Figure 3-7 Herringbone weave

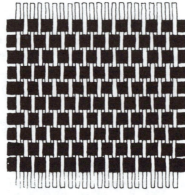

Figure 3-8 Rib weave

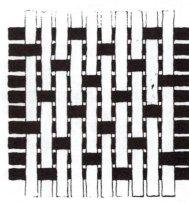

Figure 3-9 Satin weave

Figure 3-10   Pile weave

Figure 3-11   Jacquard weave

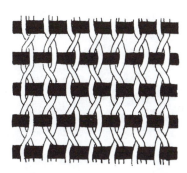

Figure 3-12   Gauze weave

Jacquard weave.   This is a patterned weave created by a specific jacquard attachment, which controls the warp and weft yarns individually in order to create individual and specific designs. A similar but simpler pattern structure called a dobby creates geometric patterns. Brocades and damasks are typically created with a jacquard attachment.

Gauze weave.   This is an open mesh in which the weft threads are twisted in figure 8 fashion around the warp threads.

KNIT FABRICS

Knit fabrics are constructed with a series of interlocking loops resulting in a natural give or stretch to the final fabric.

Common Knits

Plain jersey knit.   This is a single-yarn construction in which all loops are pulled to the back, leaving the surface smooth. The stretch in a plain jersey knit is greater in width than in length.

Purl knit.   This is a single-yarn construction in which loops are pulled in alternate rows to the front and back of the fabric, creating a looped appearance on both sides. Like the jersey knits these fabrics stretch more in width than in length.

Rib knit.   This is a single-yarn-construction arrangement of alternating knit and purl sections which create a lengthwise ribbed effect on the front as well as the back of the fabric. Ribbed fabrics are capable of extensive

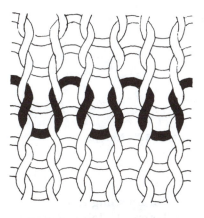

Figure 3-13   Plain jersey knit

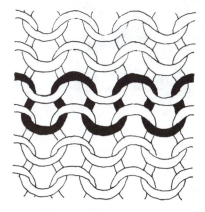

Figure 3-14   Purl knit

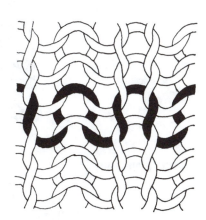

Figure 3-15   Rib knit

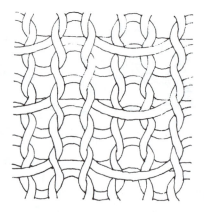

Figure 3-16 Double knit

stretch in width, and because they pull back with elastic ease they are commonly used in necklines, cuffs, and waistbands.

Double knit. This is produced by two yarn and needle sets working together. Stretch capacity is limited, and the appearance of the front and back may differ.

OTHER FABRIC CONSTRUCTION SYSTEMS

Specialty fabrics and interfacings may be created with nonwoven or non-knitted techniques.

Felting. This is achieved by applying heat, moisture, and pressure to short fibers to produce a matted, interlocked layer. Wool is the easiest fiber to felt because it mats naturally, but many synthetic fibers and blends also have been successfully felted.

Fusing. This resembles felting except that a bonding agent is used to hold fibers together. Many nonwoven interfacings are created in this way.

Bonding. This is a method of joining two or more fabrics together with an adhesive.

Netting. This involves knotting yarns at the points where they intersect.

Figure 3-17 Felting

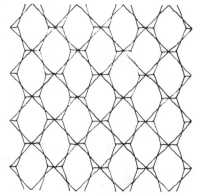

Figure 3-18 Netting

FABRIC FINISHES

The final step in fabric creation is applying a variety of finishing treatments. These must sometimes be broken down or destroyed before the fabric will suit a specific purpose. It is important to determine the finish on a fabric before you purchase it so that you may successfully judge its suitability.

Figure 3-19 Decorative fabric finishes

Finish	Process
Bleaching	Use of active bleach to whiten or strip color from fabric.
Carbonizing	Removal of vegetable matter from wool to improve texture, promote even dyeing.
Calendering	Pressing process where fabric passes through rollers to remove wrinkles and give fabric a sheen. Other calendering processes are used to create watermarking and embossed effects.
Dyeing	Fabric is unrolled into a dye trough, then rerolled at the other end. Dyeing may also take place at the fiber stage or the yarn stage.
Flocking	An adhesive is applied to the fabric by a roller printer. Cut fibers adhere to the glue, creating a raised, textured pattern.
Glazing	A calendering process which uses starch, shellac, or glue applied to the fabric before it passes through the hot rollers.
Napping	The surface of the fabric is brushed to create a soft, warm texture.
Pleating	A form of embossing where heat is used to create the pleats.
Roller printing	Engraved copper cylinders are rolled onto the fabric to create a pattern.
Screen printing	Good for large designs. Dye is forced through a screen onto which the design has been created by masking out the areas which will not be part of the pattern.
Transfer printing	Process by which the design is first applied to paper, then transferred with heat and pressure to the fabric.

Figure 3-20 Functional fabric finishes

Finish	Purpose/Result
Anti-bacterial	Finish used to prevent deterioration from bacteria including perspiration.
Anti-static	Especially important in man-made fabrics, this process helps to reduce static so fabrics will not cling or give off electrical charges.
Flame-resistance	Produces a slow-to-burn, or self-extinguishing quality in fabric.
Mercerization	Process which causes greater strength, absorbency, and luster in cottons and linens.
Moth-resistance	A process which chemically alters the molecular structure of the wool fiber, thereby causing moths and other insects to lose interest in the fabric.
Permanent press	Resin-finish applied to fabric which makes it resistant to wrinkling, but increases susceptibility to soiling, pilling, and weakening of the fiber.
Preshrunk	Fabric has been treated so that it will not shrink more than 2% if the user follows care instructions.
Soil-release	Finish which allows oily stains to be easily removed through machine-washing.
Wash-and-wear	Resin-finish applied to fabric which causes wrinkles to be minimized if fabric is removed from washer before the spin cycle and hung up to dry.
Waterproof	Process in which the pores of a fabric are completely closed by a film coating, causing the fabric to be totally impervious to water.
Water-repellent	Densely woven fabric in which a film coats the yarn but does not fill in all pores of a fabric. Fabric remains pliable, air can pass through it, but it resists water.

The purpose of fabric finishes to the public is to make that fabric better suited to a specific need. Often the needs of the general consumer are very different from the needs of the costumer, and it is likely that an appropriate fabric finish for one will be unsuitable or unnecessary for the other. Functional and decorative finishes alter the absorbency of the fabric, the way it wears, the way it feels to wear it, and its ability to be broken down, dyed, bleached, and softened to suit the very specific need of a predesigned costume. Figures 3–19 and 3–20 describe decorative and functional finishing processes.

FABRIC SELECTION

Having a knowledge of the composition and structure of fabric is a good basis for making the final decisions as to which fabric to select for a given project. Other considerations must come first, however.

Price

This may or may not be the most important consideration. Become familiar with stores that deal in seconds and irregulars, and look for sales. Whenever possible buy in bulk for the future. If your budget is tight accept the fact that some compromises will have to be made. Decide where compromises will be the least damaging.

Weave and Weight

Weave and weight are the most important considerations when determining how the final costume will look. The movement and drape of the costume will be determined by this factor, so this must be a primary concern for the costumer. Other qualities of fabric such as color or texture may be altered with dyes and stenciling later, but it is virtually impossible to add weight, reduce weight, or stiffen or soften to a great degree an existing fabric. In order to determine the fabric weight and drape, one must actually feel the fabric, bunch it, hold it up, watch it fall, and play with it in the store. See if the folds are crisp

Figure 3–21 Designer checking the drape of a fabric before purchasing

or soft. See whether it falls into place immediately or lingers in the air. These features will make a great difference to the finished product.

Color

Color may be altered to some extent by dyeing and bleaching. A discussion of fabric manipulation in Chapter 9 will help you to determine to what extent this will be possible. If a specific color is essential and dyeing is not possible, then naturally it is important to locate a fabric as close as possible to the color of the designed costume. Remember that any color will look different in different types of light. Fabric stores are often lit with fluorescent light, and the color you select in the store may look different to you when you bring it back to the costume shop.

Gels used in stage lighting instruments may affect the color as well. Subtleties in color may be disappointingly lost when the final costume appears under stage lights. If you have any question about the final effect of the colors on stage, talk with the lighting designer. If possible look at swatches of the fabric under the lights to be used. It is usually possible to resolve color problems by expressing concern to the director and other designers if the color will be seriously altered by the lighting.

Texture

Texture and perceived texture may be added to a fabric in the same way that color may be altered. Subtle textures and prints may blend together over a distance to appear to be a solid color. Take a look at each fabric from a distance to determine the effect of texture or pattern from an audience perspective.

FABRICS FREQUENTLY USED IN THE THEATRE

Although any fabric may be used for costuming if it suits the budget and design requirements, certain fabrics are used more frequently than others because of their price, availability, or flexibility. Such fabrics are frequently bought in quantity and stored for future use. A list of such fabrics and their characteristics follows.

> **Acetate**—a manmade fiber made from cellulose acetate. It imitates silk, drapes well, and is frequently used as a lining.
>
> **Acrylic**—a manufactured fiber which may be used to imitate wool, fur, or velvet. It dries quickly, keeps its shape, and needs little ironing.
>
> **Broadcloth**—closely woven, finely ribbed fabric. Cotton broadcloth is frequently used for inner linings to provide body for flimsy fabrics.
>
> **Brocade**—a fabric with an interwoven pattern of raised figures that give an embossed appearance.
>
> **Buckram**—coarsely woven cotton fabric impregnated with a glue sizing. Used extensively in millinery and mask-making.
>
> **Burlap**—coarse, stiff, and very textured fabric made from jute. Used for rustic garments, though rough texture can be uncomfortable next to skin.
>
> **Canvas**—cotton, linen, or synthetic; a densely woven and heavy fabric used for heavy-duty rigging and corsetry.
>
> **Cheesecloth**—a very loosely woven cotton fabric. Used for special effects and overlays.
>
> **Chintz**—a glazed cotton fabric frequently printed in brilliant large floral

patterns. Used to imitate cotton printed fabrics of the eighteenth and nineteenth centuries.

Corduroy—a cut-pile fabric with wide or narrow wales. The surface texture of corduroy creates depth and light reflection when sewn into folds. Corduroy is sometimes used to imitate velvet.

Cotton—fabric made from the cotton fiber. Used for undergarments and as linings because of moisture absorbency and comfort.

Crepe—textured fabric created by weaving crimped yarns or by calendering the final fabric. Crepes drape well and are used in costumes that must have a soft drape.

Damask—a fabric woven on a jacquard loom combining a number of different weave patterns which create pattern emphasis through varying light reflection. Fibers used frequently in damasks are cotton, linen, rayon, and acetate.

Denim—a strong, twill-weave cotton cloth usually made with colored warp and white filling.

Duck—closely woven, heavy, durable fabric in plain or basket weave.

Felt—a pressed fabric made with fibers of fur, wool, cotton, or synthetics. Felt comes in various weight and may be dampened and shaped over a form for armor or hats or cut into shape and used in appliqué work.

Flannel—fabric with a plain or twill weave and a slightly napped surface. Flannel has a soft, rustic quality when broken down.

Gabardine—a firmly woven, twill-surface fabric. Gabardine is frequently used in tailored garments.

Georgette—a heavy, sheer crepe. Georgette flows and moves beautifully on stage.

Grosgrain—a closely woven ribbed fabric. Grosgrain ribbon is especially useful for staying waist seams and trimming hats and costumes.

Jersey—a fabric knitted in tubular form. It may be used for hose and tights and other garments which require form-fitting ability.

Lace—decorative fabric or trim constructed without a ground fabric. Manufactured lace is usually constructed on a net backing. Used as trim and decoration and for undergarments.

Lamé—a plain metallic fabric or one with metallic threads woven into it. Used for period garments and a wide variety of special effects.

Linen—fabric made from flax fibers. Linen has a slightly shiny textured appearance, and wrinkles very easily.

Monk's cloth—a heavy, loosely woven fabric. It is frequently used for robes, capes, and other heavy garments.

Muslin—cotton fabrics of varying weights and finishes. Inexpensive muslin fabric is frequently used for making and testing patterns as well as interlinings.

Nylon—synthetic fiber producing a silk-like fabric. Nylon is used in modern underwear, nightwear, and draped garments.

Organdy—a sheer, crisp cotton fabric. It may be used as a lightweight stiffener.

Organza—a sheer, crisp silk fabric.

Peau de soie—a dull-luster, closely woven satin.

Pellon—a nonwoven interfacing sold in black and white and in several different weights.

Piqué—cotton fabric of medium to heavy weight with raised cords in both directions.

Polyester—a synthetic fiber which can be woven or knit into fabrics that imitate in appearance and drape silk, cotton, and wool. Polyester fabrics are very durable.

Sateen—cotton cloth made with a satin weave. Sateen is a good substitute for satin because it is washable and often less expensive.

Satin—silk or synthetic fabric with a satin weave and a lustrous finish.

Serge—a fabric with twill-weave diagonal pattern evident on both sides.

Silk—a fabric made from fibers of the silkworm cocoon. Silk has a shiny surface.

Taffeta—crisp, densely woven fabric, usually with a lustrous finish. It is used in undergarments as well as outerwear.

Terry cloth—soft fabric with a looped pile. It is used for soft-textured costumes.

Tricot—a warp-knitted ribbed fabric with great elasticity.

Tulle—a fine, machine-made net. Used for veiling and in dance costumes.

Velour—a soft pile fabric made of wool and synthetic fibers.

Velvet—silk, rayon, or polyester pile fabric with lustrous surface and light reflection.

Velveteen—cotton pile fabric woven with plain or twill weave.

Voile—lightweight, sheer fabric used for overlays and sheer sections of costumes and hats.

Woolen—fabric made from yarn spun from the fleece of sheep that has been carded but not combed. Woolens are soft and drape very well.

Worsted—a fabric created from wool yarn that has been carded and combed. Worsted fabrics are smoother, more resilient, and more durable than woolens. They also tailor better.

DETERMINING FIBER CONTENT OF FABRICS

Often the best way to determine the composition of an unknown fabric is simple visual inspection. Such factors as the sheen, body, and texture can help to eliminate some fabrics. Synthetic fibers often display many of the visual and tactile characteristics of natural fiber fabrics, however, so chemical and burn tests may be employed to narrow the field further.

Chemical testing requires the stocking of various chemicals, so burn tests are far more accessible to the typical costume shop. Figure 3–22 indicates the reactions of various fibers to a flame. Blends cannot be determined by the burn test. It is best to test warp and weft yarns separately in case they are made of different fibers. Hold the fibers horizontally and feed them slowly into a flame. Repeat this process several times; then check the results against the Fabric Burn Identification Chart, Figure 3–22.

DETERMINING YARDAGE

Because costume patterns do not supply yardage requirements as commercial patterns do, it is necessary to be able to determine yardages in a general way. Specific yardage requirements can be determined after patterns have been created by simply laying out the pattern on varying widths of sample fabrics.

When using down-scaled patterns, estimate on paper the fabric as well as the placement of these pattern pieces for an accurate yardage estimate. If this degree of accuracy is not necessary, it is best to overestimate a bit to allow for error or a forgotten pattern item.

Figure 3-22 Fabric burn identification chart

Fiber	In flame	Removal from flame	Odor
Acetate	melts	continues to melt leaving black bead	acrid
Acrylic	melts	continues to melt leaving black bead	acrid
Cotton	burns	continues to burn with gray ash	burning paper
Flax (Linen)	burns	continues to burn with gray ash	burning paper
Modacrylic	melts slowly	extinguishes leaving black bead	acrid
Nylon	melts slowly	extinguishes leaving grayish bead	celery
Polyester	melts slowly with black smoke	extinguishes leaving black bead	sweet
Rayon	burns	continues to burn with gray ash	burning paper
Silk	burns slowly	extinguishes with soft black ash	burning hair
Spandex	melts	continues to melt with soft black ash	sweet
Wool	burns slowly	extinguishes with soft black ash	burning hair

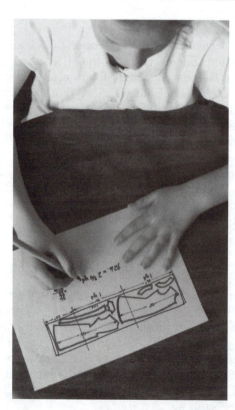

Figure 3-23 Layout of pattern pieces to estimate yardage

In general, rough and generous estimates may be made best by thinking of the lengths of the individual items and adding them up, determining as you go whether two items may be placed side by side on the fabric.

A bodice will generally require something more than the neck-to-waist measurement. Usually 20" will suffice. A fitted bodice for an average-sized woman may be able to be squeezed into one length of fabric, but if the woman is large, or the bodice is to be cut in many pieces, or if you wish to supply generous seam allowances, it is a good idea to allow two lengths of 20" for the bodice. If the sleeve is fitted it might be able to be squeezed into the same length as the bodice, or perhaps partially into the section. Allow at least a 27" length for a woman's sleeve. If it is a full or unusually shaped sleeve you will naturally need more yardage.

Continue in this way to determine the length and placement of the pattern pieces. The safest method of determining yardage is to create the patterns first and then determine yardage pragmatically—by laying out the pieces.

FABRIC WIDTHS

The fabrics typically used in costume construction range in width from 36" to 110". Naturally, it is important to know the width of the fabric you will be buying when you start to estimate yardage. Certain fabrics typically come in consistent width ranges. A list of specific types of fabrics and widths follows.

Corduroy	36"–45"
Cotton	36"–45"
Cotton/Synthetic	45"
Drapery	45"–60"
Double knits	54"–60"
Felt	36"–72"
Linen	36"
Silk and silk-like	45"
Tricot	60"–110"
Upholstery	54"–60"
Wool	54"–60"

Fabric Yardage Conversion

To estimate yardage you must, of course, consider length as well as width. The fabric conversion chart below will help to quickly convert estimated yardages from one width fabric to another. For example, 1 1/2 yards of 60-inch-wide fabric is equivalent to two yards of 45-inch fabric.

Fabric Yardage Conversion Chart

Fabric Width	60"	54"	45"	36"
Y	3/4	5/8	1	1 1/4
A	1	1 1/8	1 3/8	1 3/4
R	1 1/4	1 3/8	1 5/8	2
D	1 1/2	1 5/8	2	2 1/2
A	1 3/4	1 7/8	2 1/4	2 7/8
G	2	2 1/4	2 3/4	3 3/8
E				

OTHER CONSIDERATIONS

Although costumers frequently use and cherish fabrics most consumers would bypass, it is useful to know methods of determining fabric quality and fiber content and to be aware of the probable reactions of a piece of fabric to the wearer, to the washing machine, and to anything you plan to do to it.

Recognizing quality in fabric is easy once you study a few basic features. Check the firmness of the weave by scratching the surface to see how easily the threads move. Hold the fabric up to the light to check the regularity of the weave. Thin or thick spots indicate irregularity in weave, and this will translate into irregularity in the drape of the final costume. Check to see that the weft threads meet the selvage at right angles. Variation here will seriously affect the hang of the costume. Check the dye color along the creaseline for fading. Check to see that a geometric print is printed with the grain of the fabric; otherwise the fabric will have to be cut to suit either the printing or the grain (but not both), and neither solution will give a good result. Powdery dust on the fabric is an indication that too much sizing has been added. This is a method of making the fabric appear to be more substantial than it really is.

Naturally there are times when a flimsy fabric or one which is poorly printed or faded is exactly what the costumer is looking for. Fabric stores are grateful that someone will buy seconds and irregulars, and these can provide great savings of time and money to the theatre. The important thing is to become informed about fabric so you will actually be purchasing something which may successfully and eventually be translated into the appropriate costume for the stage.

EXERCISES

1. Analyze ten samples of fabric from your shop stock or fabric store remnants.
   (a) Determine the weave, fiber content, and yarn structure.
   (b) Describe the flow and drape of the fabrics.
   (c) What type of costume or costume accessory would you create from each selected fabric?
   (d) Look at each swatch of fabric under fluorescent and incandescent lighting and in daylight.
2. At a fabric store:
   (a) Study the drape and movement of several fabrics. How does fiber content seem to affect the drape?
   (b) Study textured and apparent textured fabrics up close and at a distance. Which fabrics look most textured from a distance? When does texture make the fabric look rich? When does it look rustic?
3. Determine the amount of 45″ yardage needed if a garment requires four yards of 36″ fabric. How much yardage is required of 60″ wide fabric?

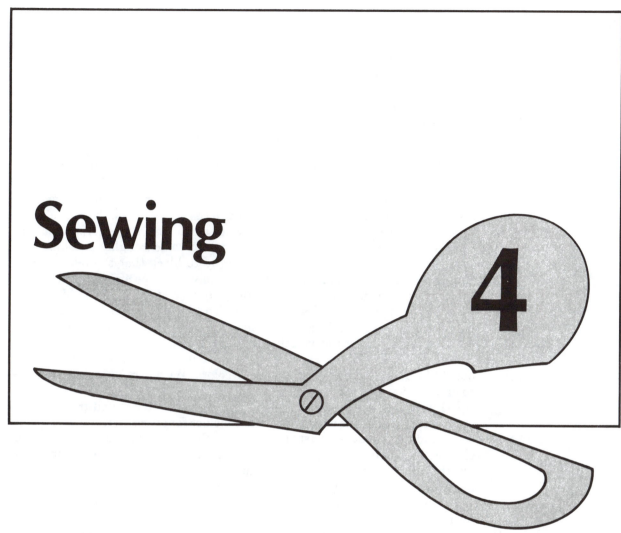

Sewing

4

COSTUME CONSTRUCTION TECHNIQUES

Much of the sewing done in costuming is similar to regular home sewing. Costumes, however, are not street clothes, and details that are important up close on clothing will likely never be seen on stage costumes. Careful layout, cutting, and fitting are as essential to costumes as to street clothing, but precise topstitching and careful matching of thread color, for example, are not. Delicate detail may not be visible from an audience point of view, but durable stitching and heavy-duty closures may be essential for quick changes. This is not to suggest that costume construction is performed with less care than the construction of everyday wear. It is merely that the care may be placed in different areas.

Many costume shops use machine techniques for hemming. Rolled hems and domestic machine blind hems save time, particularly for yards of ruffles or enormous period skirts and capes. Some costume shops have special blind-hemming machines, which produce the hem stitch found on most store-bought clothing. These are very useful since the entire hem can be removed with a pull of the right thread in the right place. If time is available, hems hand sewn by competent seamstresses will usually look nicer up close, but most hand-hemming techniques are not as strong as the machine hems, and usually the difference in appearance is insignificant, even to the first row of the audience.

Likewise, machines are frequently used for overcasting, basting, applying buttons, hook and eyes, and snaps, buttonholing, and embroidery.

Most of these processes are done by machine to save time. If your shop has more help than machinery, by all means use the hand-stitching techniques.

Because of the distance of the audience from the performer, mistakes in costume construction may be more easily disguised than those in street wear. Gussets, patches, extra gores, and trimmings are sometimes employed to save or alter a costume that would otherwise not fit or be inappropriate.

Each costume shop will likely buy some materials in bulk to save time and money. The specific items a costume shop will stock will obviously vary depending on the storage space and budget available for such purchases.

Thread colors may be limited to the basic hues, or just white, gray, and black. It saves time if each person working in the shop does not have to change thread color each time he or she sits down to a machine. By selecting a thread color that closely matches the costume's fabric value (roughly speaking, the approximate shade from white through gray to black that the fabric would photograph as in black-and-white photography), the specific hue will not be evident from the audience. This is particularly true of the stitching of interior seams, which don't show anyway, but it is also true of topstitching for the most part. A selection of some colored thread is usually kept on hand for those cases where appliqué or decorative stitching is required.

Like thread, zippers, grommets, velcro, and other closures are frequently bought in bulk quantities and standard colors. With careful installation the color variation will not be visible at all.

Linings, which are never seen, are frequently constructed from a more durable fabric than one would normally consider for street clothing. Bias tape, seam binding, and other construction materials that are applied to the interior of a costume may be used in the standard black, white, or gray colors, just like thread and zippers. Decorative trimmings such as lace, rick-rack, or braid necessarily coordinate with the design specifications.

In these ways, costume shops may save a great deal of money by buying in larger quantities: thread on cones instead of spools, for example, or bias tape by the bolt rather than in 3 1/2 yd. packages. The savings are considerable, and the final appearance of the garment will not be affected at all.

THE SEWING MACHINE

Each sewing machine threads a bit differently than other brands and models. Likewise, stitching with each machine will involve a slightly different touch and technique. It is a good idea to become thoroughly familiar with your machine, to study the capabilities and options, before beginning construction of costumes. Does your machine have a special stitch for knit fabrics, for example? Is it capable of sewing through several layers of leather? Can buttonholes be made and, if so, how? How is tension controlled? These questions are answered in the machine manual. If you are using a machine whose manual is no longer available, some experimentation is needed. Most sewing machines manufactured in the last 20 years will have obvious control dials or levers that regulate the stitch length and zig-zag width. Other buttons, dials, or levers will cause the stitching to reverse, and alter the needle position. In any case, practicing and becoming comfortable with the sewing machine may save hours of ripping seams later.

Threading the machine. Threading is slightly different on each model, but the basic procedure involves a similar set of guides and discs through which the thread is run in order for the machine to maintain proper tension and control of the thread. Thread guides are located to direct the thread in a basic pattern

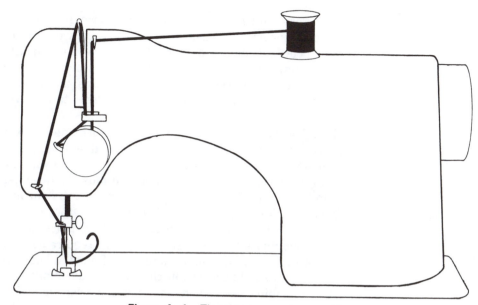

Figure 4-1   Threading a sewing machine

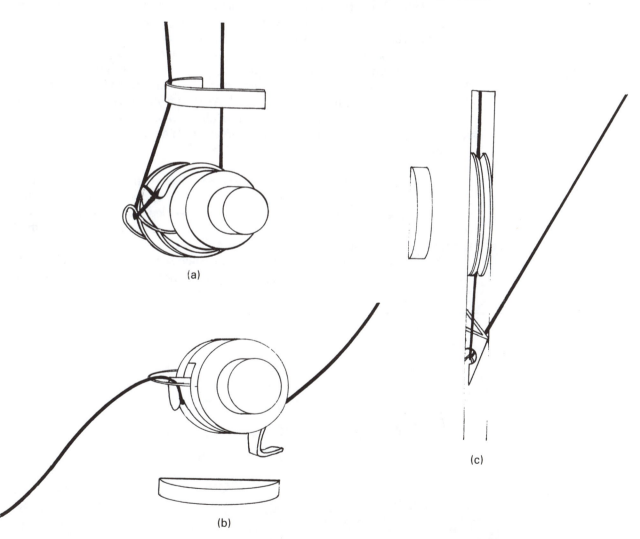

Figure 4-2 (a-c)   Three types of tension disks

first through the tension discs, then through the take-up lever, and finally through the needle. Tension discs are generally one of three types. If an instruction book is available a diagram of thread pattern will be illustrated. Check the direction of needle threading. Before threading any machine lift the presser foot to release pressure on the tension discs, and raise the take-up lever to its highest position by turning the hand wheel toward you.

Bobbins. Winding the bobbin varies with models. Check your manual for specifics. In general, the bobbin is wound on a separate spindle, though some bobbins are wound directly through the needle with the bobbin case in position. In many cases the needle action must be disengaged before the bobbin can be wound. This is usually accomplished by turning the flywheel toward you while holding the hand wheel steady. Other models automatically disengage the needle action when the bobbin is placed on the bobbin spindle.

Bobbins are made to fit the specific requirements of each machine model and are generally not interchangeable. Removal and insertion of a bobbin likewise vary with the model, but there are certain similarities. A bobbin is inserted into a bobbin case. In some machines the case is built into the machine, and in others the case is removed and inserted into the machine along with the bobbin. In all models the thread from the bobbin must pass through a tension spring in the bobbin case before the machine is ready for sewing.

After the upper and lower threads are in place it is necessary to bring the bobbin thread up through the throat plate to begin sewing. This is accomplished by holding on to the upper thread and turning the hand wheel until the needle is in its lowest position, then bringing the needle to its highest position without letting go of the upper thread. As the needle rises the upper thread brings a loop of the bobbin thread with it. Pull the bobbin thread loop to bring up the free end of the thread. Pass both threads to the back between the presser foot and the throat plate leaving at least 3″ of excess.

Machine needles. Machine needles come in a variety of sizes and point types. Sizes range from very fine (9 or 60) to heavy (18 or 120). Regular sharp pointed needles are used for most sewing, but ballpoint needles are often used for sewing knit fabrics so the needle will pass between rather than break the yarn of the fabric. Wedge needles are used for vinyls and leathers.

Needles vary in length and shank style. Each sewing machine has its own needle size and insertion requirements. In general, needles are inserted with the

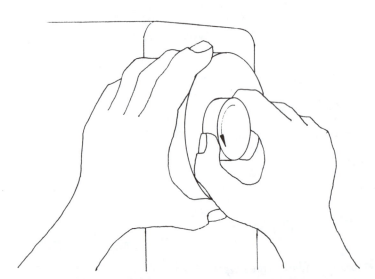

Figure 4-3 Disengaging the flywheel

flat side of the shank facing away from the needle thread guide, and tightened with a thumb screw. It is best to check the machine manual for specifics. An incorrectly inserted needle, a blunt needle, or a bent needle can affect the quality of the stitching or even the ability of a machine to sew.

Practice Stitching

After the sewing machine and bobbin are threaded correctly, begin practice stitching with scraps of cotton fabric in a color that contrasts with the thread color. The contrast will allow you to see the quality of the machine stitching more easily.

First practice straight, even stitching. Fold the fabric double so the edges match. Pull the machine threads to the back leaving about 5″ ends. With the larger amount of fabric to the left of the needle, line up the right edges with one of the marks on the throat plate. Most throat plates have guidelines etched into them at a variety of distances. Since the most common commercial pattern seam allowance is 5/8″, this marking may be the only one. (For convenience, you may wish to indicate on the machine with permanent marker or pieces of tape other useful distances such as 3/4″ or 1″.)

Lower the presser foot to hold the fabric in place while stitching. Turn the hand wheel toward you to guide the needle into the fabric. Depress the control pedal slowly to start stitching. Guide the fabric without pulling so that the right edge stays even with the guideline.

When you finish stitching, turn the hand wheel toward you until the needle reaches its highest position. Raise the presser foot and pull the fabric away from you out the back of the machine. Clip the threads.

This is the basic stitching procedure. After you are comfortable with it, experiment with more complicated stitching procedures:

1. Stitch backward for a few stitches at the beginning and end of a seam line to lock the stitch.
2. Draw a curved line on the cloth and try to stitch following the curve.
3. Practice using other stitches on your machine: zig-zag, stretch, and decorative stitches.
4. Check other presser feet and accessories included with your machine.
5. Practice until you are comfortable with the machine.

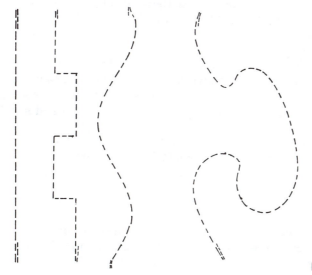

Figure 4–4   Practice machine stitches

STITCHING

Most of the costume stitching is done by sewing machine. If time is not a factor, and talented hand stitchers are available, more precise work can often be done by hand. The following sewing machine and hand-stitching techniques are commonly used in the construction of costumes.

SEWING MACHINE TECHNIQUES

Seams

A seam is formed when two pieces of fabric are sewn together. Seaming is basic to costume construction and any other sewing procedure.

Machine basting is a preliminary seam intended to be used for fittings or to hold the fabric in place while a permanent seam is made. A machine basting stitch is made with the machine set at the longest stitch length. Because basting will later be removed, do not backstitch at the beginning and end of the seam.

Straight seams are sewn by machine with a setting of 10 or 12 stitches to the inch. Seam allowances vary according to the pattern and cut. Commercial patterns are cut with a standard 5/8″ seam allowance, but many costumes are constructed with larger allowances to make them more adaptable for alterations. All seams should be pressed open flat from the inside of the garment.

Curved seams are sewn with the same stitch length as straight seams. They are a bit more difficult to pin and control and must be clipped or notched before pressing.

Dissimilar curve seam occurs when an outward or inward curved piece is sewn to a straight piece or to a piece with a different curve. Clip the inward curve piece to within 1/8″ of the seam line. Baste or pin the two pieces together and stitch the seam. Notch the outward curve before pressing.

Corner seams are made when outer and inner corners are stitched with a very small stitch, then clipped before turning.

Enclosed seams are seams that enclose the seam allowances. They are especially useful when working with visible seams in unlined jackets or capes, and when working with sheer fabrics.

Flat-felled seam is a very durable seam often used in manufactured sportswear. Stitch pieces with wrong sides together. Press open the seam, then trim away about one half of one of the seam allowances. Press the other seam allowance over the trimmed allowance, turn under the outer edge and stitch.

French seam is a finished seam often used with sheer fabrics. Stitch a 1/4″ seam with wrong sides together. Trim seam to 1/8″. Press open, then fold right sides together along the seam line. Stitch again 1/4″ from first seam edge.

Seam Finishes and Special Stitching

Overedging is a method of finishing the edges of seams and raw edges. Zig-zag stitches as well as a variety of other machine stitches may be used for finishing seams and edges.

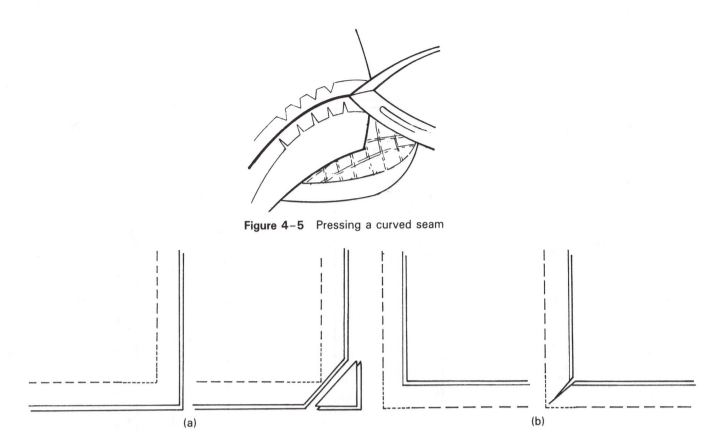

Figure 4–5 Pressing a curved seam

(a)   (b)

Figure 4–6 Clipping outer and inner corners

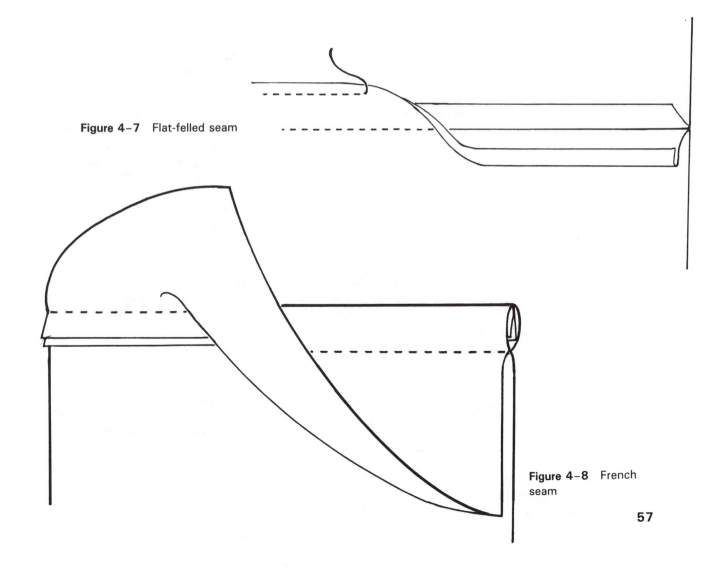

Figure 4–7 Flat-felled seam

Figure 4–8 French seam

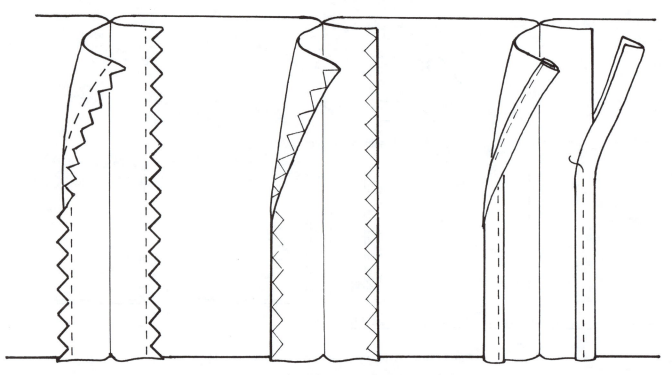

Figure 4-9 Overedging techniques

Topstitching is always done on the outside of the garment. It is a way of emphasizing construction detail; for costumes, topstitching should be done in a contrasting thread color for it to read to the audience. Topstitching is also used to sharpen the edge of a faced garment or emphasize a seam by holding the seam allowances and facings securely in place.

Cording seams is a good way to emphasize seams on stage. Cording may be purchased in various colors, or made by covering cotton cording with bias strips of fabric. The cording is pinned or basted along the seam line with the raw edges of the cording toward the seam allowances of the garment. The raw edges of the cording should be clipped to accommodate curves and angles, then stitched with a zipper foot to one side of the garment. Then, using the stitching line as a guide, sew the seam into the garment with the cording between the two pieces. Corded seams add structure and emphasis to costumes. They are especially nice finished for the waist seam of a bodice.

Seams with ease or fullness occur when one side of a seam is cut with a bit more fullness than the other. This is frequently the case with shoulder seams and curved bodice seams. These seams should be carefully pinned and may be stretched slightly when sewing to distribute the fullness without causing puckers when stitched.

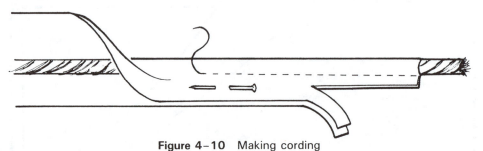

Figure 4-10 Making cording

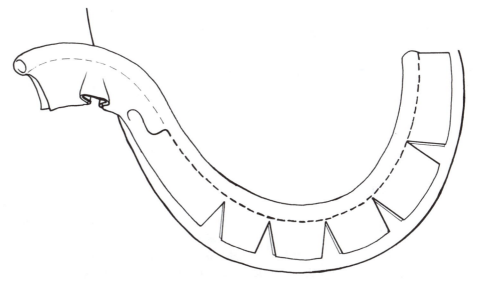

Figure 4-11 Cording clipped and stitched to a curved edge

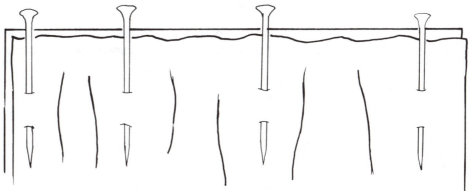

Figure 4-12 Easing a longer edge into a shorter one

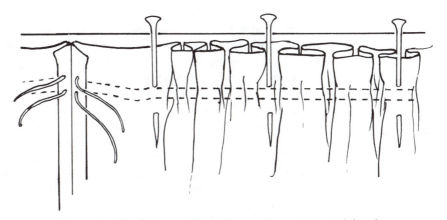

Figure 4-13 Gathers pinned for sewing onto a straight piece

Seams with gathers occur when one or both sides of the seam are gathered before the seam is stitched. There are numerous ways to create gathers in fabric. Zig-zagging over a heavy thread and then securing one end while you pull up the other is a very simple and effective method. Some machines have a ruffler attachment or may be adjusted by tightening the tension button to automatically create a gathering stitch. Additional methods of gathering are discussed in Chapter 8.

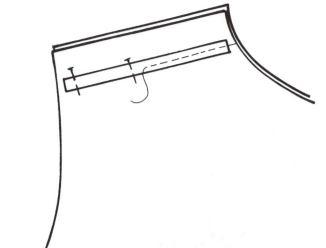

Figure 4–14 Seam reinforced with seam tape or twill tape

When attaching a gathered edge to a flat edge adjust the fullness of the gathers as desired, then pin the pieces together so that the raw edges match up. Check to make sure the fabric above and below the gathering line has not been caught up into the stitch line. Stitch the seam in place, and remove any visible gathering stitches.

When both edges are gathered it is necessary to reinforce the seam with seam binding or twill tape (see Taped seams and Figure 4–14).

Taped seams are seams that require extra strength or stability to keep from stretching. For these seams a narrow piece of twill tape is actually sewn into the seam. This technique is used for loosely woven and stretchy fabrics such as knits, and may also be employed wherever the seam is likely to be subject to much stress, or where at least one edge of the seam has been eased or gathered.

Shaping, Finishing, and Decorative Techniques

Darts are a basic structural element of garment shaping. To make a dart, fold the fabric along a center line, forming a triangle, then stitch from the wide end to the point. Darts are pressed toward the center of a garment, or cut along the fold line and pressed open. Contour darts, which taper to points in two directions, are clipped at the widest point to the seam line, then pressed.

Zig-zag stitching has numerous uses. By varying stitch length and zig-zag width the costumer expands the structural and decorative possibilities. Narrow zig-zag stitching may be used to seam stretchy knits, since it will not easily break when pulled. Zig-zag stitching is frequently used to quickly finish a raw edge of fabric to keep it from raveling, or to finish seam edges. Topstitching and appliqué are other uses of zig-zag stitches. Most decorative stitching possibilities on machines are based on the sewing machine's ability to go sideways as well as forward and backward.

Machine blind hems can be performed by most zig-zag sewing machines. The process is described in the next chapter.

Machine buttonhole capabilities vary with specific machines. Any machine that can do a zig-zag stitch is capable of making a buttonhole. Some machines have separate attachments for making buttonholes. More information on machine buttonholes can be found in the next chapter.

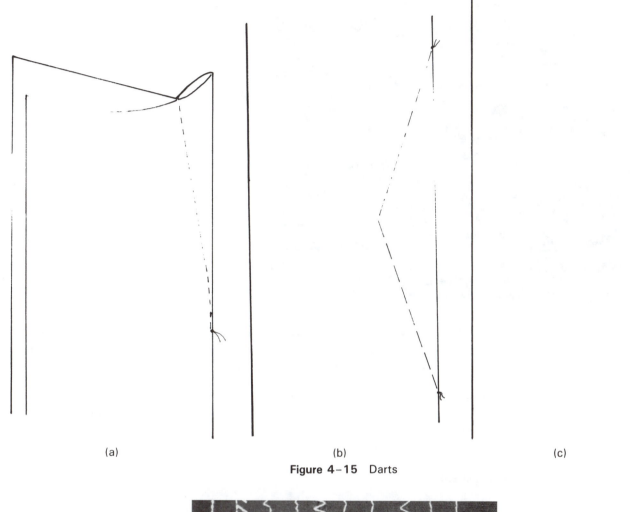

(a)   (b)   (c)

Figure 4–15   Darts

Figure 4–16   Functional machine stitches

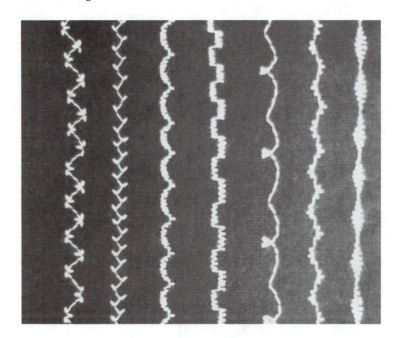

Figure 4-17 Decorative machine stitches

Sewing buttons, snaps, and hooks and eyes onto fabric can be done by machine, using the zig-zag stitch when the feed dogs are lowered. A description of this process will be found in the next chapter.

Decorative stitching is usually too small to be seen very successfully from the audience. Some of the thicker stitches that rely on satin stitching produce a nice decorative edging that is visible if you use a contrasting thread.

HAND-STITCHING TECHNIQUES

Certain procedures must be done by hand, and many volunteers enjoy hand work and can do it very quickly. The following is a compilation of basic hand-stitching techniques commonly used in costume construction.

Hem Stitches

Slant hem stitch—a quick but not particularly durable stitch. This stitch is easy to remove for later adjustment to the hem. Bring thread through hem edge. Move from right to left catching a tiny bit of the garment fabric, then returning the needle up through the hem edge again. Make stitches 1/4" to 1/2" apart (Figure 4-18).

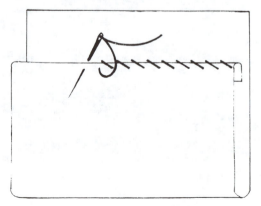

Figure 4-18 Slant hem stitch

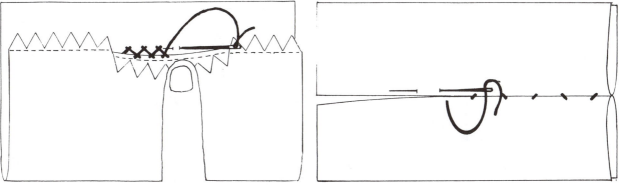

Figure 4–19 Catchstitch   **Figure 4–20** Slipstitch

Catchstitch—durable hem stitch for use on a pinked hem edge. Working from left to right, bring needle and thread up through hem edge. Catch a tiny bit of the garment fabric above the hem edge with needle passing from right to left. Move 1/4″ to 1/2″ to the right and take a tiny stitch in the hem fabric with needle passing again from right to left. Continue this pattern of tiny crossed stitches (Figure 4–19).

Slipstitch—nearly invisible stitch used in hemming and appliqué. This stitch is durable since very little thread is exposed. Working from right to left, bring needle and thread up through the hem edge. Take a tiny stitch in the garment fabric directly above the stitch in the hem edge. Insert the needle back into the hem fold directly below the stitch and run the needle and thread within the fold for 1/4″ to 1/2″. Repeat this process (Figure 4–20).

Tailoring and Millinery Stitches

In the processes of tailoring and millinery, certain hand stitches produce results that are not easily imitated by machine stitching.

Hand basting is at times necessary or preferable to machine basting. Seams in garments that tend to stretch or move during stitching may be held firmly in place by hand basting. It is also useful to hand baste portions of hats or boots in place for fittings. A basting stitch is a long running stitch that is easy to put in and easy to remove when the final stitching or gluing is done (Figure 4–21).

Pad stitching is a technique used to shape and mold under collars and lapels. The stitch is accomplished by making a small horizontal stitch through the fabric, then repeating the stitch directly below the first. The shape may be

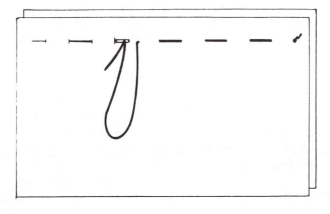

Figure 4–21 Hand-basting

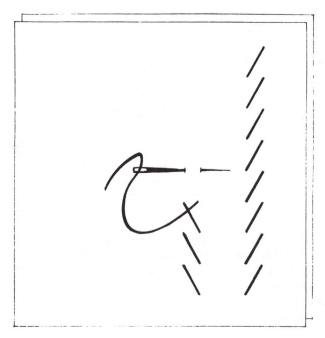

Figure 4-22 Pad stitch

developed by holding the collar or lapel over the finger or knee while stitching (Figure 4-22).

Stab stitching is necessary when the layers of a garment are too thick for the sewer to bring the needle in and out of the fabric in one operation. The stitch is accomplished by inserting the needle through the garment and pulling it through to the other side, then reinserting it on the second side and pulling it through the first. This stitch can be made nearly invisible on the right side of the fabric if you insert the needle at an angle from the wrong side and reinsert it in nearly the same place, but at an opposing angle.

CLIPPING, TRIMMING, AND GRADING

Clipping is necessary whenever you are using curved seams. If the curve is concave, you will need to notch the seam in order for it to lie flat. If it is convex, clipping is enough (Figure 4-24).

Trimming and clipping may be necessary when installing facings, or any time you stitch a seam and then fold the fabric back along the seam line. First trim the seam allowance to 3/8", then clip to the seam line.

Grading is used whenever the fabrics making up the seam are heavy. To do this, trim each layer at a different distance from the seam line. If you are using an interfacing, trim it very close to the seam line; the next layer will be trimmed to about 1/4", and the last to about 3/8". Clip all layers before pressing if you are working with a curved seam.

PRESSING

Pressing is critical in costume construction. Each seam and dart should be pressed before another seam is sewn across it.

Use the pressing rolls and hams to press open clipped or notched curved seams. Darts are generally pressed down and toward the center of a garment. Gathers are generally pressed away from the gathered section, and facing seams are pressed open and then folded back when the final seam line is pressed.

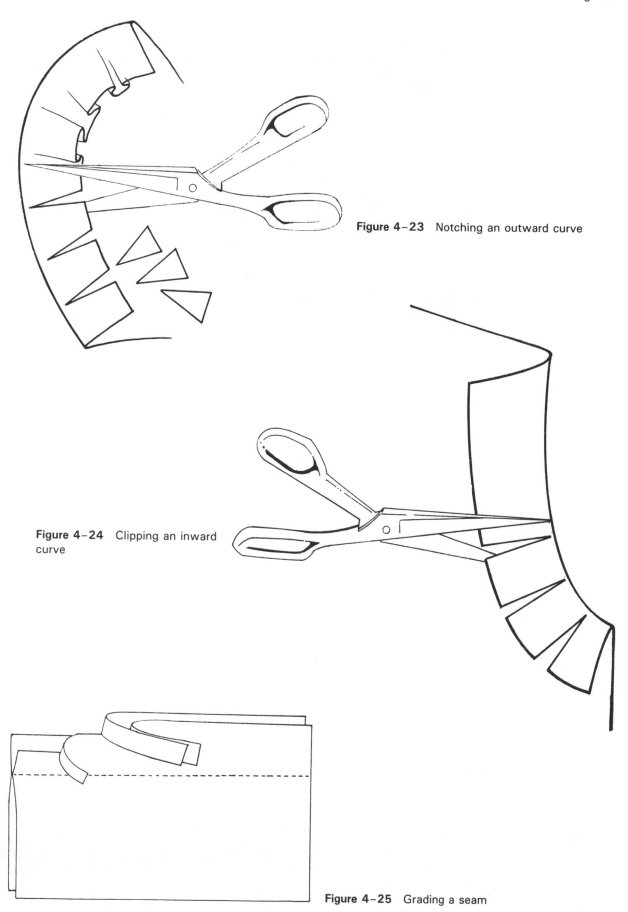

Figure 4–23 Notching an outward curve

Figure 4–24 Clipping an inward curve

Figure 4–25 Grading a seam

EXERCISES

1. Practice the following stitches (if applicable) on your sewing machine by working with the instruction manual.
   (a) Straight stitches
   (b) Basting stitches
   (c) Zig-zag stitches
   (d) Blind hem
   (e) Buttonhole
   (f) Decorative stitches

2. Create the following seams. Then clip and press them.
   (a) Straight seam with 5/8″ seam allowance
   (b) Straight seam with 2″ seam allowance
   (c) Curved seam
   (d) Dissimilar curved seam
   (e) Inner and outer corner seams
   (f) Flat-felled seam
   (g) French seam

3. Execute the following hand-sewing techniques:
   (a) Slant stitch
   (b) Catchstitch
   (c) Slipstitch
   (d) Pad stitch

Creating a Garment

By now you should be familiar with the tools, materials, and processes involved in costume construction. Now it is time to learn the steps in creating the basic costume.

We will assume that you have a well-organized space in which to work and the sewing equipment you will need. You will have the pattern developed and the fabric prepared for cutting. You understand the basic stitches by machine and by hand. It is time to pick up a pair of scissors and commit yourself to the fabric before you, to begin to cut and construct a garment.

Layout and cutting is one of the most frightening steps for beginning costumers. It is easy to look at a paper pattern and decide that it looks fine, but quite a different matter to believe in it enough to transfer it to an unblemished and costly piece of fabric. Perhaps it will help if we reemphasize one of the significant differences between costuming and the construction of street wear. The fact is that almost any mistake you may make in the initial cutting and stitching for a costume can probably be corrected. With a costume it is fairly easy to add a gusset, or an extra panel, or to cover an error with a patch or piece of trim. This is not true with street wear, since others will see your garment at a closer range.

This is not to suggest that layout and cutting are not important. Almost no aspect of the costume construction process will affect the final appearance of the costume in such a significant way. The way a costume hangs and moves on stage is determined by the cut. Distance will likely emphasize rather than diminish mistakes in cutting.

On the other hand, it is not wise to have an unnatural fear of these processes. All cutters have made mistakes and profited by them. Sometimes wonderful discoveries are born from these mistakes, but more often than not, the mistake will be seen as a mistake to be corrected. Fortunately costumers are in a good position to learn from mistakes and to correct them with time and patience.

LAYOUT AND CUTTING

Although certain shortcuts may be made in costume processes, there are no shortcuts for layout and cutting. One must pay close attention to the grain of fabric, seam allowances, and the specific requirements of a piece of fabric (stripes, plaids, nap).

The following is a general method for typical layout and cutting of each costume. Naturally, each costume has unique features, just as each costume shop varies slightly in specific procedures.

Making a Mock-Up

Theatre costumes are often flat-lined or underlined with muslin for added durability. This means that each pattern piece is cut from both muslin and the outer fabric. These pieces are sewn together flat and treated as one before any construction begins. If the costume you are constructing is to be underlined, or if you are uncertain about the pattern you are using, a muslin mock-up of the garment should be constructed and fitted to the actor before the actual fabric is cut. After the muslin mock-up is corrected, it can be used for both the pattern and the underlining for the final costume.

Straight of Grain

Straight of grain refers to the direction of the warp threads on a piece of fabric. Commercial patterns clearly indicate placement of each piece in regard to

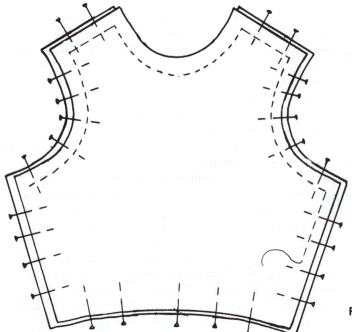

Figure 5–1 Flat lining or underlining

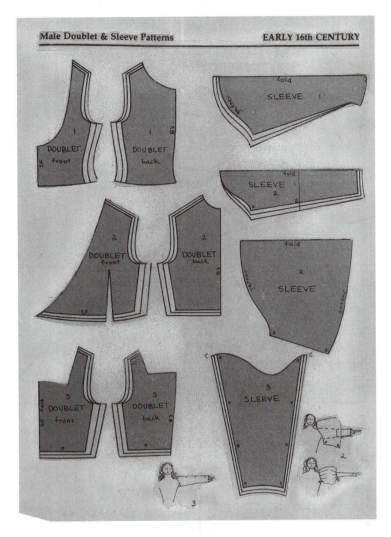

Figure 5-2 Layout of patterns in a book

straight of grain with a long arrow. It is just as important to think about straight of grain for historical patterns as for commercial patterns intended for street wear.

With patterns found in historical pattern books, the straight of grain is usually indicated by the placement of pattern pieces on the book page. The edges of the page correspond to straight of grain, and the way the pattern is laid out on the page is usually an indication of the way it should be laid out on fabric.

Authentic layout diagrams from early sources may occasionally surprise you because of the odd placement of pattern pieces. Garments were sometimes cut compromising the logical straight of grain in order to keep from wasting fabric. Cutting in this way may be authentic, but it is unlikely that your audience will appreciate the research. More likely the effect will be distracting. Since you may not always have your book or other pattern source to refer to when cutting the fabric, it is wise to mark straight of grain on each pattern piece as it is being developed.

Preparing the Fabric

Chapter 9 talks about ways of changing and manipulating fabric to closely resemble the designer's sketch. Frequently this type of manipulation (dyeing, aging, decorating, etc.) will take place before the garment is cut.

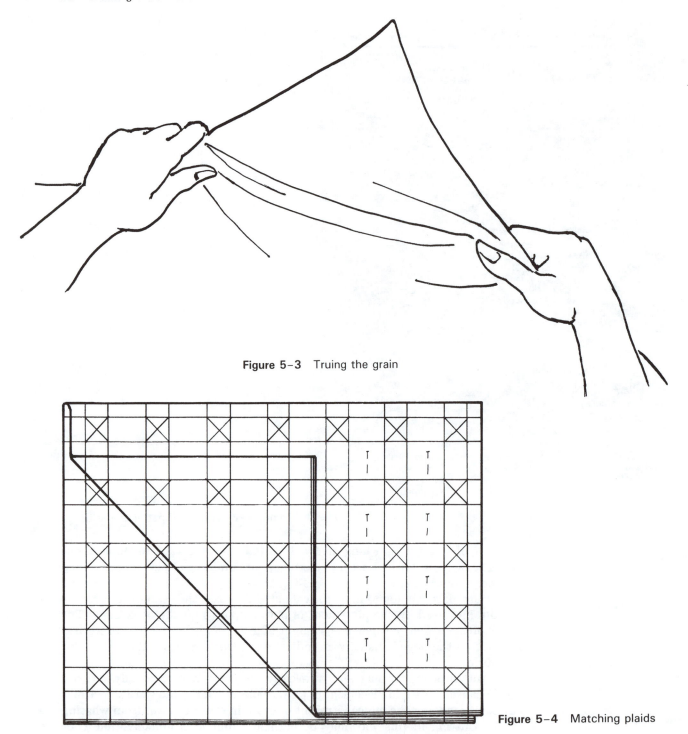

Figure 5-3 Truing the grain

Figure 5-4 Matching plaids

If a fabric is machine washable, and you plan to wash the costume eventually, or if the fabric is filled with a sizing or finish you wish to soften, prewash the fabric, dry it, and press it before you cut.

Many pattern pieces may be cut with the fabric folded selvage to selvage, though very wide pieces and bias-cut pieces will need the full width of the fabric.

In order to fold a piece of fabric evenly the ends of the piece should be cut along the cross grain. If a fabric is tightly woven you may be able to tear a straight line on the cross grain. With loosely woven fabrics pulling a thread may be the best way to determine the cross grain line.

The next step is to correct, if possible, any misalignment that may have occurred during the manufacturing process. Fabrics that have permanent-press or water-repellent finishes will not be correctable if they are off-grain. Otherwise, fold the fabric lengthwise, bringing the selvage edges together. If the ends do not line up the fabric will need to be realigned. With the fabric damp, stretch it gently on the bias to correct the problem.

If the fabric has a pattern, stripe, or plaid to be matched, fold the fabric carefully so that the pattern is lined up on both sides. If the fabric has a nap, be sure to line up the pattern pieces in one direction only.

Seam Allowances

Theatre costumes are usually constructed with larger seam allowances than the standard 5/8″ allowance found in most commercial patterns. This way a costume may be modified later to fit someone else. Different shops use different standard seam allowances, but generally at least 1″ is allowed at side, front, back, waist, and shoulder seams. Curved seams, such as necklines and arm-scyes, are generally no more than 1/2″ to 3/4″.

Laying Out the Pattern Pieces

The specific efficient layout of the pattern will be determined by the costume being used. Generally it is a good idea to place the large pieces first (skirts, breeches, capes) and then try to fit smaller pieces into the remaining spaces.

Pattern pieces are arranged on the fabric to accommodate seam allowance and appropriate straight of grain and specific fabric requirements.

Pin each pattern piece in place when you are sure the layout is the way you want it. Mark seam allowances with tailor's chalk to indicate the cutting lines.

Cutting and Marking

Cut through both layers of fabric along seam allowance lines.

Mark with a tracing wheel, tailor's chalk, or tailor tacks any necessary darts, seam lines, or other construction markings before you remove the pattern.

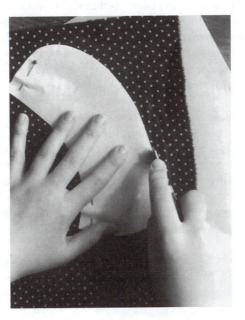

Figure 5-5 Tracing wheel marking

Stitching

Stitch the garment together along seam lines. Do not set in sleeves yet or add waistbands, collars, knee bands, closures, or hems. All major construction seams may be put in with a machine basting stitch if you are unsure of the pattern or size of the actor.

FITTINGS

Even with the best set of measurements and perfectly drafted or altered patterns, at least two fittings are necessary to insure proper fit of the costume. The first fitting will occur after the major seams of the garment have been stitched or basted in place, but before collar, sleeves, waistbands, or peplums have been added. The next fitting will occur when the costume is totally put together from the markings of the first fitting. At this point the closing plackets may be marked as well as the hemlines for sleeve, skirt, trousers, and waists.

The First Fitting

Upper-body garments.   Start first with the upper-body portion of the costume. Have the actor put the costume on right side out. Pin along the marked closing line if possible. Otherwise pin on a line parallel to that line.

Check the neck and armhole curve for the fit. If the seam allowance is binding (as it will with a high-neck or small-armscye garment), clip the seam allowance enough to release the pulling. Do not clip into the body of the garment, but only enough to correct the smooth fit of the pattern. If the neckline or armscye needs to be enlarged, you may clip a bit beyond the seam line to create a new seam line.

Check the placement of seams while fitting the garment. Make sure that whatever is done to one side of the garment is also done symmetrically to the other. Alter seams and darts with regard to the silhouette of the costume and the function of that seam or dart. Seams may be let out or taken in unevenly; that is, more seam allowance may be removed from the back side or shoulder seam, for example, than from the front. Any adjustment you wish to make is acceptable so long as the fit is corrected and the silhouette remains consistent.

After the upper-body garment has been fitted, mark the location of the neckline, waistline, armscye, and closing line with tailor's chalk. It is also a good idea to make chalk marks, notches, or clips in fabric to indicate the matching of one piece to another. This is particularly important with curved seams or seams that require easing.

Sleeves.   Slip a sleeve onto the arm while the upper-body garment is still in place, and pin it in place at the shoulder seam, underarm seam, and front and back armscye. Make sure the arm movement will not be restricted by the sleeve, and that the dart or curve for the elbow is located in the right spot on a tight-fitting sleeve. Carefully mark the sleeve and armhole with chalk or clip into the fabric to indicate the accurate positioning of the sleeve cap. You may mark the length of the sleeve at this time, or the placement of cuff or trim, or wait until after the sleeve has been set in for these details.

Skirts.   Skirts may be pinned to a waistband or bodice for the first fitting to check fullness and to distribute gathers, pleats, or ease, to hang properly. Adjusting the pleats and gathers in a skirt might well be done on a fitting form,

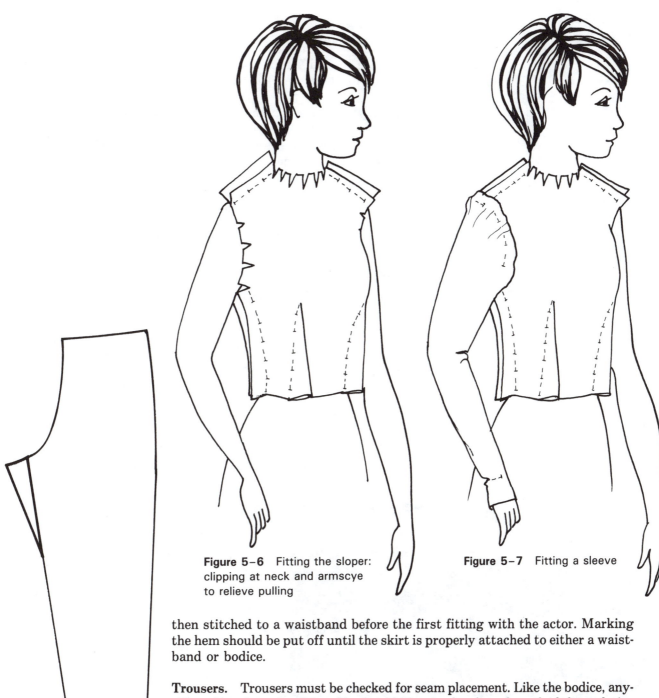

Figure 5–6 Fitting the sloper: clipping at neck and armscye to relieve pulling

Figure 5–7 Fitting a sleeve

Figure 5–8 Adding a gusset to the inseam

then stitched to a waistband before the first fitting with the actor. Marking the hem should be put off until the skirt is properly attached to either a waistband or bodice.

Trousers. Trousers must be checked for seam placement. Like the bodice, anything altered on the right side should likewise be altered on the left, and vice versa. A crotch seam that is too low may be raised by raising the entire waist seam on the trousers. A crotch seam that is too high usually is not correctable unless the legs of the trousers are very full, since lowering the crotch seam may make the pant leg smaller through the thigh. If this happens, you may be able to solve the problem by adding a gusset to the inseam.

Collars, cuffs, knee bands, belts, and peplums. These items and all other costume pieces may be fitted separately at this time and carefully marked for placement on the costume. It is a good idea to supplement markings with written notes.

Evening Up the Pattern

After the garments have been fitted, but before they are removed, make sure that all pin positions are marked. The pieces of the pattern should then be taken apart and the alterations clearly marked with the corrected continuous pattern lines.

At this point you will correct any asymmetrical or uneven fitting. Although most bodies are not perfectly symmetrical, it is desirable to correct human flaws and make the costumes as even as possible. Of course if the actor is supposed to be deformed, you may ignore these directions.

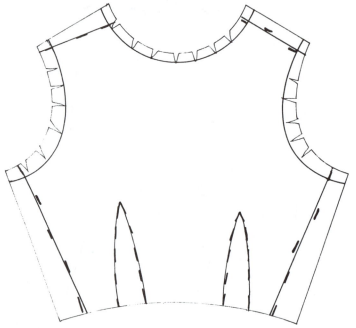

Figure 5-9 Alterations marked on the fitted pattern from the pin markings

Figure 5-10 Evening up a pattern after first fitting

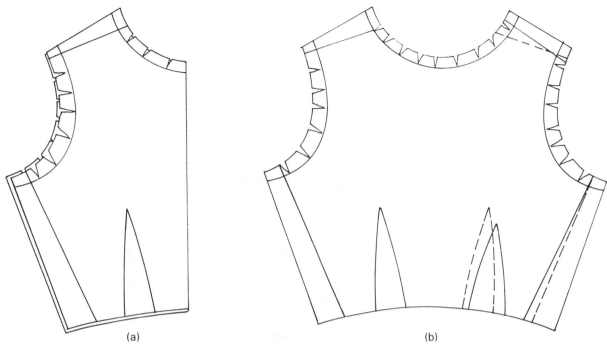

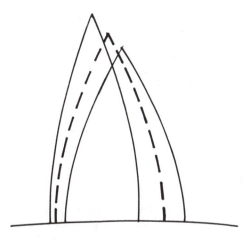

Figure 5–11 (a–b)   Fitting marks transferred from one side of the pattern to the other.

Figure 5–12   Creating a dart halfway between the right and left side markings

Pattern pieces may be evened up by transferring the alteration marks from one side of the pattern to the other. If the alteration lines fall on top of each other, you have managed to fit the costume very evenly. If they do not, simply draw a line halfway between the two sets of marks and consider this line to be the final seam line. This final seam line may then be transferred back to the original pattern piece with a different marking color. (It is a good idea to keep all of your final markings in a specific color to avoid the confusion of multiple lines.)

Necklines, waistlines, closing lines, and darts can all be evened up in this fashion, and the resulting garment should fit well and beautifully.

The garment should then be reassembled to the new markings. Sleeves, collars, peplums, waistbands, and so on will be added at this time based on placement markings from the first fitting.

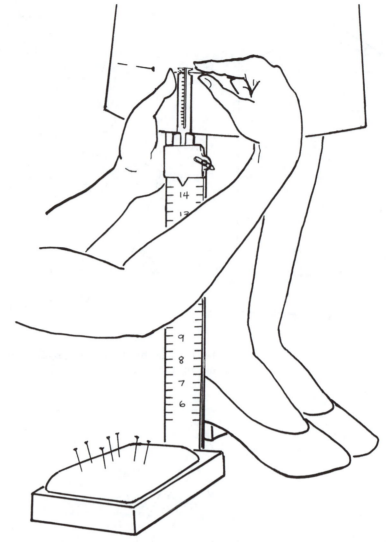

Figure 5-13 Marking a hem

The Second Fitting

If the garment fits correctly after having been pinned along the closure line, the hem lines may be marked. For this process you may use a hem marker or yardstick for skirts and gowns to make sure that the distance from the floor is constant. Make sure that the actor is wearing the shoes that will be worn in the production, and that he or she stands still with arms comfortably at the sides of the body while you are marking the hem.

If the garment does not fit correctly, repeat the processes for the first fitting by letting out or taking in seam lines. You will need a seam ripper for this. If the first fitting was done properly, however, there should be very few problems with the second fitting.

FINISHINGS

Hemming, facing, and adding closures are the last steps in finishing a sewn costume. These occur after the final fitting and may or may not precede trimming of the costume.

Facings

Facings are used to finish the raw edges of necklines, armholes, and any decorative curved area of a costume where hemming would be difficult. A facing may be a separate pattern piece that follows the same edge curve as the original garment, or simply a narrow bias strip of fabric. Sometimes facings are cut as extensions of the original garment and then folded back.

Shaped facings. Shaped facings should be cut with the original garment to follow the same pattern lines. Finish the outer edge of the facing with a small roll hem or zig-zag edge to prevent fraying. Place the facing on top of the gar-

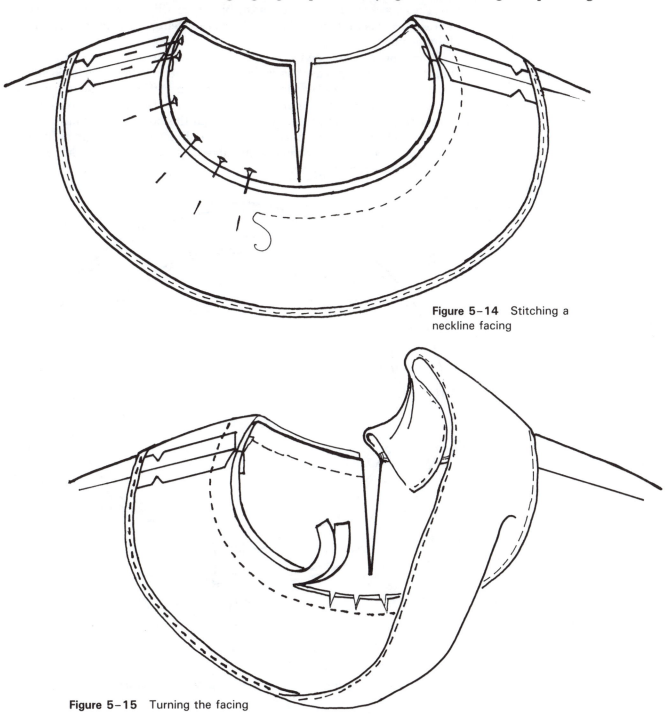

Figure 5–14 Stitching a neckline facing

Figure 5–15 Turning the facing

ment edge with right sides together; match seams and curves exactly. Stitch the seam line, then trim or grade and clip the curve and any corners. Press the seam open, then toward the facing. Stitch through the facing and seam allowance to prevent the facing from rolling out. Turn facing to the inside and press.

Bias tape. Bias tape may be used in much the same way as the shaped facings. Bias strips of the fabric may be used in place of commercial bias binding. Using a narrow strip (1/2″ folded commercial bias tape), press one folded edge flat. Pin the bias tape along the raw edge of the garment to be finished so that the original fold line of the bias tape lies over the final seam line. Stitch the seam. Grade the excess seam allowance to the bias edge. Clip the curves and corners and press the bias tape to the inside. Stitch the facing to the garment by hand or by machine.

Bias tape may also be used to encase and add a decorative border to an unfinished edge. In this case the seam allowance of the edge to be faced should be trimmed away before the bias tape is sewn on. After the edge is trimmed, the bias tape is pressed so that one fold is flat. Pin the flattened edge of the bias tape to the raw edge of the garment so that the two raw edges meet. Stitch the seam in place along the bias tape fold line. Press the bias tape away from the seam line; then fold it around the raw edges to encase them. Stitch the folded edge of the bias tape in place.

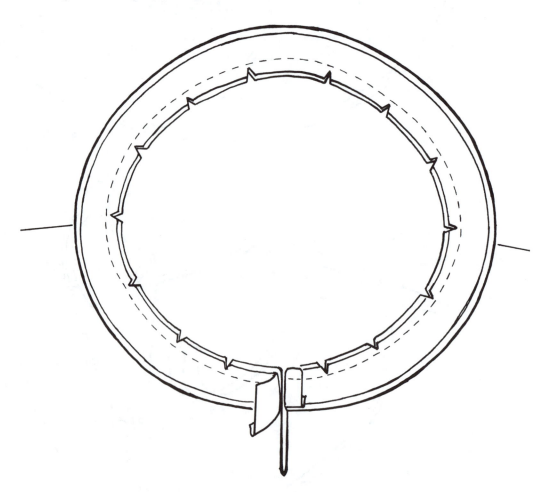

Figure 5-16 Stitching bias tape as a facing

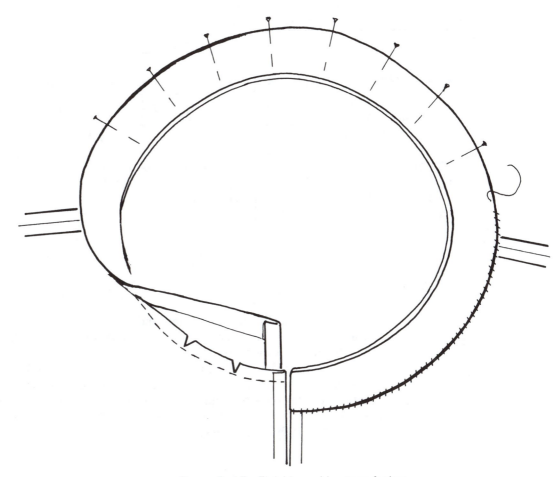

Figure 5-17 Finishing a bias tape facing

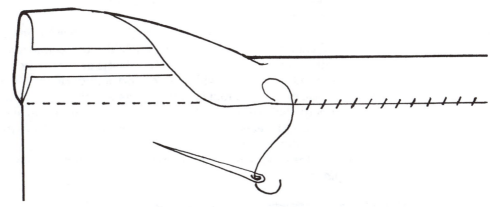

Figure 5-18 Bias tape used to encase a raw edge

Cording. This may be used to finish an edge as well as to emphasize a seam. Cording gives a subtle decorative edge to necklines, waistlines, and armscyes. Pin the cording on the right side of the costume, matching the seam line with the stitch line of the cording. Sew the cording to the garment. Trim and clip all raw edges except the outermost cording allowance. Press the allowance to the inside and stitch through the cording allowance to encase the raw edges.

You may wish to combine a facing or bias tape with the corded edge for a more durable finish.

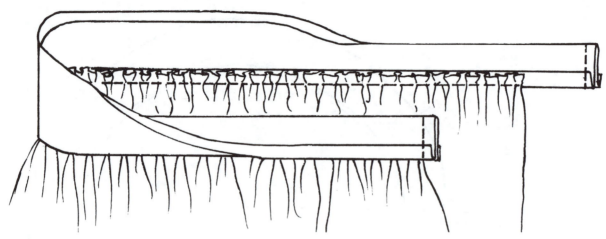

Figure 5-19 Application of a waistband

Waistbands and Cuff Bands

Interfacing is usually added to waistbands and cuffs, especially if the garment fabric is very light or flimsy. With right sides together pin the waistband to the garment, making sure that center-fronts match. Adjust gathers, pleats, or ease to correct the fit. Stitch along the seamline. Trim and press seam allowances toward the band. Finish the other long edge of the band, then fold the band right sides together and stitch the ends together. Trim the ends of the band then turn to the inside and press the fold and ends. Hand- or machine-stitch the inner band in place.

Casings

A casing is used to enclose an elastic or drawstring. These are commonly found at neck edges, waistlines, sleeves, and knees. Mob caps and drawstring pouches also employ casings.

Fold-down casings are commonly used when the fabric raw edge is straight and enough seam allowance is available to accommodate the elastic or cord width. Determine the width of the elastic or cord to be used. Waistline elastic is usually 3/4" to 1" wide for comfort and durability. Finish the raw edge of the garment, then fold it over to form a casing slightly larger than the elastic or cord that will be used. Stitch the casing in place, leaving a small opening to insert the elastic or cord. For a crisper finish topstitch the upper edge of the casing as well.

Insert elastic or cord by pulling it through the casing with a large safety pin. Stitch elastic in place at the proper length.

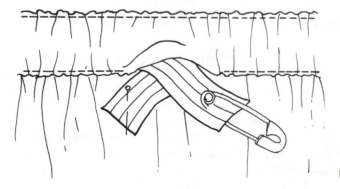

Figure 5-20 A fold-down casing

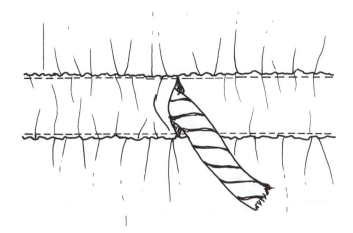

Figure 5-21 An applied casing

Applied Casings

Applied casings are appropriate when the casing does not come at an edge of the costume. Casings may be made from bias strips of the garment fabric or commercial bias tape. Pin the folded under edges of the bias tape in place on the costume. Stitch both edges of the tape close to the folds, leaving a small opening on one side. Insert the elastic or cord and adjust the size to fit.

Plackets

Openings that must be created where seams don't exist can be structured with a simple placket. Such plackets are frequently seen at necklines, skirt openings, and cuffs of sleeves.

Cut a piece of the costume fabric twice the length of the cut opening and twice the width plus 3/8″ seam allowance of the desired finished placket. Placing right sides together, pin the placket piece along the opening in the garment opened to a straight line.

Stitch a 3/8″ seam through the placket and cut edge, bringing the end of the cut close to the stitching.

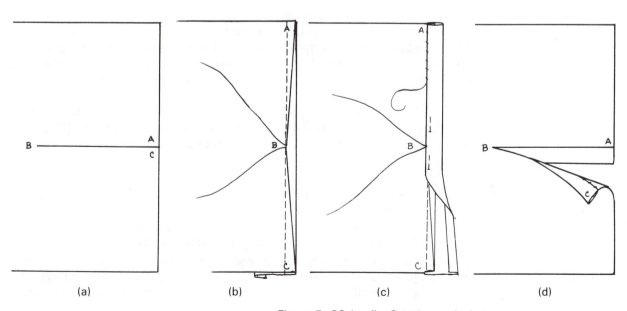

(a)   (b)   (c)   (d)

Figure 5-22 (a-d) Creating a placket

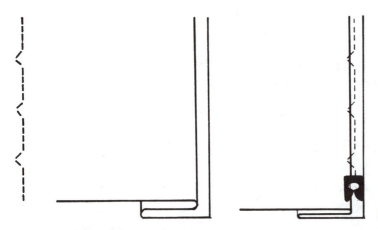

Figure 5-23 Machine hemming

Press the seam allowances toward the placket piece. Finish the other side of the placket and fold the placket in half lengthwise so that the opposite edge covers the original seam line. Topstitch through all layers. Press the placket, then fold it to the inside of the garment.

Hemming

Facing and hem edges may be stitched in place by using one of the hand hemming stitches described in Chapter 4 or by machine hemming or topstitching.

Machine blind hems are stitches which go straight for about five stitches, then perform a single zig-zag before returning to five more straight stitches. Most zig-zag sewing machines have blind-hem capabilities. This stitch is especially useful for putting in quick and relatively invisible hems. The hem edge is finished, then pinned, to allow about 1/4" hem allowance to be exposed. The garment is placed under a special presser foot that allows the sewing machine to sew straight on the hem allowance, then zig-zag over to catch a tiny bit of the body of the garment (Figure 5-23).

Closures

For historical garments it is often desirable to imitate the appropriate type of closure if at all possible. Lacings, buttons, brooches, and hooks and eyes have long been used as garment fasteners. Zippers and velcro are products of the 20th century. If these fasteners are used in period garments they should be hidden or disguised in order to maintain the proper illusion.

Hook and Eye Tape. Hook and eye tape is a good and very durable standard fastener for period costumes. It provides a flat, very strong closure. It is easy to install and after a bit of practice can be as easy to work with as a zipper.

1. Fold back both sides of the garment along the closing edge and press in place.
2. Pin the hook tape along the folded edge on the left side of the costume so that the tape runs just inside the fold.
3. Line up the eye tape on the right side of the opening so that the eyes just reach beyond the fold. Make sure that the hooks and eyes are properly aligned by hooking the two sides of the tape together before you stitch.

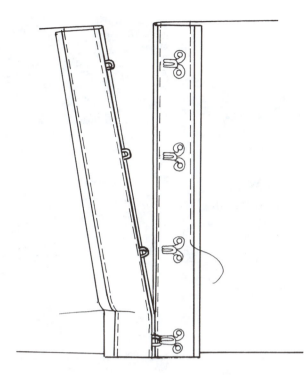

Figure 5-24 Hook and eye tape installation

4. Using a zipper foot, stitch the tape on both edges through the garment.
5. If your sewing machine is able to sew over pins, it should be possible for you to sew directly over the eyes if you are careful. Otherwise stitch around each eye as you go.

Zippers. Zippers are useful in modern-day garments and in costumes that require a very quick change. The lapped zipper placket described below looks most like the placket formed with hook and eye tape and is the least obvious if it becomes necessary to use a zipper in a period costume. (Avoid using zippers in period costumes if at all possible.)

1. Baste the seam where the zipper will be installed and stitch with a regular construction stitch the seam from that point on.
2. Press the seam open and extend the right-hand seam allowance away from the seam.
3. Place the zipper face down on the right-hand seam allowance so that the teeth of the zipper are arranged directly above the seam in the costume.
4. Stitch the zipper to the costume through the right-hand seam allowance using the zipper foot attachment.
5. Turn the zipper face up to create a fold in the right-hand seam allowance. Bring the fold up to the outer edge of the zipper teeth and press or pin in place.
6. Stitch along the fold through the seam allowance and zipper.
7. Turn the costume to the outside and flatten the fabric and seam over the zipper below.
8. Pin or baste the zipper to the costume at about 1/2″ from the seam line.
9. Topstitch the zipper in place using the zipper foot; then remove the basting threads.

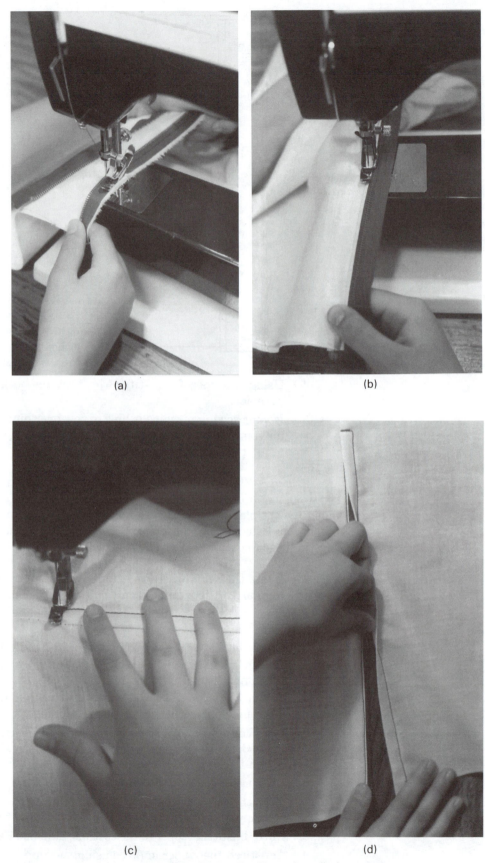

(a)

(b)

(c)

(d)

Figure 5-25 (a-d) Zipper installation

Velcro. This tape consists of tiny nylon hooks on one side which fasten to tiny loops on the other. When closed this type of fastening is a bit bulky. It is particularly useful for quick changes or in the construction of breakaway costumes, particularly if you don't object to the characteristic sound it makes when being ripped open.

1. This type of closure requires enough overlap in the seam to accommodate the width of the tape.
2. Press under the outer edges of the closing, allowing half the width of the tape beyond the closing mark.
3. Stitch the hook side of the tape to the underlap along both edges of the tape. Stitch the loop side of the tape to the overlap along both sides.

Hooks and Eyes. Hooks and eyes are useful as strong single-point fasteners. There are several types of hooks and eyes and a variety of sizes. They are all attached in much the same way.

1. The hook is sewn on the inside of the garment by sewing around each loop, then securing the end of the hook in place.
2. The eye comes in two different styles depending on the specific need of the costume. If the closure overlaps, the bar eye may be used. If the two edges merely butt together, the loop eye should be used.
3. An eye should be lined up by first looping it into the hook, then carefully placing the hook and eye pair in place on the garment.
4. The eye is sewn carefully around each loop to the underlap of the garment or, if the edges butt together, simply to the other edge of the garment.

Snaps. Snaps are not as strong as hooks and eyes. Snaps are comprised of two sections, one with a "ball" and one with a "socket." The socket section is sewn to the underlap through each hole, and the ball section is lined up and likewise sewn to the overlap.

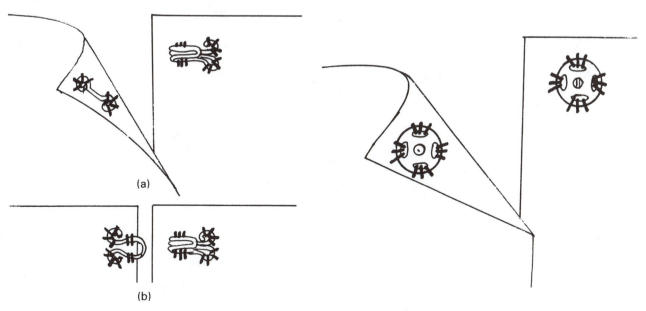

(a)

(b)

Figure 5-26 Sewing a hook and eye

Figure 5-27 Sewing a snap

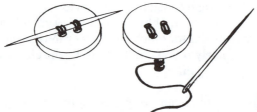

Figure 5–28 Creating a shank for a button

Buttons. Nearly everyone has sewn a button on at one time or another by sewing through the holes in the button to the garment itself. For costuming the thread used is often a heavy-duty thread.

1. Shanks may be created for buttons that must go through very thick fabric by sewing the button to the costume with a toothpick laid on top of the button.
2. Remove the toothpick, lift the button away from the garment, and wind the thread around the stitches to create a thread shank.

Sewing Buttons and Hooks and Eyes by Machine: The zig-zag stitch is used to sew buttons and hooks and eyes to costumes by dropping the feed dogs so the fabric will not move forward during the stitching process. The width of the zig-zag is determined by the specific fastener being applied. Simply place the button, snap, hook, or eye under the foot, then stitch in place to lock the thread. Set the zig-zag to the proper width, then sew back and forth six or seven times. Stitch in place again to finish the process.

Buttonholes: Buttonholes may be made by machine or by hand. Each sewing machine has its own buttonhole procedure. Some have separate attachments

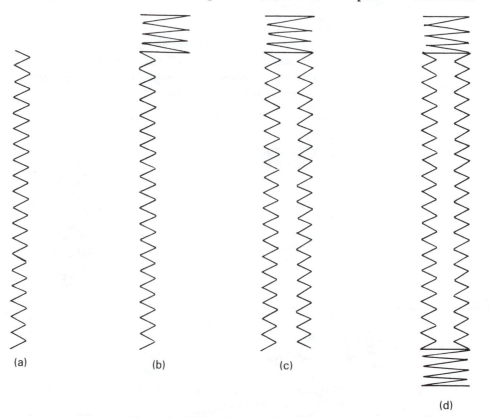

(a)   (b)   (c)   (d)

Figure 5–29 (a–d) Making a buttonhole

for buttonhole making. Basically any zig-zag machine can make buttonholes by running a narrow zig-zag along the line of the buttonhole, running a wide zig-zag stitch in place to secure the end of the hole, running a narrow zig-zag down the other side of the buttonhole, and running a similar wide zig-zag stitch in place at the other end. To do this easily your machine should have a variable zig-zag width and be able to change needle position.

The instruction book for your sewing machine should give more specific instructions for the intended system for perfect buttonholes on that particular machine.

To determine the proper length of the buttonhole, measure the diameter of the button and add to that the measurement of the thickness of the button. If your button is 3/4″ across and 1/4″ thick, the buttonhole should measure 1″.

Eyelets and Grommets and Lacings. Eyelets are small finished holes which may be made by hand or machine, or finished with tiny metal shanks. Grommets are large metal reinforcements for larger holes, and are often constructed in two pieces rather than one. Eyelets and grommets are used when one part of a costume is to be tied to another, as in the case of a Renaissance sleeve to a doublet, or when a costume is to be laced together through a series of openings. Grommets are frequently used in costume accessories such as boots, corsets, belts, and armor.

1. A grommet placket must be reinforced with belting or interfacing, depending on how tightly the costume will be laced. Mark the placement of the grommets so that they line up exactly on both sides of the garment.

2. Punch or clip a hole at each marking somewhat smaller than the grommet opening. If you do not have a punch, an easy way to cut a hole is to fold the fabric in quarters, then clip a tiny bit of the corner. Large grommets come with a tool for punching the proper-size hole.

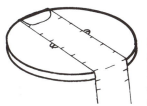

Figure 5-30
Measuring a button to determine the length of a buttonhole

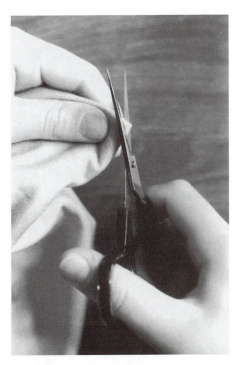

Figure 5-31 Cutting the grommet hole

3. Place the grommet side with the longer shank on the outside of the costume; then slip the smaller piece over the shank from the other side.

4. Using a hammer and the tools provided with the grommets, set the grommet in place by pounding the larger section to create a lip, which will hold the two sections of the grommet together.

EXERCISES

1. Make a sloper in muslin from the commercial pattern that most nearly fits your measurements. Cut, stitch, fit, even, and finish the sloper.
2. Practice installing the following closures:
   (a) hook and eye tape
   (b) zipper
   (c) grommet
   (d) shank button and buttonhole
   (e) snap
   (f) hook and eye

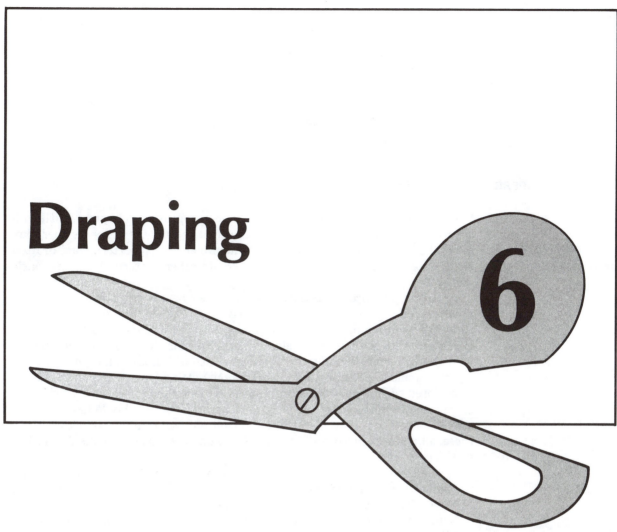

Draping

Draping is a truly expressive and creative method of pattern making. With this method the designer works in three dimensions with the help of a fitting form or the human body. Draping is like sculpture in that the draper builds a form in fabric, sees the results immediately, and can correct, change, and recreate right then and there.

Although many drapers use the actual costume fabric during the draping process, beginning drapers should probably experiment with an inexpensive substitute fabric similar in drape and weight to the fabric to be used in the final costume.

Principles of draping may be applied to all historical, ethnic, and fantastic garments. It is a good idea to understand the development of historical pattern and to look at illustrations of cutting diagrams or pattern shapes for a given period in order to understand the silhouette of an era and how it relates to flat pattern.

MATERIALS NEEDED

1. Fabric similar in weight and drape to the final costume fabric
2. Scissors
3. Pins
4. Tailor's chalk

5. Fitting form or human body
6. Tape measure
7. French curve
8. Right angle
9. Tracing wheel and tracing paper
10. Pattern paper

DRAPING SLOPERS

We have discussed the use of the basic sloper in previous chapters. Although the sloper is usually not the form of the final costume, a draped sloper may be used in exactly the same way as commercial fitting patterns and drafted slopers. In chapter 7 you will learn to create other patterns from this basic garment.

The draping process is basically the same when working on a fitting form as when working on a human being, except that you will have to be more sensitive about smoothing fabric and pinning on an actor than on a fitting form. Using a fitting form is easier also because you may pin directly into the inanimate form and need not worry about the time you are taking or the body squirming underneath. If you are working on a fitting form, it should be padded or corseted to simulate the actor's measurements and silhouette for the specific production. If you are draping on an actor, he or she should likewise wear the silhouette-altering understructures that will be worn in production. Over these, a high-necked leotard and tights should be worn so that the draper has a surface to pin into.

The draping process for the upper-body sloper is the same for men and women, although the size of the front dart is normally larger for the woman's sloper to follow the shape of the bust line.

For all standard sloper patterns use a plain-weave cotton fabric such as muslin. Gingham also is a nice fabric to use for draping because the straight of grain and cross grain are boldly indicated in the weave.

Draping the Front Upper-Body Sloper

1. Begin with a length of muslin 5" longer than the neck-to-waist measurement and 5" wider than the distance at chest/bust level from center front to the side seam (approximately 1/4 chest/bust measurement plus 5").
2. Pin the muslin so that the straight of grain runs along the neck-to-waist line and the fabric overlaps the center front by about 1". Make sure that enough fabric is available to cover the shoulder and extend below the waist.
3. Clip to the neckline and work fabric around the base of the neck so that the straight of grain is not disturbed.
4. Smooth the fabric from the center front, across the chest, and over the shoulder without stretching the muslin or changing the straight of grain.
5. Pin the muslin along the shoulder line from the neck to the armscye. On a fitting form the shoulder line is frequently indicated with a seam in the fabric covering the dummy. If your actor is wearing a leotard, you may wish to follow the shoulder seam of that garment.
6. Clip to the armscye as you smooth the fabric from the shoulder seam down across the chest and around the armscye.

Figure 6–1 (a–h) Draping the front upper-body sloper

7. Pin under the arm.

8. Allow the muslin to fall naturally from under the arm, then smooth from underarm to waist and pin at the waist.

9. Pin the side seam from underarm to waist.

10. Remove the excess fabric at the waist by forming a dart halfway between the center front and side seam, or directly under the fullest part of the chest. The side seam, like the shoulder seam, may be taken directly off the fitting form or the actor's leotard. (If the actor's waist is as large as the chest measurement, you will not have excess fabric at the waist, and consequently no dart will need to be made.)

11. Pin the dart from the waist to the fullest part of the chest.

12. Mark the neckline, shoulder seam, armscye, side seam, waistline, dart, and center front with tailor's chalk before removing the front chest sloper pattern from the body.

13. Remove the muslin pattern from the form and remove pins from the dart. Correct and smooth the neckline and armscye curves with a French curve, and straighten the seam lines with a ruler. The waist seam line may be corrected by pinning the dart in place, then drawing a continuous straight line with a ruler with the dart in place.

14. Trim away the excess seam allowance, and re-pin the front chest sloper pattern to the fitting form or body, matching center front lines, shoulder seams, underarm, and waistlines.

Draping the Back Upper-Body Sloper

1. Prepare a length of muslin 5″ longer than the center back neck-to-waist measurement and 5″ wider than the distance between center back to side seam at bust line.

2. Pin the fabric along the center back of the form from neck to waist, keeping the straight of grain in line with the center back line and making sure that there is enough fabric to cover the shoulder seam and extend below the waist.

3. Smooth the muslin from the center back across to the underarm, keeping the crosswise threads of the fabric parallel to the floor.

4. Pin under the arm to the front chest sloper.

5. Allow the fabric to hang naturally below the armscye, then pin the back to the front sloper from underarm to waist, following the line established from the front side seam.

6. Create a dart with the excess fabric at the waist directly below the shoulder blade.

7. Clip and smooth the fabric at the neckline to the shoulder without disturbing the straight of grain.

8. Clip and smooth the fabric around the armscye, up and over the shoulder.

9. Create a dart with the excess fabric at the shoulder halfway across the shoulder seam.

10. Pin the back sloper to the front sloper along the shoulder line established on the front sloper.

11. Mark the center back, neckline, shoulder, armscye, waistline, and darts with tailor's chalk before removing the back chest sloper from the body or form.

(a)

(b)

(c)

(d)

(e)

(f)

Figure 6-2 (a-f) Draping the back upper-body sloper

12. Remove all pins from the back chest sloper and correct the curves and lines of the pattern with ruler and French curve.

Draping a Basic Skirt Sloper

The skirt sloper is sometimes referred to as a hip sloper since it is as useful for creating men's garments and peplums as for women's skirts. The draping of the skirt sloper is done over the hips of a human or fitting form. Below the

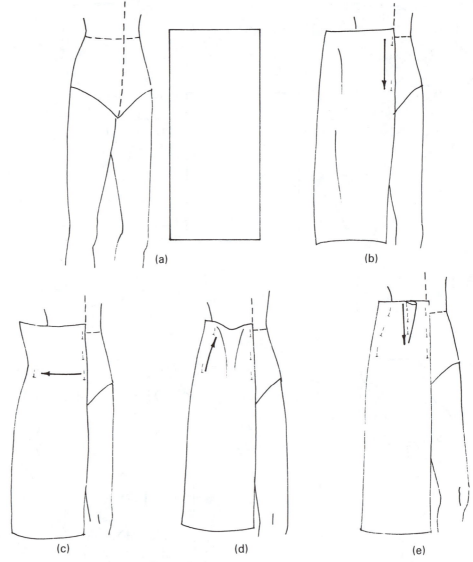

Figure 6–3 (a–e) Draping a skirt

hip line the lines of the skirt sloper simply continue straight to the desired length.

1. Prepare a length of muslin at least 3″ longer than the desired skirt length and at least 3″ wider than the center front-to-side seam measurement of the hip.
2. Pin the muslin with the straight of grain along the center front of the body or fitting form from the waist to the hip.
3. Smooth the muslin at the hip line from the center front to the side seam, keeping the crosswise grain of the fabric parallel to the floor.
4. Pin the skirt front sloper at the hip.
5. Smooth the muslin from hip line to waistline and pin in place.
6. Create a dart with the excess fabric at the waistline halfway between the center front and the side seam.
7. Mark the waistline, side seam, and dart before removing the sloper from the body or fitting form.

8. Correct the curves and seam lines with ruler and French curve as illustrated for the front chest sloper.

9. Trim away the excess fabric to the seam allowance, then pin the corrected skirt sloper with dart in place back on the fitting form.

10. Create the back skirt sloper as you did the front, pinning into the front skirt sloper along the established side seam.

Draping a Basic Sleeve Sloper

A sleeve sloper is easily draped on a human form since dress forms generally have no arms. For the draping procedure it is best for your model to wear a leotard or other snug-fitting garment with evident armscye.

1. Prepare a rectangle of muslin 3″ longer than the arm and 3″ wider than the bicep measurement.

2. Pin the top center of the fabric to the shoulder seam of the chest sloper or leotard with the straight of grain parallel to the length of the upper arm.

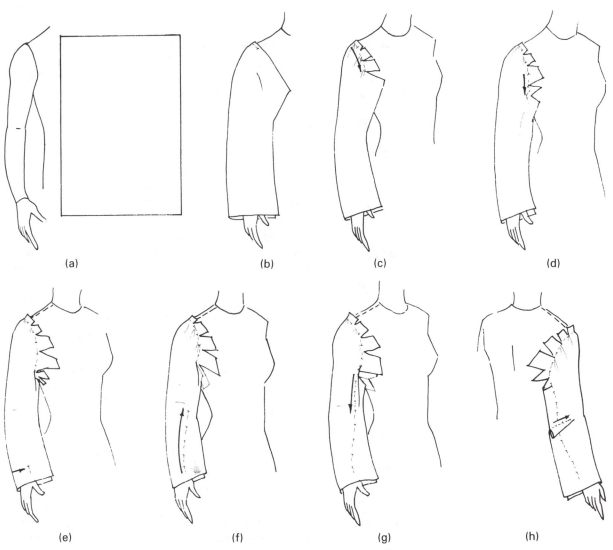

(a)   (b)   (c)   (d)

(e)   (f)   (g)   (h)

Figure 6-4 (a-h)   Draping a sleeve

3. With the model's arm in a relaxed position slightly away from the body (slightly bent at the elbow), smooth the muslin around the armscye by easing, pinning, and clipping as necessary, and without disturbing the straight of grain on the upper arm.

4. Pin the muslin under the arm, clipping the curve of the sleeve sloper around the armscye to achieve a smooth fit.

5. Allow the fabric to fall naturally from the armscye. Position the arm in a comfortable position as before, slightly away from the body.

6. Smooth the fabric around to the inside of the wrist just as it lies naturally on the arm.

7. Pin at the inside of the wrist.

8. Pin the sleeve seam from the wrist up to the elbow, smoothing the fabric snugly over the lower arm. Make sure that the actor is able to move and flex the muscles of the lower arm without the sleeve binding.

9. Smooth and pin the fabric from underarm down to elbow. The fit should be comfortable and allow the actor to flex the muscles of the upper arm without binding.

10. Create a dart by removing excess fabric along the back seam line at the elbow.

11. Mark the armscye seam, underarm seam, dart, and wrist line before removing the sleeve sloper from the body.

12. Correct the curves and lines of the sleeve sloper with ruler and French curve as described for the front chest sloper.

Draping a Basic Pants Sloper

1. Prepare muslin 3″ longer than outseam measurement and 3″ wider than the thigh or half of the hip measurement (whichever is larger).

2. Measure crotch-length on the pants fitting form or actor and make a cut in the muslin 2″ in from the side at the crotch-length distance plus 2″ from the top edge.

3. Pin the muslin from waist to hip along the center front 2″ in from the edge along the straight of grain, so that the cut in the muslin will fall between the legs and 2″ of excess muslin will extend above the waist.

4. Smooth the fabric around the hip line from the center front to the center back along the crosswise grain. Pin the fabric at the hip line to the center back, keeping the crosswise grain of the fabric parallel to the floor.

5. Gently remove some of the fullness at the waist with a dart at the side if needed. Do not disturb the straight of grain or the crosswise grain at the hip line. If the difference between the hip and waist measurements is negligible, there may not be a need for a dart at this location.

6. Form waistline darts halfway between center front and side seam and center back and side seam by pinning the remaining fullness.

7. Clip the excess fabric away from the center back seam line to allow the remainder to wrap freely around the leg to the front piece.

8. Pin inseam at crotch, clipping excess fabric as necessary to prevent fabric from pulling, while maintaining straight of grain and crosswise grain.

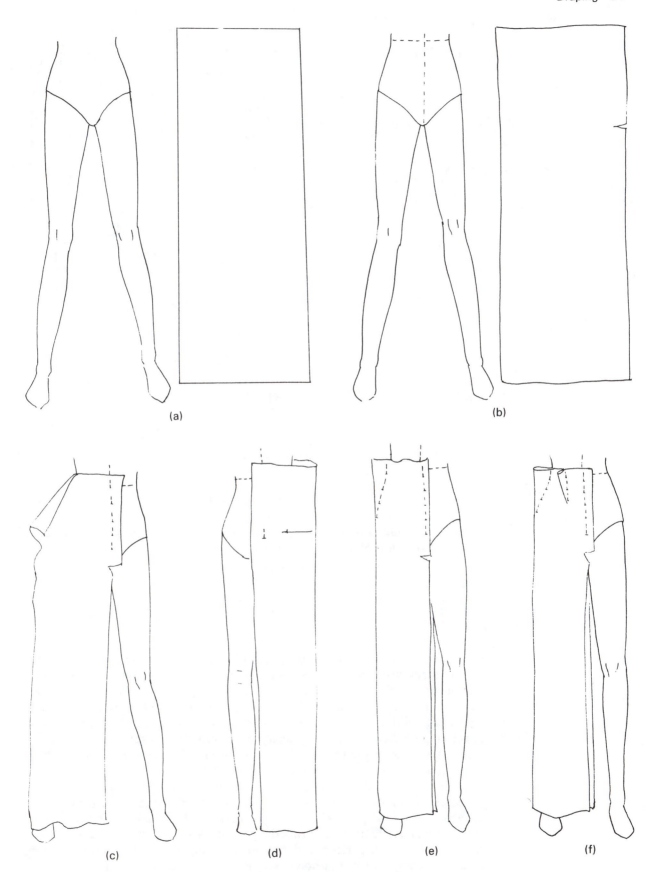

Figure 6-5 (a–i) Draping pants

 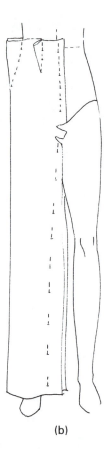 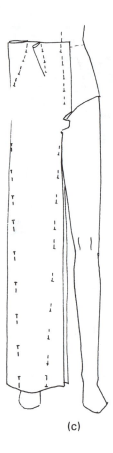

| (a) | (b) | (c) |

Figure 6-5 continued.

9. Taper inseam to fit leg while maintaining straight of grain over the back and front of leg.
10. Remove excess fullness on the outer leg by tapering from the ankle to the hipline to form an outseam.
11. Mark and correct the pattern.

DRAPING PERIOD COSTUMES

Basically any garment may be draped once you understand the nature of fabric and the structure of the finished garment. To create authentic period garments it is necessary that draping take place over the proper understructures. Corsets, hoops, bustles, padding—all must be considered in the creation of an accurate silhouette. Likewise, a study of the flat pattern and cutting diagrams of actual period garments is essential before effective draping can take place. Once a structure is understood, the trick is to reproduce it for a modern body wearing appropriate silhouette-changing devices.

Dress forms may be padded, and some may be reduced, to create new silhouettes. A small form is more easily changed than a rigid larger form. As always, draping may take place on the person who will wear the costume if that person has the time. Accurate draping of period costumes may be successfully achieved with altered dress forms shaped to the actor's altered measurements. Corset and hoop construction are discussed in chapter 10.

Bodice Variation

The variation in upper-body garments has evolved through a series of draped and fitted garments. The shape of the flat pattern determines the look of the final bodice.

It is always a good idea to know the flat pattern shape before the draping process takes place. This will help in the establishment of the proper grain line as well as the hang of hidden portions of the garment, for example. The more you understand about historical patterns, the better you will be able to drape them.

Since we have determined a system for developing a fitted bodice pattern in our basic sloper, variations on fitted bodices follow basically the same procedure. Dart placement and seam lines may vary. Bodices may be longer, shorter, and in more or fewer pieces than the basic sloper, but the smoothing

Figure 6–6 A Victorian bodice

and pinning process is all very much the same. Consideration of the straight of grain and crosswise grain remains important no matter what is being draped. With practice, patience, and care you will be able to drape pleats, gathers, and tucks right into a bodice as you go.

Draping Skirt Variations

A look at the development of skirt patterns in western history will reveal a variety of effects. It is important to understand how the cut of a skirt in relation to the bias and straight of grain will affect the drape of that skirt.

It is sometimes useful to begin with a basic flat pattern and drape for subtlety in fit. This is true of 20th century skirts, which hug the hips and in-

Figure 6-7 An 1890s skirt

volve complex pleating or pieced effects. The skirt in Figure 6–7 is cut with the straight of grain swung to the front of each gore. This is because of the way the bias reacts in movement. A skirt cut in this way will swing gracefully to the train in movement and fall in soft pleats to the back at rest. The actual pleating of this skirt should be carefully draped on a fitting form or an actor but it is probably a good idea to cut the gores ahead of time with this straight of grain in mind.

Skirts that are asymmetrically swagged or draped to the waistline can be successfully draped directly on a dress form, provided a large enough piece of muslin is used to account for the fullness of drape.

EXERCISES

1. Drape an upper-body sloper on a fitting form or another person.
2. Drape a skirt sloper on a fitting form or another person.
3. Drape a sleeve sloper on another person.
4. Working from an illustration or period pattern, drape a period bodice, doublet, or sleeve on a fitting form or another person.

Flat Pattern Drafting and Manipulation

7

PATTERN DRAFTING

Pattern drafting is a method of creating a pattern directly from an individual set of measurements. Because of this, each pattern is developed uniquely to fit each actor. It is important when using the drafting technique of pattern development that measurements be taken very carefully and that the resulting patterns be drawn very accurately. A small error in measurement may result in a rather large error in the final pattern. There are books of pattern drafts that can be used to develop tailored garments as well as basic slopers. Here, we will learn the process of drafting by creating an upper-body sloper.

MATERIALS NEEDED

1. A large flat table or drawing surface
2. T-square or right angle
3. Yardstick
4. Tape measure
5. Pencil and eraser
6. Craft paper
7. Scissors
8. Set of measurements
9. French curves

CREATING AN UPPER-BODY SLOPER

The following is a set of instructions for creating an upper-body sloper by drafting. You will need to refer to an accurate set of measurements and the illustrations in this book as you proceed.

1. Start with a piece of paper at least 5″ longer than the neck-to-waist (back) measurement, and at least 5″ wider than 1/2 chest or 1/2 waist measurement (whichever is larger).

2. Draw a rectangle and construction lines on the paper, labeling all points with appropriate letters by following the illustration and specific measurement chart so that:

   AB and CD = 1/2 chest or 1/2 waist (whichever is larger).
   Place AB 1″ below the top edge of the paper.
   AC and BD = neck-to-waist (back) plus 1″.
   EF divides the rectangle ABDC in half vertically.
   GH is parallel to and 2 1/2″ below AB.
   IJ is parallel to, and underarm-to-waist measurement above CD.
   (If underarm to waist is 7″, IJ will be 7″ above CD.)
   KL divides rectangle GHJI in half horizontally.
   MN is parallel to and 1/2 bust/chest span measurement to the left of BD
   OP is parallel to and 1/2 bust/chest span measurement to the right of AC

   Make sure all points are labeled before you continue.

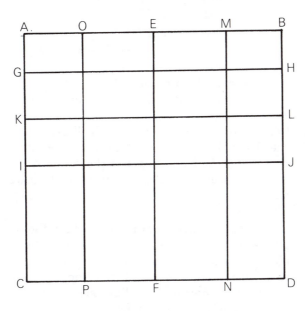

Figure 7–1 Construction lines for upper-body sloper draft

3. Create the outer lines of the sloper by finding the following points while referring to the illustration.

   a   is 1″ below A on line AC
   b   is 3″ to the right of A on line AB
   Gc = 1/2 across shoulders (back)

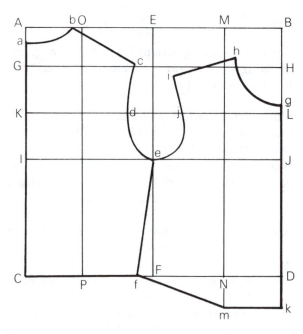

Figure 7-2 Outline of upper-body sloper

Kd = 1/2 width of back

Ie = 1/4 chest

f is 1″ to the left of F on line CD if waist measurement is at least 5″ smaller than the chest measurement. Otherwise f and F will be the same point.

g is 5″ below B on line BD

h is 2″ below line AB and 3″ to the left of BD

i is 1/2 across shoulders (front) to the left of BD and 1/2″ below line GH

Lj = 1/2 width of front

Je′ = 1/4 chest. If chest is larger than waist, e and e′ will be the same point.

gk = neck to waist (front)

km = is parallel to and the same length as ND

4. Connect points as indicated in the illustration to form the outline of the sloper. Back sloper is the connection of points a, b, c, d, e, f, C, and a, and the front sloper is the connection of points g, k, m, f, e (or e′), j, i, h, and g. A French curve may be used to create the neckline and armhole curves.

5. If the waist measurement is smaller than the chest measurement, plot all the points for the darts by referring to the measurement chart and illustration 7-3 and the following instructions. If the waist is equal to or greater than the chest, the sloper will have no waistline darts. In this case refer only to illustration 7-4, and points p, q, r, and s in the following instructions.

n and o Subtract 1/4 waist measurement from line Cf.
Divide that distance equally on each side of point P.

p is the intersection of line IJ and OP.

q bisects line bc. Draw a line from p to q.

r is 3″ below q on line pq.

s is 3/4″ to the right of q (sq is parallel to AB).

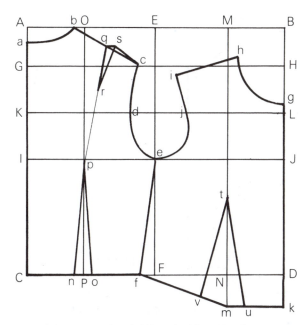

Figure 7–3 Adding the darts to the upper-body sloper

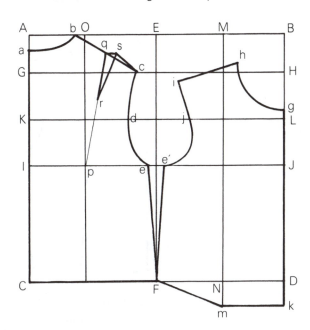

Figure 7–4 Upper-body sloper draft when waistline is larger than chest

t   is height-of-dart measurement above m on line Mm.

u and v   Subtract 1/4 waist from distance fmk. Mark 1″ of that distance to the right of m on line mk, and the remainder to the left of m on line mf. Extend or shorten line tv to equal line tu.

6.   Connect all lines to form the darts: qrs, npo, and vtu.

The back sloper will be the connection of points a, b, q, r, s, c, d, e, f, o, p, n, C and a, and the front sloper will be the connection of points g, k, u, t, v, f, e (or e′), j, i, h, g.

Drafting seems very complicated at first, but once you are familiar with the system the process is quite quick. Drafting is a way of coming close to an accurate fit for those actors who do not easily fit into standard sizes. Books of pattern drafts for other garments are listed in the Bibliography.

FLAT PATTERN MANIPULATION

Flat pattern manipulation begins with the sloper, which we discussed in earlier chapters. This simple, perfectly fitted basic garment may be used to create almost any other garment pattern. Creating patterns by manipulating a basic sloper is often the easiest way to get the shape of the pattern needed for a specific design. The basic sloper changes with the silhouette of a given period since the undergarments, which mold the body, change with each period (see chapter 10). The sloper, then, is a garment snugly fitted over the undergarments of a given period.

Development of the Basic Sloper

As mentioned earlier, commercial pattern companies often include a sloper pattern in the collection of patterns. This pattern is a fitted skirt, bodice, and sleeve and will be found in all adult women's sizes. Men's sloper patterns must be

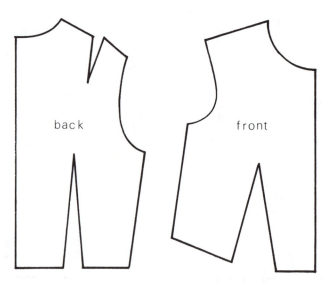

Figure 7–5 Upper-body
sloper pattern

developed through draping, drafting, or serious alteration of commerical shirt
and pants patterns. Whether the basic sloper came from a pattern envelope,
was draped on a fitting form, or was drafted to a specific body's measurements,
it is essential that all slopers be checked and fit to the actor before flat pattern
changes occur.

Fitting the Basic Sloper. Fitting the basic sloper is no different from fitting any garment except that the sloper is always fitted very snugly to the
body while other garments are fitted according to the style of a specific design
(see chapter 5). If you have been following the exercises in this book, you have
already fitted a sloper to a dress form or another individual. (It is nearly impossible to fit a sloper to your own body.)

Transferring the Sloper to Paper. After the sloper has been fitted and the
new marks made on the cloth pattern, the sloper pieces should be carefully taken
apart and pressed. The pattern should then be transferred to brown paper. Cut
the pattern with no seam allowance and the darts removed as in Figure 7–5.

Upper-Body Sloper Manipulation

Dart Manipulation. Darts are the stitched triangular folds that shape and
fit a flat piece of fabric to a three-dimensional form. Darts may originate from
any outer edge of a pattern piece without changing the original fit as long as
the dart points toward the fullest part of the body (in a front sloper this will
be the chest or bust; in the back it is usually the shoulder blade). Dart fullness
may be managed in a number of ways, including: tucks, gathers, pleats, or seam
lines.

Movement of darts allows the designer a greater range of decorative possibilities. The costume constructionist can easily build these construction details
into the costume by understanding the simple principles of dart manipulation.

Making a One-Dart Sloper Into a Two-Dart Sloper.

1. Determine where the second dart will be located.
2. Draw a line from the origin of the new dart to the pivot point. The
   pivot point will be at the fullest part of the chest or bust, and is located
   at the end of the sloper dart.

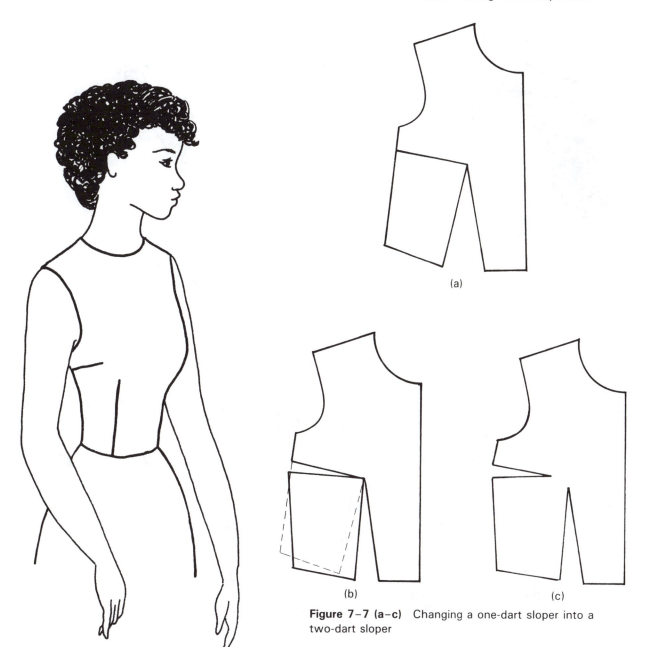

Figure 7–7 (a) label

Figure 7–6 A two-dart bodice

(b)   (c)

Figure 7–7 (a–c) Changing a one-dart sloper into a
two-dart sloper

3. Cut the new line and open the pattern on this line, closing out some
    of the fullness in the waist dart and keeping the center front on the
    straight of grain.
4. In the actual costume these darts may be shortened to within 1″ of
    the actual bust point.

This same system may be used for any number of darts in any position
on the bodice or vest.

Creating Stylized Darts.   Stylized darts are decorative as well as functional
(Figure 7–8). They are treated in much the same way as regular darts.

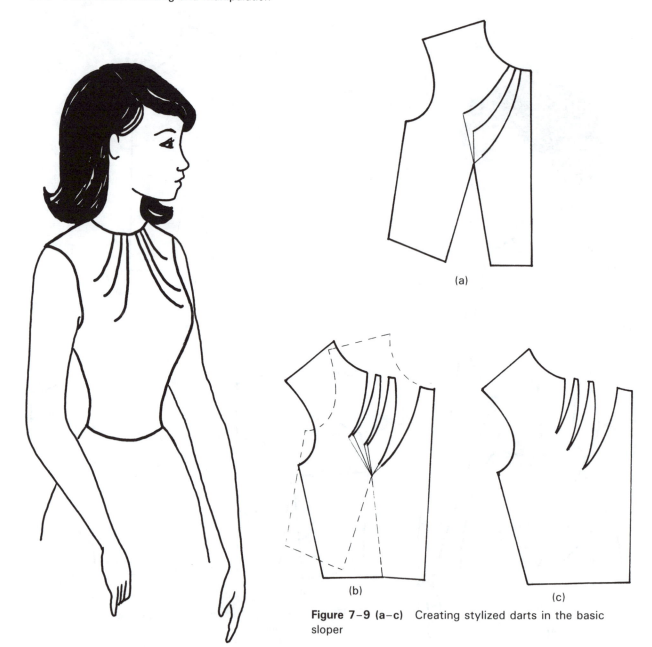

(a)

(b) (c)

Figure 7–9 (a–c) Creating stylized darts in the basic sloper

Figure 7–8 Bodice with stylized darts

1. Draw lines on the sloper where the stylized darts will be placed (Figure 7–9a).
2. Cut the dart lines and extend to the pivot point (Figure 7–9b).
3. Open up the stylized darts and close out the original sloper dart, keeping the center front on the straight of grain (Figure 7–9b).
4. Redraw the darts on the pattern so that they come to an end before reaching the pivot point (Figure 7–9c).

Gathering and Shirring to Control Dart Fullness. Gathering, or multiple rows of gathering called shirring, can replace functional darting to shape fabric into a three-dimensional form. Functional gathers may occur wherever darts appear on a costume (Figure 7–10).

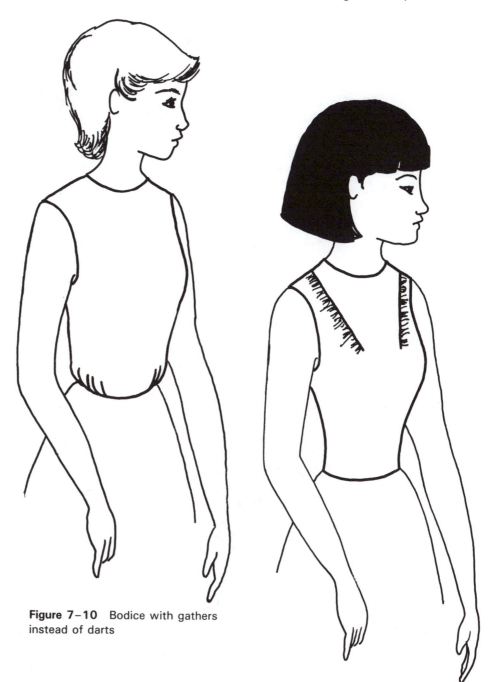

Figure 7–10 Bodice with gathers
instead of darts

Figure 7–11 Bodice with decorative
shirring

Adding Fullness for Decorative Shirring.   For decorative purposes, additional
fullness may be added to the pattern first, then re-gathered for a decorative
effect (Figure 7–11).

1. Move dart to appropriate position on basic sloper.
2. Make evenly spaced cuts through the pattern where the shirring will
    occur.
3. Spread the cut sections to open where the shirring will occur.
4. Redraw the pattern to connect the slashed and spread pieces.

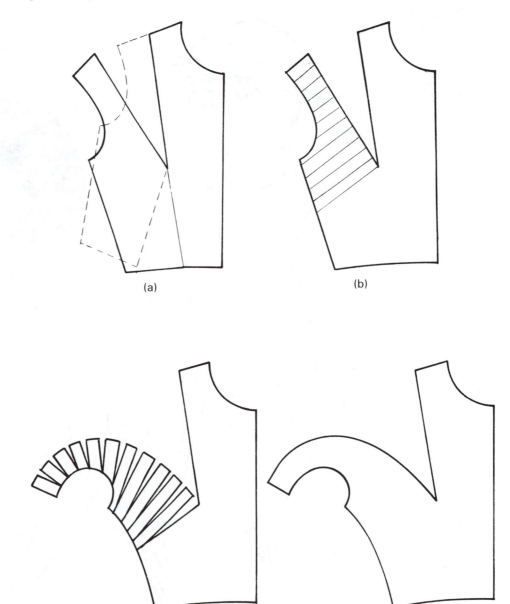

Figure 7–12 (a–d)   Creating a pattern with decorative shirring

Creating a Multi-Pieced Doublet

1. Draw a line on the basic pattern to suit the specific style of the costume (Figure 7–14a).
2. Cut along this line and separate the pieces (Figure 7–14b).
3. Close out the dart (Figure 7–14c).
4. Redraw the cut section to smooth the curves (Figure 7–14d).

Fitted upper-body garments may be cut into as many pieces as are desired as long as the darts are accounted for and the pieces are resewn in the proper sequence.

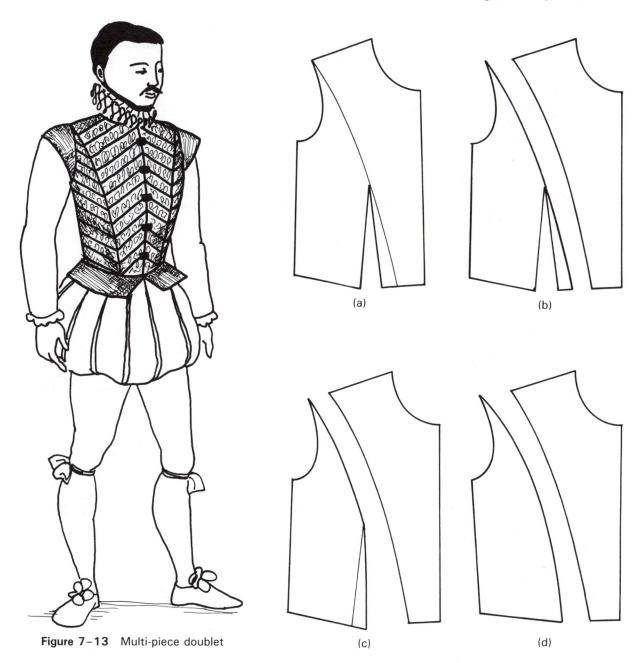

Figure 7–13 Multi-piece doublet

Figure 7–14 (a–d) Creating a multi-piece doublet pattern from the basic sloper

Manipulation of Skirt Slopers

The skirt is often the primary element in defining the female costume silhouette. A study of patterns for historical garments will help to create appropriate skirt patterns from a skirt sloper. It is often easier, however, to begin at a different point for skirts with a great deal of fullness at the waist and skirts that rely on shifting the bias to perfect the proper drape and flow. Manipulation of the skirt sloper is especially useful in the creation of skirts with some degree of fitting.

Gored Skirts. A gored skirt is composed of any number of tapered sections called gores. Gored skirts may be fitted to the waist and hips or may be very full and gathered or pleated at the waist.

1. Separate skirt sloper by cutting pattern from the dart down along the straight of grain.
2. Create flare to the skirt by extending the waist dart lines.

Peg-Top Skirt. A peg-top skirt is one with fullness at the waist but not at the hem.

1. Cut slash lines from the waist to the hem of the skirt sloper.
2. Spread sections at the waist line, keeping the center front and center back of the skirt on the straight of grain.
3. Redraw the waistline.

Figure 7–15 A gored skirt

(a)

(b)

Figure 7–16 (a–b) Creating a gored skirt from a basic skirt sloper

Figure 7–17 A peg-top skirt

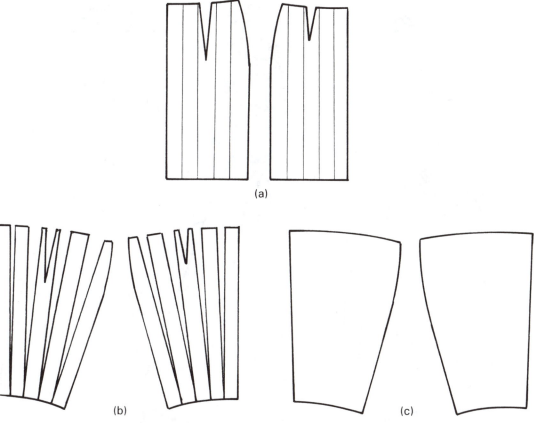

Figure 7–18 (a–c) Creating a peg-top skirt from a basic skirt sloper

Skirts from Period Patterns. Most historical skirts do not closely conform to the body. They are fitted loosely over petticoats, hoops, paniers, and bustles or are cut very full and gathered into a bodice. With these skirts it is best to begin with a picture of how that skirt was originally cut.

Full hemmed skirts are cut in three basic ways: rectangular cut skirts, circular cut skirts, and gored skirts. Rectangular cut skirts have as much fullness where they join the bodice, or at the waist, as they do at the hem. Circular skirts have considerably more fullness at the hem than at the waist. Gored skirts are also fuller at the hem but are more structured, with control of the

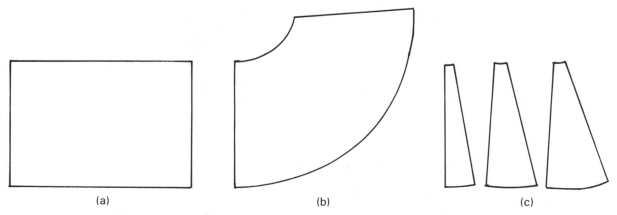

Figure 7–19 (a–c) Three basic patterns for full skirts: rectangular, circular, and gored

(a)   (b)   (c)

Figure 7–20 (a–c) Skirts cut with rectangular, circular, and gored patterns

seams and bias. Much can be done with gored skirts to affect drape and movement of the skirt.

Patterns for rectangular and circular skirts are easy to understand. Circular skirts are sometimes hard to cut because the fabric is not wide enough. There are two solutions to the problem. The first is to piece the fabric first and then cut the pattern; the second is to divide the fabric into gores and piece the skirt together after the gores have been cut. By using gores rather than a single flat circular piece, you will be altering the drape of the skirt, however.

Adapting and altering historical skirt patterns is not difficult. Lengthening or shortening the skirt requires very little instruction. Making the skirt larger, smaller, or increasing the flare at the hem are logical processes. Moving the straight of grain will change the way a skirt hangs.

In general, skirts are not as difficult to fit and adjust as bodices are. Making sure hems are marked evenly over structured hoops, bolsters, and bustles may be the most difficult task presented by a skirt.

Manipulation of the Pants Sloper

Changing the Leg of a Pants Sloper.   The easiest thing to change on a pants sloper is the length and shape of the leg. Adding fullness to the ankle or creating breeches is a fairly simple matter. Adding fullness or moving darts on pants is similar to making those adjustments on skirts.

Making Breeches from a Pants Sloper

1. Cut the pants pattern below the knee or wherever the breeches are to end.
2. Slash pattern and spread to accommodate desired fullness.
3. Redraw the pattern (Figure 7–23c).

   (Figures 7–23, 7–24, and 7–25 indicate breeches which are, respectively, full at the knee, full at the waist, and full at both the waist and the knee.)

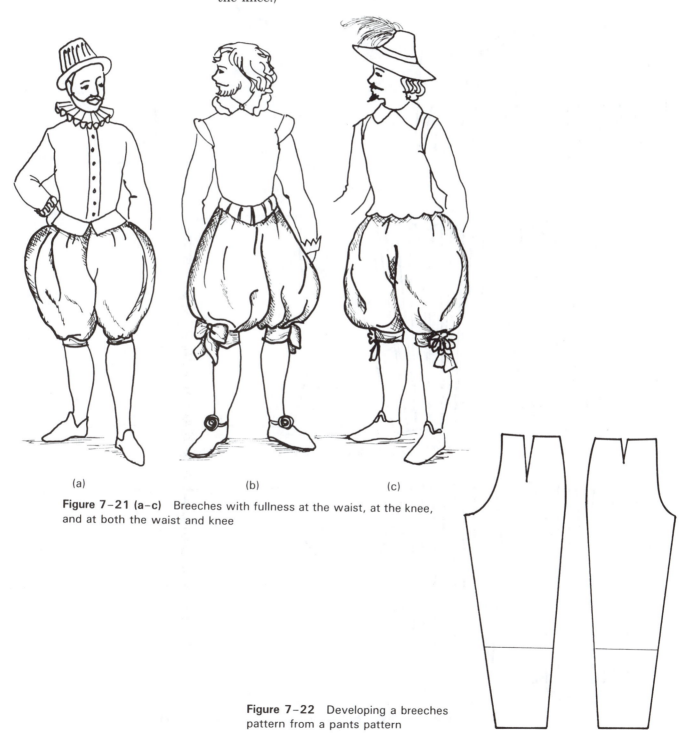

(a)   (b)   (c)

Figure 7–21 (a–c)   Breeches with fullness at the waist, at the knee, and at both the waist and knee

Figure 7–22   Developing a breeches pattern from a pants pattern

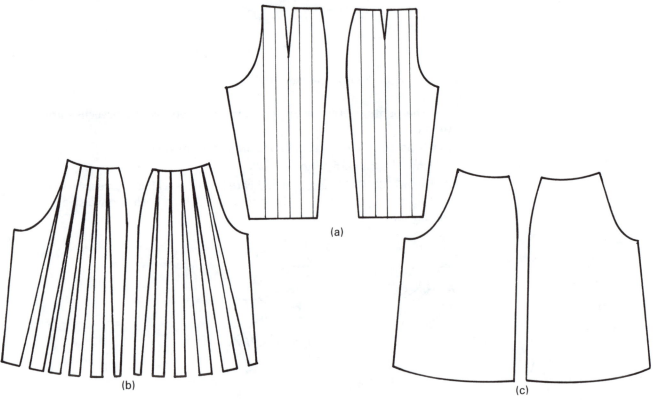

(a)

(b)

(c)

Figure 7-23 Pattern for breeches with fullness at the knee

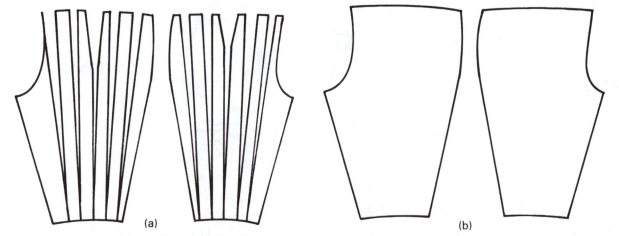

(a)

(b)

Figure 7-24 Pattern for breeches with fullness at the waist

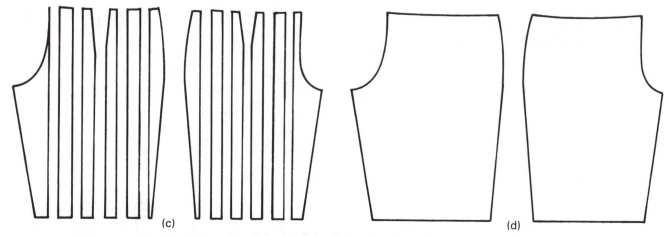

(c)

(d)

Figure 7-25 Pattern for breeches with fullness at both the waist and knee

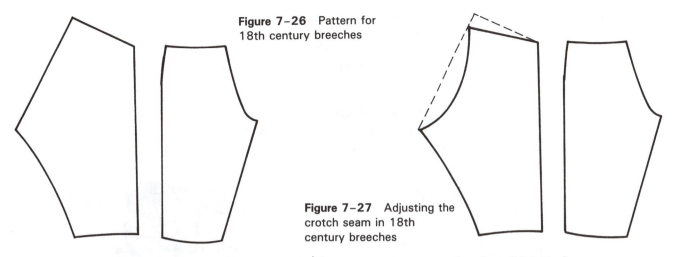

Figure 7-26 Pattern for 18th century breeches

Figure 7-27 Adjusting the crotch seam in 18th century breeches

Adapting Historical Pants Patterns. Patterns taken from historical sources often have peculiar crotch seams that create fullness in the seat of the pants. Although this is quite authentic, the look is somewhat odd to today's audiences. If you wish to change this effect, cut the back crotch curve as you would a modern pants sloper by lowering the center back waist, and curving the crotch line rather than cutting it on the bias.

Manipulation of the Sleeve Sloper

Creating a Bell Sleeve. A bell sleeve is one with more fullness at the wrist than at the bicep (Figure 7-28). The amount of fullness may vary.

1. Move the elbow dart to the wrist (Figure 7-29a, b).
2. Slash the pattern from hem to cap (Figure 7-29c).
3. Open the sleeve at the wrist along the slash lines (Figure 7-29d).
4. Redraw the pattern (Figure 7-29e).

Figure 7-29 (a-e) Creating a bell sleeve from a basic sleeve sloper

(a)　　　(b)　　　(c)

(d)　　　(e)

Figure 7-28 A bell sleeve

Developing a Leg-o-mutton Sleeve. A leg-o-mutton sleeve is one that has more fullness through the bicep and cap than at the wrist. Leg-o-mutton sleeves may taper gradually to the wrist or be reduced abruptly at the elbow and become tight-fitting over the forearm (Figure 7–30).

1. Slash the pattern from the cap to where the sleeve will be fitted to the arm (Figure 7–31a).
2. Spread the slashed sections to the desired fullness (Figure 7–31b).
3. Redraw the final pattern (Figure 7–31c).

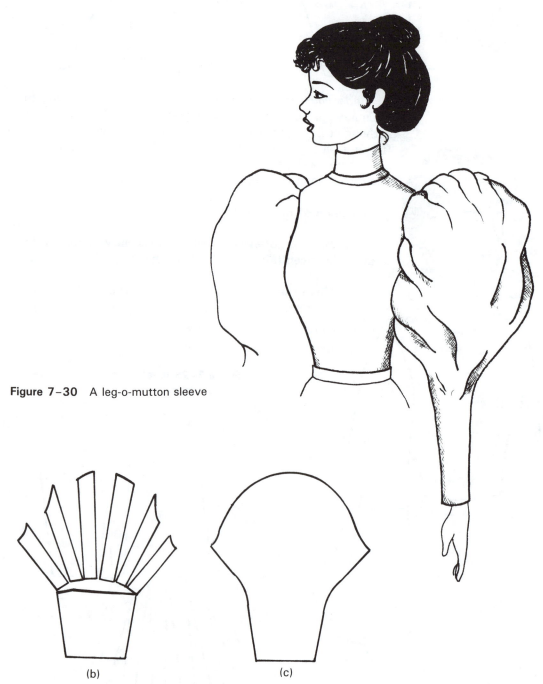

Figure 7–30 A leg-o-mutton sleeve

(a) (b) (c)

Figure 7–31 (a–c) Creating a leg-o-mutton sleeve from a basic sleeve sloper

Manipulation of Collars and Cuffs

With collars and cuffs there is really no sloper to begin with. For some collars you may use the bodice sloper as a starting point. Most collars are fairly easy to develop by draping (see chapter 6).

Simple shirt cuffs are often mere rectangles cut to go around and overlap at the wrist. Naturally, the slash method pertains to collars and cuffs as well as to any other garment pattern and may be employed whenever a pattern can't be developed more simply in other ways.

Developing a Flared Cuff

1. Slash the cuff pattern to, but not through, the wrist edge.
2. Spread the pieces to the desired fullness (Figure 7–33b).
3. Redraw the pattern.

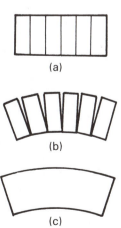

(a)

(b)

(c)

Figure 7–32 A flared cuff

Figure 7–33 (a–c)
Developing a flared
cuff pattern

Figure 7–34   A ruffled collar

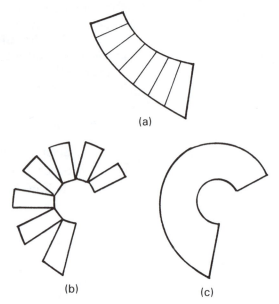

Figure 7–35 (a–c)   Developing a ruffled collar pattern

Developing a Ruffled Collar

1.   Slash the collar from the outer edge to, but not through, the neck edge.
2.   Spread the pieces to the desired fullness. If the pieces begin to overlap, you may have to cut the collar in more than one piece.
3.   Redraw the final pattern.

You have probably begun to notice the similarities among these methods of pattern manipulation. We could go on to discuss more examples, but by now the processes should be quite clear.

There is never only one way to arrive at the pattern for a specific garment. In all choices of pattern development it is important to arrive at the best solution to the pattern in the most expedient manner.

EXERCISES

1.   Draft an upper-body sloper to your measurements. Compare it to the commercial sloper and the draped sloper. Which one fits you best?
2.   Create a pattern for the bodice shown in Figure 6–6 by using flat pattern manipulation techniques.
3.   Design a bodice, doublet, sleeve, or collar and create the pattern from your basic sloper.

Dressmaker Details

8

DRESSMAKER DETAILS

Dressmaker details are stitched decorative elements applied to garments and costumes, including tucks, pleats, topstitching, slashing, shirring, embroidery, and smocking. These details may be done by hand or machine, or their illusion may be created by paint, felt-tipped markers, or glue. Depending on the distance of the viewer from the costume, these details may require more or less time and effort. They are important in creating specific period authenticity, such as metallic embroidery effects on costumes of the Renaissance, or cartridge pleating on 16th century German gowns, or smocking on medieval bodices.

DETAILS THAT CONTROL FULLNESS

Some dressmaker details serve a dual purpose of controlling fullness of a garment as well as adding decoration. Pleating, shirring, and smocking are processes that also reduce fullness.

Pleating

Pleats are folds in the fabric which reduce and control in a precise manner a quantity of fabric. Pleating schemes are numerous. The most common pleat methods used by the theatre costumer are knife pleats, box pleats, cartridge pleats (or padded pleats), and primitive pleats.

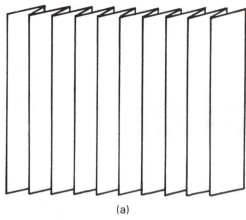

(a)

Figure 8-1a Knife pleats

Figure 8-1b Knife pleats on apron hem. Costume designed by James Berton Harris (David W. Fathauer).

(b)

Knife pleats. These pleats are made by folding the fabric back and forth consistently in the same direction (Figure 8-1). They may be pressed into place by an iron to achieve a crisp formal appearance or left to hang softly. Typically, a fabric is reduced to one third of the original length with this method of folding the fabric back and forth upon itself, but if the fabric is overlapped even more, or if spaces of open fabric are left between the pleats, more or less fabric may be worked into a set finished length.

Box pleats. Like knife pleats, box pleats are usually constructed with three times the final pleated length of fabric. In this scheme the fabric folds first one way and then the other to create folds in both directions (Figure 8-2).

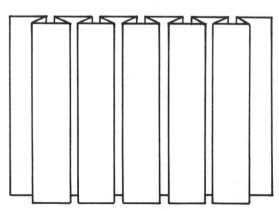

Figure 8-2 Box pleats

Figure 8-3 Cartridge pleating

Cartridge pleats.   Cartridge pleats, padded pleats, bullet pleats, and organ pipe pleats are all basically the same. These pleats must be sewn in place by hand, and usually are sewn into the final garment by hand also in order to maintain the structure of the pleat. This kind of pleat is seen most frequently today in the body and sleeves of choir robes and graduation gowns. In the 15th, 16th, and 17th centuries, this type of pleat was seen across the front and back of robes, in sleeves and skirts of gowns, and jerkins (Figure 8-3).

Cartridge pleats must be carefully marked for the most satisfactory results. Cartridge pleating allows you to reduce large amounts of fabric in a very orderly fashion. Variations on the size of the pleat depend in part on the distance between stitches and in part on the material used to pad the pleats.

Pellon, felt, lightweight polyurethane foam, and dacron fiberfill may all be used to pad the pleats.

1. Pin a strip of the padding material close to the top of the fabric to be pleated.
2. Finish the raw edge of the fabric with a strip of lining fabric brought over the padding and stitched in place, or fold the fabric itself over the padding and secure it.
3. Mark two rows of dots at regular intervals on the inside lining (Figure 8-4a). The distance between dots will determine the size of your pleats. Usually these will vary from 1/4" to 1 1/2". The farther apart the dots are, the larger the final pleats will be. If thick padding is used, and large quantities of fabric need to be reduced, you will need to space the dots farther apart. It is a good idea to experiment with padding and spacing beforehand to see if the final result will be appropriate.
4. Run a heavy-duty thread in and out from one dot to another along the top row of dots. Using another thread do exactly the same thing with the lower row of dots (Figure 8-4b).

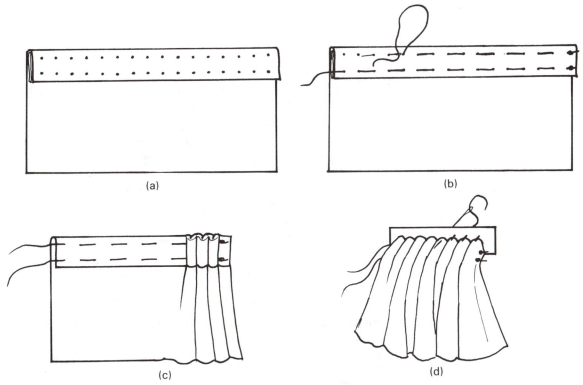

(a)

(b)

(c)

(d)

Figure 8-4 (a-d)   Cartridge pleat construction

5. Sometimes for security or for very long pleats, several rows of stitching may be used instead of the standard two rows. Each row must follow the exact stitching pattern as the first for the scheme to work.
6. Pull all rows of threads together until the pleating is reduced to the desired measurement (Figure 8-4c).
7. Sew pleated piece into the garment by hand (Figure 8-4d).

Primitive pleating. Primitive pleating is a method of creating fine, irregular pleats for use in garments from ancient cultures.

Primitive pleating will work easily with any fabric which can be naturally wrinkled. It can also be achieved with wrinkle-resistant fabric by setting the pleats with heat. In this century fabrics are occasionally created with a primitive pleating heat-set into them.

1. Wet the fabric to be pleated.
2. Twist the fabric very tightly until it begins to twist back on itself.
3. Wrap the fabric around a pole or tie the ends together and allow the piece to dry completely.
4. When fabric is completely dry unwrap the piece and it will fall into fine, irregular pleats.

For a finer pleat, gather both ends of the fabric by hand stitching before wetting and twisting the fabric.

Figure 8-5 Primitive pleating

Shirring

Shirring is decorative gathering. Shirring can be created in single or multiple rows.

Shirring may be done in a number of ways depending on the fabric being used, the amount of shirring, and the need for durability of the piece.

Methods of Shirring

a. Set your sewing machine at the longest stitch length and the loosest upper-thread tension. Allow the fabric to feed through without pulling from the back. The fabric will gather naturally.
b. Set your machine for the longest stitch length and make two parallel rows of stitching about 1/2″ apart. Pull both bobbin threads together as you gently push the fabric into a gather (Figure 8-6).

This method produces a very fine and easily controlled gather stitch for short distances. It is good for sleeves, shirt fronts, and skirt waists. For pieces longer than two yards, or that require greater reduction than 300 percent, it is usually better to use another shirring method, since stress on the bobbin threads may cause these threads to break.
c. Place a piece of heavy-duty thread under the presser foot of the sewing machine, and do a wide zig-zag stitch over the thread. Pull the heavy thread to the desired length (Figure 8-7).
d. Hand-wind the bobbin loosely with elastic thread. Using elastic thread in the bobbin and regular thread for the top thread, sew the piece to be gathered. The piece will automatically gather because of the elastic thread in the bobbin.

This method produces a flexible shirring stitch. It is useful when multiple rows of gathers are used to create a fitted bodice or sleeve,

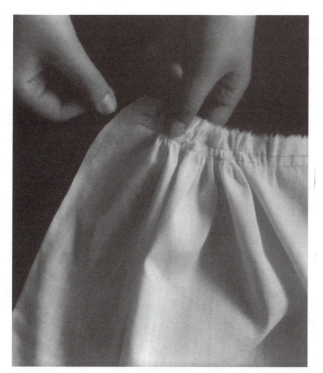

Figure 8-6   Shirring by pulling loosened machine stitching

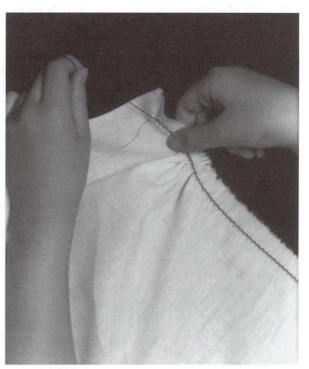

Figure 8-7   Shirring by pulling a heavy thread held in place with a zigzag stitch

Figure 8-8   Crossed shirring creating a smocked effect on the bodice and sleeve

since the elastic allows the piece to fit snugly yet comfortably (Figure 8-8).

Variations and creativity in shirring can produce many functional and decorative effects. By substituting a metallic elastic thread in the bobbin, the shirred line is emphasized. Crisscrossing shirred lines gives a honeycomb smocked effect.

Smocking. Smocking is a method of controlling fabric by multiple rows of precise tacking or gathering. Smocking is often done by hand. Few theatres have the time to create many smocked garments by hand, although occasionally small details may be employed. Multiple rows of machine shirring and criss-cross shirring create from a distance the effect of hand smocking. Collars, cuffs, and yokes of garments are the common place for smocking detail.

Hand Smocking

1. Create a grid of dots at intervals of 1/2″.
2. Pull the first two dots on the top row together as illustrated.
3. Drop down to the next row and connect the second and third dots as illustrated.
4. Go back to the top row and connect the third and fourth dots. Continue this way until all dots are connected.

You may wish to display colorful threads and reveal the stitching with this method. Sometimes pearls or tiny beads may be attached at the connecting points to enhance the smocking even more (Figure 8–10).

Machine Smocking

1. Create several rows of machine shirring.
2. Using a decorative machine stitch, or pieces of trim, sew directly on top of the gathered stitch to emphasize the line.

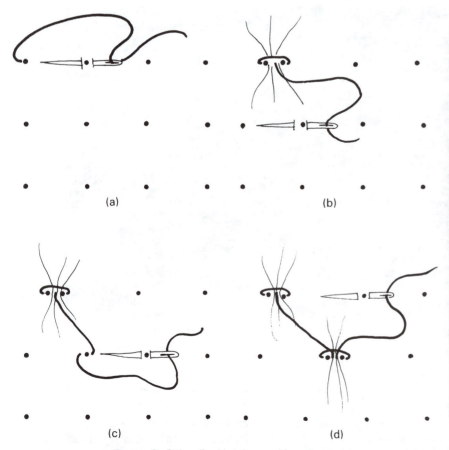

(a)　　　　(b)

(c)　　　　(d)

Figure 8–9 (a–d) Hand smocking steps

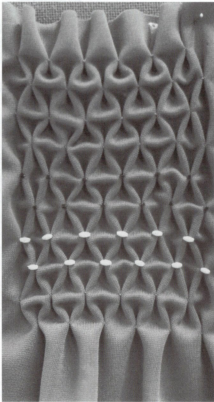

Figure 8–10 Hand smocking with beads

DECORATIVE DETAILS

Embroidery

Embroidery is an ornamental needlework. Threads sewn into the fabric create patterns and pictures. Embroidery is one of the oldest forms of fabric decoration, probably dating back to before 1200 B.C. Examples of embroidered garments have been found in ancient Egyptian tombs and depicted in Roman wall paintings.

In the 19th century girls were routinely taught this form of textile ornamentation. Today embroidery is found primarily in wall hangings, tablecloths, pillow cases, and dresser scarves.

In costuming, hand embroidery is still employed when the luxury of time is available. Otherwise the effects of embroidery may be created with paint, crayons, pens, and glue (see chapter 9).

Embroidery may be done with embroidery floss, yarn, or heavy thread and a large-eyed needle. An embroidery hoop may be used to hold the fabric in place during the stitching.

The following are descriptions of the basic embroidery stitches that are most useful to the theatre costumer:

Backstitch.   This is an outlining stitch. Historically it was used in blackwork embroidery. It is worked from right to left. Bring the needle through the fabric, reinsert it to the right of the entry point, then bring it up again to the left of the original entry point (Figure 8–12).

Figure 8–11   Hand embroidery on an 18th century costume stomacher

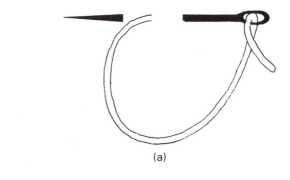

(a)

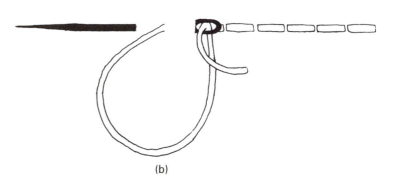

(b)

Figure 8–12   Backstitch

Stemstitch. This is a heavy outlining stitch frequently used in embroidery to create the stems of flowers and plants. Working from left to right, bring the needle through the fabric and reinsert it to the right of the point of entry. Bring the needle through the fabric again at a point halfway between the entry point and the place where the needle was reinserted. Continue in this fashion (Figure 8-13).

Blanket stitch. This stitch was a method of finishing the edges of blankets but today is used to make handworked buttonholes and eyelets as well as for a decorative treatment for edges. Working from left to right, bring the needle up through the fabric, then reinsert it to the right and at an angle above the point of entry (Figure 8-14). Bring the needle up again through the fabric directly below the point it just entered and to the right of the first entry point. Before pulling the yarn through, slip it under the needle so that a right angle is formed with the yarn. Continue in this fashion.

Chain stitch. A chain stitch forms a heavier outline than the stemstitch or backstitch. Bring the needle through the fabric, then reinsert it at the same point bringing it out a short distance away while carrying the yarn under the needle while you pull it through (Figure 8-15).

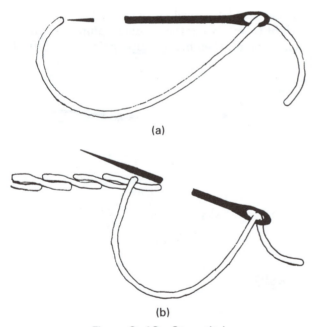

(a)

(b)

Figure 8-13 Stemstitch

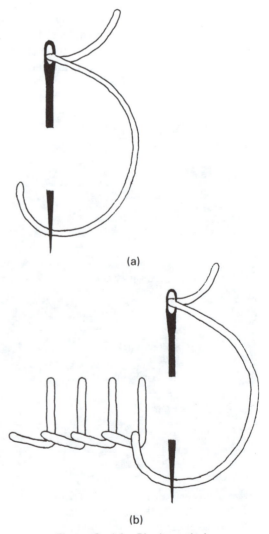

(a)

(b)

Figure 8-14 Blanket stitch

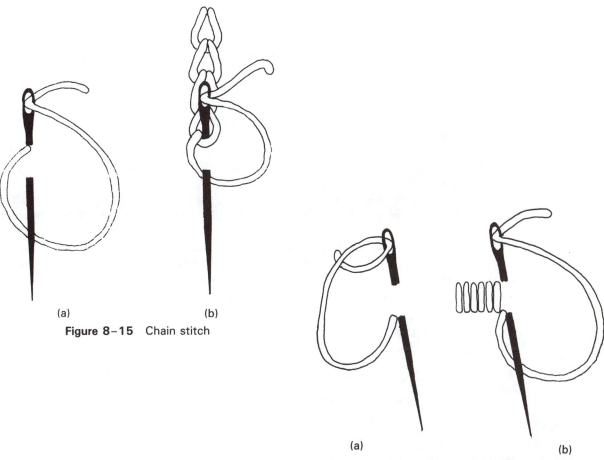

(a) (b)

Figure 8-15 Chain stitch

(a) (b)

Figure 8-16 Satin stitch

Satin stitch. A satin stitch creates a solid block of color with long straight stitches placed close together. Working from left to right, insert the needle into the fabric, then reinsert it directly above the point of entry. Pull the needle through again right next to the first entry point to form a line and begin the next (Figure 8-16). Continue in this fashion with a series of lines.

Tucking

Tucks are simply small decorative pleats. They are used to add detail to a garment rather than to control fullness. Often tucks are stitched in place (Figure 8-17).

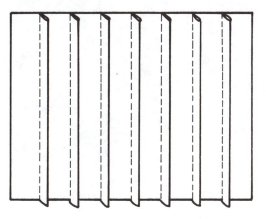

Figure 8-17 Tucking

Quilting

Quilting is the process of sewing through two pieces of fabric with a filler in between. Quilting is more practical than decorative, though occasionally it may be seen as an ornamental detail in undergarments. Padded and quilted doublets in the 14th and 15th centuries served to protect the body from armor but were attractively quilted and worn as outer garments as well.

Quilting patterns may be very regular and geometric, or they may follow a pattern established by the texture or pattern on the fabric itself.

Quilting may be done by hand or by machine. Either way all layers should be securely pinned or basted before the final stitching is done in order to prevent movement and slipping.

Usually a light, inexpensive fabric is used for the backing. On top of this the filler is placed. Dacron fiberfill and lightweight polyurethane foam are good filler materials. The fiberfill will produce a softer padded effect and the foam a rather rigid look. The top layer will be the visible fabric.

When all layers are securely pinned, the pattern is drawn on the top layer. Stitch through all layers in the desired pattern. If layers tend to shift, baste the pieces together with a long running stitch.

Figure 8–18 Designer's rendering showing quilted skirt for Mistress Quickly in the opera FALSTAFF. Designed by James Berton Harris, Krannert Center for the Performing Arts, University of Illinois.

Figure 8–19 Finished costume for Mistress Quickly showing a pieced and quilted skirt

Figure 8-20 Quilting used with polyurethane foam filler to create dagged edge

Figure 8-21 Quilting on stomacher

Figure 8-22 Felt appliqué used to create King and Queen of Hearts costumes for *Alice in Wonder* at Eastern Michigan University.

Appliqué

This is a process of applying a cut-out fabric pattern to a larger piece of fabric. Appliqué work may be glued in place or stitched. The slipstitch, described in chapter 4, is a good hand stitch to use for appliqué since the stitching is nearly invisible. Zig-zag machine stitching may be used with appliqué to create a defined border for the pattern being applied.

Figure 8–23 Hand beading used to decorate bodice and belt

Beading

Beading by hand is very time-consuming but the effects are spectacular. Beads may be sewn on individually or by using a special beading hook, which resembles a crochet hook. With the beading hook the work is done with the beads already strung. Loops of the beading string are pulled with the hook to the wrong side of the fabric, then interlocked with a chain stitch.

OTHER USEFUL NEEDLEWORK

Almost all needlework processes have application to costuming. Handwork, if carefully done, can add immeasurably to the beauty of a costume and the pride an actor and artist take in the garment. Among the most useful skills for a costumer to learn are knitting, crocheting, and macramé. Crocheting is especially useful to a costumer. One can make costumes, caps, belt loops, and armor with a very simple crochet stitch.

Crocheting

Crocheting may be applied in several ways to create or decorate costumes. Chain-stitch crocheting may be done with or without a hook. It is often employed in the creation of belt and button loops, sashes, and ties.

Chain Stitch

1. Hold the crochet hook with the hook facing down, as shown in Figure 8–24a. Left-handed crocheters will do the same, using the left hand, and may look at this series of illustrations in a mirror for more clarification.
2. Make a slipknot in the yarn about 4″ from the end of the yarn and insert the hook (Figure 8–24b).
3. Pulling both ends of the yarn, make the loop smaller but large enough so that the hook still moves freely back and forth within it (Figure 8–24c).
4. Wrap the yarn around the little finger of the hand not holding the hook, then over the top of the index finger, which will control tension on the yarn (Figure 8–24d).

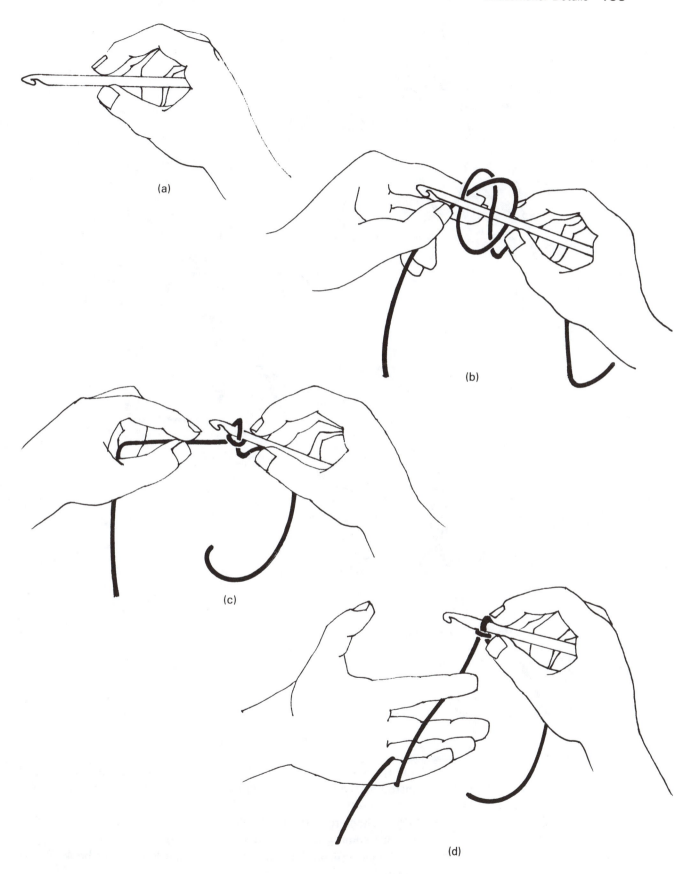

Figure 8-24 Crochet series

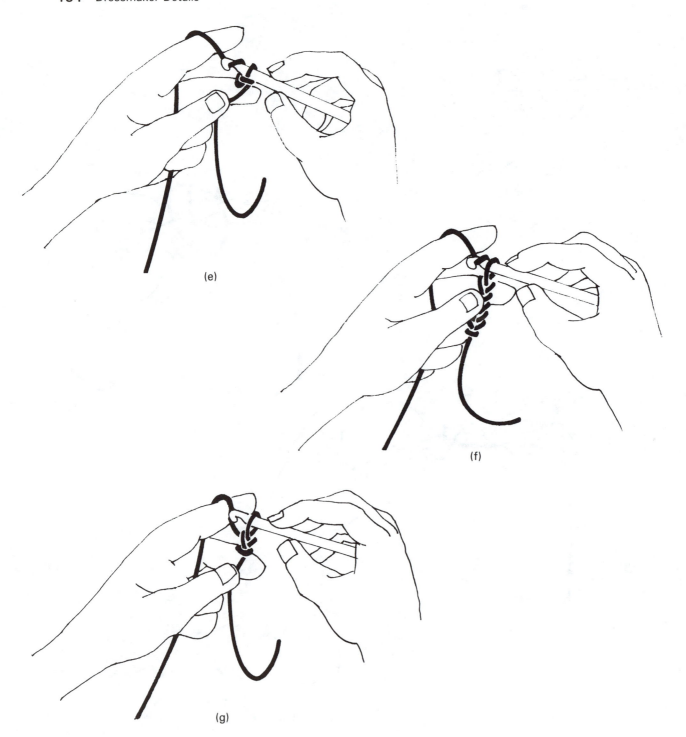

Figure 8-24 continued.

5. Hold the slipknot between the thumb and middle finger of the hand controlling the yarn, while keeping the yarn taut over the index finger (Figure 8-24e).

6. Push the hook forward and twist it toward you so that the hook grabs the yarn coming over the index finger (Figure 8-24e).

7. Pull the yarn through the loop to form a new loop on the hook (Figure 8-24f).

8. Repeat the process until the chain is as long as you wish. Continue to hold the last loop formed with the thumb and middle finger, and keep the yarn taut as it is pulled over the index finger (Figure 8–24g).
9. To complete the chain, cut the yarn over the index finger, then pull the yarn through the loop on the hook.

Single Crochet.   This is the basis for chainmail armor. The pieces are crocheted with a very large hook, then sewn together with yarn or thread.

1. Create a chain as long as one dimension of the piece you wish to crochet.
2. Insert the hook in the second chain from the hook and catch the yarn and pull it through the chain. You should now have two loops on your hook.
3. Grab the yarn with the hook by looping it under the yarn, and pull that yarn through both loops.
4. Repeat this process in each chain across the row.
5. At the end of the row make one chain stitch, then turn and insert the hook in the last stitch of the previous row to begin the single crochet procedure for the second row.
6. To finish off a piece, cut the yarn and then pull the cut yarn through the loops on the hook.

EXERCISES

1. Practice creating the four basic types of pleats.
   a. knife
   b. box
   c. cartridge
   d. primitive
   Where would it be appropriate to use each type?
2. Practice the following dressmaker details:
   a. smocking
   b. shirring
   c. tucking
   d. quilting
   e. embroidery
   Where might you use such details in costume construction?

Fabric Modification

It is not always possible to find the perfect fabric for a costume. Even when it is available, the perfect fabric may cost more than a limited costume budget will allow. Fortunately, there are many ways of enhancing and changing existing fabrics to turn them into near-perfect choices for costumes. Painting, dyeing, dressmaker details, and the distance of the audience from the costume all work together to create marvelous illusions and theatre magic.

FABRIC QUALITIES

Some things cannot be changed. The way a fabric drapes, the weight and movement of a fabric, remain more or less constant beyond the removal of sizing or severe beating. For this reason certain factors should be considered before attempting to change one fabric into another.

As mentioned in chapter 3, the important qualities to consider when buying fabric are: weave, weight, color, texture, and price. As weave and weight (or price, for that matter) may not be easily altered by the theatre designer, these are the factors to first consider when buying fabric. Although it is possible to build up fabric with sizing and inner lining, or to soften it through repeated washings, weave and weight, like price, are difficult for a costumer to change much.

Figure 9-1 Elizabethan dress created from dyed, stenciled, painted, sprayed and highlighted fabrics for *Elizabeth the Queen* at Eastern Michigan University

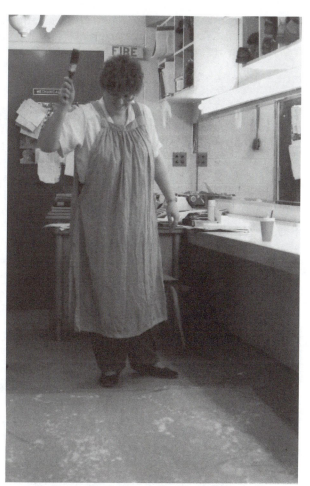

Figure 9-2 Splatter painting technique for nontoxic paints

Qualities that can be altered through dyeing, painting, and stitching are color and texture. Fiber content will determine which dyes or paints can be used and the procedures to follow.

Much experimentation has been done with fabric manipulation, and many happy accidents have achieved beautiful results, but it is important to understand the dangers of using dyes, markers, and laundry additives that may in themselves or in combination be toxic. Naturally, following package directions is a start, and working in a well-ventilated area with mask on and hands protected is also wise. Beyond this, common sense must prevail.

DYEING

Fabric dyeing can be very confusing without clear directions for dealing with specific fabrics. A good manual on fabric dyeing is valuable, though it often goes beyond the capabilities and limitations of a typical costume facility.

Different fabrics will react differently to different types of dyes. It is therefore important to test a small swatch of any fabric before immersing the entire yardage in a dye bath.

Other factors influencing the acceptance of dye into a fabric are the temperature of water, the time allowed in the dye bath, and chemical assistants added to the bath.

Dye Equipment

If dyeing is to be done on a regular basis, it is a good idea to set aside a regular space away from other costuming activity. This space should be well-ventilated and separate from materials that might be damaged by dye spills. It is useful to have a washer, dryer, sink, and table in the dye area, though dyeing may be done in reduced spaces as well, with a hot plate and metal pots. Commercial soup kettles or dye vats will provide increased dyeing options, but most costume shops are not set up to do such extensive dyeing.

Materials Used in Dyeing

1. Hot plate
2. Spoons and dyesticks
3. Measuring cups and spoons
4. Old dress forms
5. Stainless steel or enamel pots and vats
6. Rubber gloves
7. Candy thermometer
8. Paint brushes
9. Detergent
10. Bleach
11. Water softening agent
12. Dyes (union, acid, and basic)

Types of Dye

There are ten types of dye commonly used by costume designers. Each requires following a precise procedure and involves different risks. Lists of these dyes and their uses may be found in books devoted specifically to dyeing. Many costume shops are not equipped to safely use a wide range of dyes. We will discuss two common and easy-to-obtain dyes in this book. Additional information on fabric manipulation through dyeing and painting may be found in Deborah Dryden's *Fabric Painting and Dyeing for the Theatre.*

Union Dyes. These are household dyes available in supermarkets and drug stores and capable of easy use by beginners. They are designed to dye a wide range of fabrics because they are composed of a blend of many types of dyes. Rit, Tintex, and Putnam are common household union dyes. This type of dye may be used without additional chemicals and extensive safety precautions and is therefore the most commonly used staple dye in most costume shops.

Specific instructions for dyeing appear on individual packages.

Procedure for using union dyes

1. Wash and cold rinse fabric to be dyed.
2. If dye is in powder form, mix with a small amount of water to dissolve into a paste.

3. Add dye to water.

4. Add fabric to dye bath.

5. Bring bath to boil and simmer, or maintain high temperature of water and move fabric in bath for the first 15 minutes. The intensity of color will increase with extended time in the dye bath, though the majority of color will enter the fabric within the first 15 minutes.

6. Rinse fabric with cold water and dry.

7. The union dyes will remain fast longer if the fabric is dry cleaned rather than washed. If material is to be machine washed, do so with cold water and wash separately.

Fiber-Reactive Dyes. These dyes are particularly popular with fiber artists. The colors are extremely fast since the dye molecules actually bond to the fiber chemically during the dyeing process. These dyes are used with cold to lukewarm water. They may be purchased in art supply stores. They are especially effective in dyeing cotton, linen, rayon, silk, and wool.

Procedure for using fiber-reactive dyes

1. Fill dye bath container with water. Allow enough room in container for fabric to move freely in bath.

2. Dissolve dye powder in a small amount of hot water and add to dye bath.

3. Add salt according to package instructions.

4. If water is hard, add a tablespoon of a water-softening agent (such as Calgon).

5. Place washed and evenly wet fabric in the dye bath and stir for ten minutes.

6. Remove fabric.

7. Add dissolved washing soda to dye bath.

8. Return fabric to bath and stir for an additional 15 minutes.

9. Remove fabric from the bath and rinse in cold water.

10. Allow fabric to dry in the air.

11. After fabric is dry, rinse again in cold, then warm water.

12. Remove excess dye by running fabric through a hot wash cycle with mild detergent.

Discharge Dyeing. Discharge dyeing is the process of removing color from, or bleaching, fabric. It is commonly used in the theatre for aging costumes and fabrics.

Procedure for discharge dyeing

1. Test fabric to determine proportion of bleach or color remover and water. (Start with a 1-to-10 proportion bleach to water solution and add more bleach if necessary, bearing in mind that bleach can begin to destroy the fiber if it is too concentrated.)

2. Place cool, dampened fabric into the bleach solution for the predetermined time. The solution may also be applied to the fabric directly by brush or spray, depending on the desired effect. Make sure you have protected your clothing and work in a well-ventilated area.

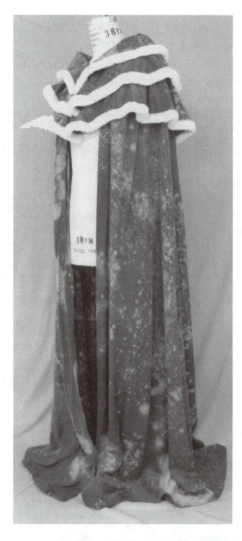

Figure 9-3 Discharge dyeing on robe velour cape

3. If the fabric is to be washed, rinse it in a weak solution of hydrogen peroxide (1 to 20) to stop the action of the bleach. If you are using color remover, rinse thoroughly in clear water.

FABRIC PAINTING

Painting is another way of changing the appearance of fabric either before or after it is made into a costume. Costumers use several types of paints on fabrics. Some are actually made to be applied to textiles, and others, which are not strictly textile paints, have qualities that make them particularly useful to costumers.

Types of Paints and Markers That Can Be Used on Fabric

Acrylic Paints. These multifaceted paints are very popular with costumers for several reasons. First, they are readily available at art supply stores in a large range of colors and metallics. (Many designers use acrylic paints to paint costume sketches.) These paints may be diluted with water and used with airbrush or applied directly to a surface with a paintbrush. When dry the paints remain flexible, although the more thickly the paint is applied, the more the fabric will be stiffened.

Acrylic paints will cover synthetic and natural fibers and remain permanent despite machine washing and dry cleaning if they are set by pressing with a hot iron. Be sure to use a press cloth rather than placing the hot iron directly on the painted surface.

Dye Pastes. Unlike acrylic paints, dye pastes will not stiffen fabrics. Almost all dyes may be thickened to a paste for controlled brush and print application. Dye pastes are set by steam heat.

Dye pastes are built from dye and a thickener. For fiber-reactive dyes (see previous section), sodium alginate is used as a thickener. Four teaspoons of sodium alginate are mixed with one teaspoon of a fabric softening agent and four cups of water in a blender. The mixture should be allowed to thicken before use and may be stored in the refrigerator until needed.

Glycerin, acetic acid, and urea are all agents used in creating thickeners for other types of dyes. Specific recipes for thickeners as well as additional hints on painting with dyes may be found in textile painting books.

Enamel Spray Paint. These paints are available in hardware stores at inexpensive prices and in a wide range of colors. They dry quickly and if used sparingly will not stiffen fabric much. They are especially popular for their metallic colors and for overall aging and general light painting. As with all paints and dyes, adequate ventilation is essential during use. It is very important to wear a mask while spray painting.

Acrylic Medium. Acrylic medium comes in matte and gloss finishes. It is the binder for acrylic paint and therefore may be used like acrylic paint. The medium is especially useful for applying metallic bronzing powders to create a relatively brilliant metal effect on fabric. The bronzing powder may be added to the medium, then painted directly onto fabric. Like acrylic paint, the medium will stiffen fabric a bit, but it will not crack or peel off when dry.

Textile Paints. A number of textile paints exist with a variety of solvents and procedures for use. They are available at art-supply stores in brilliant colors. Follow label directions for best results.

Felt-Tip Markers. Although costumers have long used permanent felt-tip markers as painting tools on fabric, in the last decade markers designed especially for fabric painting have been developed in a range of colors. Markers will not stiffen fabric, and they provide direct control over pattern and use. This is especially nice for detail and creating highlights and shadow. Depending on the specific marker and fabric being used, the color may or may not withstand washing or dry cleaning. It is therefore wise to test fabric before cleaning. It is particularly important to use markers in a well-ventilated area.

Fabric Crayons. Crayons have been developed specifically for fabric use in the past few years. Some can be used to draw the pattern directly onto the fabric, while others are used to draw the pattern paper (the pattern is then transferred to fabric with a hot iron). Specific instructions are listed on crayon boxes. In all cases, the results look very much like crayon applied to cloth, and are effective if that is the desired look.

Liquid Embroidery. These are ballpoint tubes of paint, which are applied to fabric the way one would draw. The paints are colorfast and good for detail work, and the imitation of fine embroidery may be achieved quite successfully with them.

Methods of Painting on Fabric

Much fabric painting is done by direct application. Because a pattern is frequently confined to a small area and because detail fades over distance it is often the most efficient method of creating or enhancing a pattern.

Creating a regular, repeated pattern involves stenciling or printing procedures that are more complicated but, if a repeated pattern is needed to cover a large amount of fabric, probably desirable.

Stencils. Stencils can be cut from stencil paper, cardboard, or heavy craft paper treated on both sides with several layers of shellac after the stencil is cut to resist deterioration from the paint.

Procedure for stenciling

1. Cut the pattern with a utility or X-acto knife, leaving sufficient sections of the paper intact to hold the pattern in place. If the pattern is to be continuous, cut the stencil with a portion of the repeated pattern to use in lining up the stencil.
2. A particularly delicate pattern may be reinforced with netting.
3. Lay the fabric to be painted on a hard, smooth surface. Smooth the fabric so that no wrinkles are present. If spray paint is being used the fabric should be pinned to a vertical surface and the stencil should be pinned over it. If you are using an airbrush, the material to be painted can be laid out on the floor. In either case, fabric not being painted should be masked to prevent light, accidental dusting.
4. Mark the fabric with chalk to indicate placement of the stencil.
5. Place the stencil on the fabric and secure it so it will not be moved during the painting period.

Figure 9-4 Stencil pattern used to create embroidered effect on ruffle

(a)

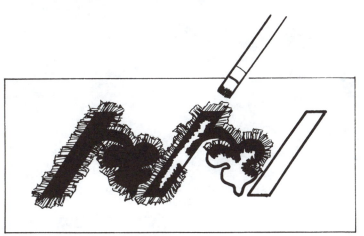

(b)

Figure 9–5 Cutting a stencil; painting with a stencil brush

6. Paint the pattern with brush, airbrush, or spray paint. With a stencil brush, make short strokes in from the sides of the stencil, then fill the center portion of the pattern. With the airbrush and spray paint, use careful, even spray application, making sure that you begin and end pressure on the applicator off the fabric to avoid blotching effects.

7. Allow the paint to surface dry before moving the stencil to the next position. Make sure that the back of the stencil is kept free from paint drips, which can cause smears on the fabric. From time to time, you may have to clean both surfaces of the stencil to keep the pattern sharp and clear. This is true especially if the pattern is to be used repeatedly.

8. If appropriate, set the paint with a press cloth and a hot iron.

Other materials may be used as stencils for overall repeated patterns and textures. Pieces of lace, metal screening, and loosely woven drapery fabric may be used as stencils themselves. The effects of painting through these open-weave materials will generally be an effective but nonspecific breaking up of the fabric surface.

Emphasizing an Existing Pattern. Sometimes it is desirable to pull out or emphasize a pattern that already exists on a fabric. Either paint or felt-tipped markers work well in this process. By underlining below and to one side of the

Figure 9-6 Using a piece of lace for a stencil

Figure 9-7 Using marker to shadow an existing pattern

Figure 9-8 Stencil used with puff paint

Figure 9-9 Puff paint heated with an iron to create "puffed" effect

pattern, the shapes are made to appear raised from the surface of the fabric and the texture will seem to be more three-dimensional. In this way a flat printed fabric can acquire the appearance of a more luxurious brocade.

Puff paints. Puff paints have the capability of creating actual rather than merely visual three-dimensional effects on the fabric to which they are applied. These paints are children's craft items which are used as textile paints with stencils or by direct application. They are found in toy stores and hobby stores with other paint and craft items.

Puff paint is applied and mixed just like acrylic paint. When the paint is thoroughly dry, the fabric is placed in a warm oven, or pressed from the back with a hot iron. The painted areas will "puff" up and create an embossed appearance.

Colors of puff paint will lighten when heat is applied, and the paint itself will take on a flocked appearance. Stripes of this paint look something like velvet ribbon.

PRINTING ON FABRIC

Printing on fabric has taken several forms in the past few years. Wonderful effects have been achieved through screen printing, photocopying, and blue-printing processes. By far the easiest and most trouble-free method to learn and apply is block printing.

Block Prints

These print patterns may be cut in wood or linoleum blocks, which are available at art-supply stores, or from other common items, including the grade-school favorite, the potato. Plastic erasers make good, though small, printing blocks. Styrofoam meat and vegetable trays also work well for this process.

Wood or linoleum block-cutting tools may be used to cut the pattern into the block or, if erasers or potatoes are used, an X-acto knife will work well. All types of fabric paints, inks, dye pastes, and acrylic paints may be used in block prints. Rollers, brayers, brushes, or stamp pads are used to transfer paint or dye to the block.

Printing process

1. Transfer the pattern to a block, remembering that the pattern will be a mirror image when printed.

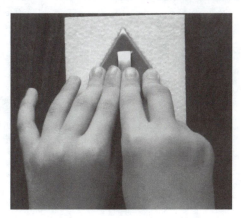

Figure 9–10 Pressing a cookie cutter in a styrofoam block to create a pattern

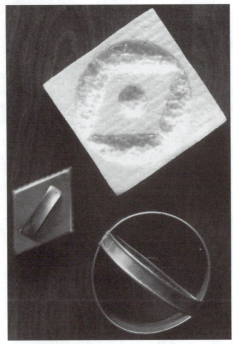

Figure 9–11 Cutting away the excess styrofoam

Figure 9–12 Transferring paint to the block with a roller

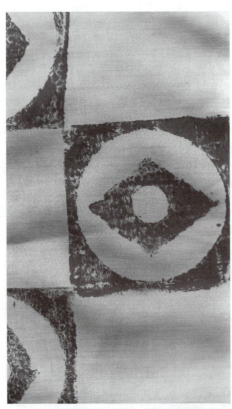

Figure 9–13 Styrofoam block print

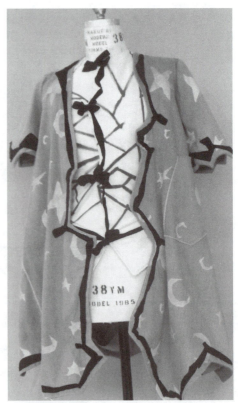

Figure 9–14 Stars and moons printed on fabric from a block print

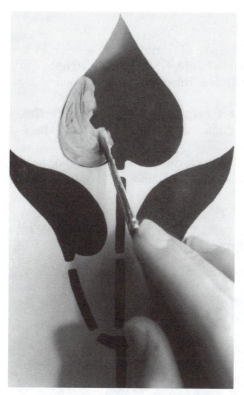 

Figure 9–15 Paint on glass which has been laid over the pattern

Figure 9–16 Pattern transferred to fabric from glass plate

2. Cut the pattern into the block, removing negative spaces with wood-cutting tools or knives. It is important to work away from the body since these tools are sharp and can easily slip.
3. Transfer paint or dye paste to the block with a brush, roller, or stamp pad.
4. Press the block into the fabric to create the image. Tapping the block with a rubber mallet will create a clearer image. For repeated images make sure the fabric has been marked with chalk for proper block placement.
5. Clean the block whenever paint starts to obscure the pattern definition or whenever a color change is desired.

Monoprint process

Single and repeated prints may also be created easily with a monoprint process. The definition of the design is not as clear in this process, but the procedure is very simple to learn and apply.

1. Place a piece of glass or acetate on top of the pattern to be reproduced.
2. Paint the pattern on top of the glass with acrylic or textile paint.
3. Before the paint dries, quickly press the fabric onto the painted glass to pick up the paint.

Printing, like stenciling, may be created in a more general fashion by painting the surface of a textured object and pressing that into the fabric. Sponges, textured fabric, and plastic packing materials are among the suitable items for this type of printing.

OTHER DECORATIVE TREATMENTS

Flexible glue. A variety of flexible white glues may be used to decorate directly or to apply trim to fabric. Glitter sprinkled onto wet glue will create a beaded effect from a distance. Black glitter is a good substitute for jet beading on costumes.

Sequins or trim may also be applied with flexible white glue, but washing and most dry-cleaning processes will dissolve the glue.

Hot-melt glue. Direct drawing with hot-melt glue or hot-melt caulking provides a raised embroidery effect. Enamel spray paint may be used to pull out the

Figure 9-17 Painting with flexible glue

Figure 9-18 Sequins applied to fabric with flexible white glue

Figure 9-19 White caulking used to create embroidered effect on Roman tunic

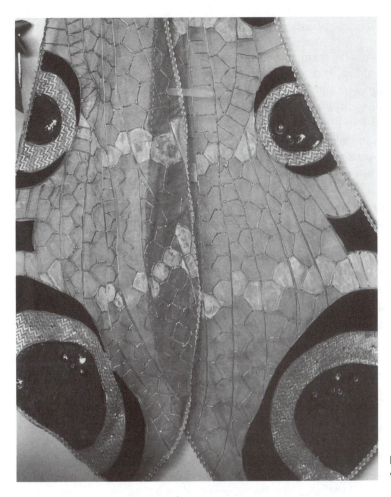

Figure 9-20 Hot glue used to create veining for dragonfly wings

pattern created by the glue or caulking. Hot-melt glue and caulking come in white, off-white, translucent honey-colored, and clear sticks. If any of these are suitable they may be used without painting. Hot-melt glue dissolves in dry cleaning, but is safe to wash in cool or warm water.

DISTRESSING FABRICS AND COSTUMES

Breaking down and aging costumes is an essential part of realistic costuming. This may be done with painting and dyeing processes as well as actual physical attacks on the fabric itself. Though the procedures vary, the techniques are lumped together into the category of costume distressing or aging.

Creating Realistic Aging

Realistic aging is creating the look of a naturally old, worn, and faded garment. It is important to realism that the distressing of the costume reflect the way clothing ages naturally. Think about what areas get thin first: the knees and seat of breeches; the elbows of a shirt or jacket. Think about which areas become sun bleached. Where is built-up dirt likely to occur? Where might spots of wear occur from constant rubbing? Study actual old garments and observe the frayed hem edges and accumulation of grime. Note how the fabric itself becomes limper and softer. All of these factors may be incorporated into the realistic aging of costumes.

Methods of Distressing Costumes

1. Physical destruction of the fabric may occur with general washing and bleaching, but more vigorous breakdown of the fabric requires more vigorous methods. Sanding the surface and edges with sandpaper, files, or wire brushes is a good way of creating realistic thinning and fraying.

2. Shapelessness may be achieved by wetting and weighting a garment to speed up a natural breakdown and gravity effect on clothing. Stuffing pockets while the garment is damp will provide a natural look of age.

3. Resilient permapress and colorfast fabrics are the most difficult to age. Very hot water and tying garments into knots may eventually break down these protected fabrics.

4. Applications of paint and dye may be used to create realistic dirt and sweat stains. Naturalistic built-up dirt and sweat is best achieved with subtle spraying procedures.

5. General shadowing and texturing may be accomplished with spraying to emphasize construction details and to give a costume more depth and interest.

6. Blood, mud, and exceptional specific dirt may be applied through splattering, if the blood or dirt is to appear splattered. A wet-blood look may be achieved by painting clear nail enamel over acrylic blood stains. Commercial stage blood makeup may stain a costume.

7. If dirt is to look rubbed in, why not actually "rub" the paint where the worker would likely have wiped his hands? This kind of aging and distressing should look specific, and it should make sense.

8. Airbrushes and spray paints are most useful for aging. Both subtle and dramatic effects can be achieved, depending on the dilution of the paint or dye and the size of the spray nozzle being used.

EXERCISES

1. Experiment with direct application of the following materials on different types of fabrics. Keep track of what works and what doesn't work.
   (a) Dyes
   (b) Bleach
   (c) Crayon
   (d) Paints
   (e) Felt markers
   (f) Glues
2. Design and cut a stencil. Try the stencil with several types of paints on a variety of fabrics. Keep track of the results.
3. Experiment with one of the printing techniques described in the chapter.

Understructures 10

Controlling the body, especially the female body, by the use of restrictive and silhouette-altering understructures dates back to the ancient civilizations of Crete and Sumeria. As understructures changed, so changed the fashion line of the costume. Without the proper undergarment, a style or period is not accurately displayed. With the proper understructures the actor will not only look appropriate to the period, he or she will also be able to get a feeling for the posturing and movement of that period.

RESEARCHING UNDERGARMENTS

It is essential that the pattern lines of both outer and inner garments be re-created accurately for the silhouette of a period garment to properly emerge.

Most costume and fashion history books give information on the understructures that have affected the silhouette of high fashion throughout history, and in addition there are books that concentrate specifically on undergarments.

Patterns for undergarments may be found in many books of period patterns, notably Norah Waugh's *Corsets and Crinolines*.

ADJUSTING PATTERNS TO THE MODERN BODY

Adjusting corset patterns is much like adjusting a period pattern to fit today's body. Because corsets derive their shaping ability from the structure of the pattern pieces, it is important when altering the pattern to maintain the essential integrity of the shapes.

If the pattern you are using is taken from an original corset, it is important to enlarge carefully and without destroying the significant structural and style lines. If the pattern must be made larger than the original intended size, it is a good idea to evenly spread the extra allowance to all seams.

Remember that the corset is made to control (distort, if you will) the figure from the norm. A new structure is taking the place of the natural human form. Flesh from the waist is likely to be pushed down or up, increasing the rib cage or hip measurement. It is best to make the necessary adjustments at the waist and follow the seam lines at the same measurement both above and below the waist. If these areas must be adjusted after the corset is finished, do so carefully so as not to change the proper silhouette line.

The corset waist measurement on the final pattern is usually about 2″ smaller than the actual waist. This allows the corset to cinch the body at this point. If the waist is to be cinched more than 2″, the corset should be so adjusted.

Hoops, paniers, bustles, and pads are far easier than corsets to adjust. As these are extensions to the body rather than devices to enhance and restrict the body, they can easily be adjusted by manipulation of the waist measurement. These undergarments can therefore be used and reused for years to come.

CORSETS

A corset is a body-control device that cinches, pushes, and redistributes the flesh of the torso into the current stylish mode. Corsets have been made with wood, whalebone, and steel stays, and even cast iron for problem figures. Corsets for the theatre are usually made of 100% cotton fabric and sprung-steel corset stays for comfort and maintenance. The process for corset construction

Figure 10–1   Corsets

is the same for any period, though some corsets involve a more complex set of pattern pieces and a variety of trimming and structural materials.

Developing and Adjusting the Pattern

1. As with most book patterns it is a good idea to enlarge the pattern pieces before attempting any size adjustments.
2. Check the bust, waist, and hip (if applicable) measurements of the wearer against those on the corset pattern. Make sure that the waist of the corset pattern is 2″ to 4″ smaller than the waist measurement of the wearer.
3. If adjustments must be made to the waist, spread them over all of the pattern pieces. Remember, you are working with a pattern that will be doubled, so the measurements at this point will reflect only half of the adjustment.
4. Following the lines of the original corset pattern, make adjustments above and below the waistline. Note: Since the body will be shifted under the corset, the bust and hip lines will not necessarily end up the same measurement as on the uncorseted body. Further adjustments in these measurements may be made during the fitting process if necessary.
5. Mark all pattern pieces to indicate center front, center back, fold lines, bone placement top and bottom, and order in which the pieces are to be assembled. It is important to mark corset pieces carefully since frequently they do not resemble other garment pieces and are easily turned upside down or reversed. A simple system for avoiding this is to mark the upper corner of each piece to match the upper corner of a corresponding piece.

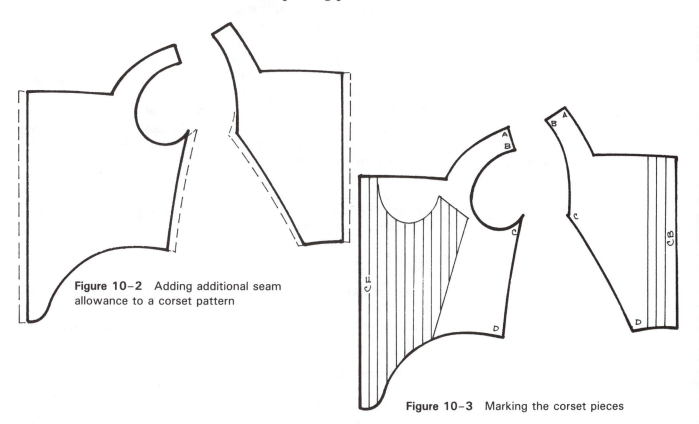

Figure 10-2   Adding additional seam allowance to a corset pattern

Figure 10-3   Marking the corset pieces

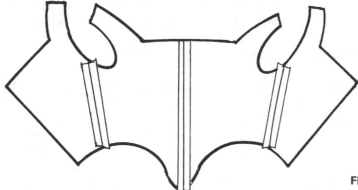

Figure 10-4 Corset basted together

Layout, Cutting, and Fitting the Inner Corset

The corset will be constructed with an outer and inner layer. The inner layer should be constructed of a heavy, densely woven cotton fabric. Canvas duck and pillow ticking are good fabrics for both outer and inner corsets. If the corset will be seen, the outer corset may be cut from any decorative fabric that suits the design. If the fabric of the outer corset is not a heavy, densely woven fabric, each piece of the outer corset may be flat-lined with cotton duck before the undergarment is assembled.

The amounts of fabric needed varies with the specific corset, but most corsets may be constructed with a yard and a half of 45″ fabric.

1. Cut the inner corset first. Lay the pattern pieces on washed, folded cotton fabric to allow for 3/4″ seam allowance on all edges, and a 2 1/2″ seam allowance in the center back.
2. Cut and carefully mark all pattern pieces.
3. Machine baste all pieces together along seam lines. Leave the center back open.
4. Fit the corset to the wearer by pinning the corset snugly in the back. The center back seam line will not come together at this point, but you should be able to get an idea of an approximate fit by pinning the corset through the excess fabric allowed at the center back.
5. Make adjustments as needed by dividing the alterations symmetrically and using several seam lines so as not to radically alter the basic line of the corset. Check the upper and lower edges of the corset and make adjustments if necessary.
6. Remove the corset, carefully mark all adjustments, remove basting threads, and correct pattern lines. Make sure corset curve lines are maintained as you even up the pattern.

Creating the Outer Corset

1. Using the fitted inner corset as a pattern, lay out, cut, and mark the outer corset.
2. Stitch the outer corset along all seam lines, leaving the center back open.

Putting the Outer and Inner Corsets Together

1. Stitch the inner corset back together along the new seam lines, leaving the center back open.

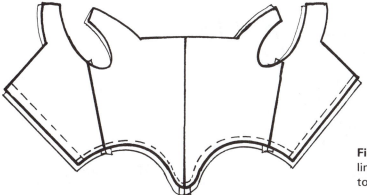

Figure 10-5 Outer and inner corsets lined up and stitched wrong sides together

2. Press open all seams of the inner and outer corsets.
3. Place the outer corset directly on top of the inner corset with WRONG SIDES TOGETHER, matching seam lines, center front, center back, top and bottom. The raw edges of the seam lines will be inside the corset at this point.
4. Stitch along all seam lines and along the bottom edge and center back finish lines.
5. Check the fit again on the wearer. The corset now has a bit more structure, and the final effect should be more evident.

Boning the Corset

The corset may be boned with plastic, steel, or woven wire boning. Steel strapping used in binding crates makes an acceptable boning material if other types of boning are unavailable. Bones may be cut with metal shears and the ends finished with tape or liquid plastic.

Figure 10-6 Finishing the ends of boning with liquid plastic

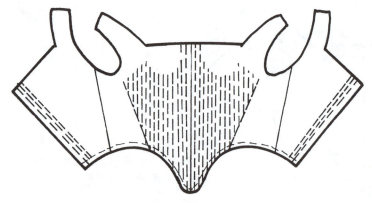

Figure 10–7 Stitching casings for corset bones

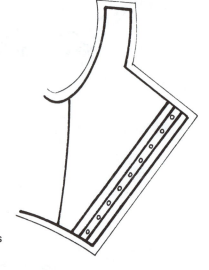

Figure 10–8 Adding grommets to the corset

1. Stitch through both inner and outer corsets to create pockets or casings for the corset bones. Placement of the bones may be indicated on the original pattern pieces, and varies according to the specific style of the corset.
2. Determine the length and cut a bone for each pocket, making sure that the top edge of the boning is below the top seam line. If the corset has armholes, cut the bones under the arms at least 2″ below the armhole seam line for comfort.
3. Finish the ends of the bones if necessary to keep them from poking through the fabric; then insert each bone into its pocket.
4. For structural integrity it is wise to have boning on both sides of the lacing grommets as well as a piece of grosgrain ribbon or belting along the grommet line.
5. Insert grommets, eyelets, or machine eyelets in the lacing area every 2 1/2″.
6. Check the fit by lacing the wearer into the corset. Any final adjustments may be made now before the outer edges are finished. With the bones inserted, the fit is now accurate.

Finishing the Corset

1. Cut away excess seam allowance in the center back; then finish all edges of the corset with bias tape, turning the tape to the inside for hand stitching in place.
2. Add ribbons, lace, and other decorations to the finished corset by hand stitching.
3. If the corset has shoulder seams, connect them with elastic for the comfort and security of the actress.

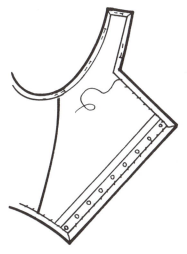

Figure 10-9 Hand stitch bias tape around edges of corset

Figure 10-10 Trimmed and laced corset

HOOPS, PANIERS, BUSTLES, AND ROLLS

A variety of devices have been used to extend and shape the torso. Manipulations of pleats, tabs, and ruffles have altered the shoulder, neckline, and waistline; padded rolls and pieces have extended hip lines, chests, and bellies, and have squared shoulders; and finally, boned and wired cages have been employed to provide a framework for an array of skirts, collars, and sleeves.

Unlike the corset, whose purpose was to control and minimize the upper body, these figure distorters were intended to expand, enlarge, and boldly display portions of the body or the costume.

Making a Hip Roll

Hip rolls are usually worn halfway between the waistline and hip line. They are used to extend skirts and breeches. The hip rolls or bolsters vary in size and shape, but the construction techniques are the same for all rolls.

1. Develop or find appropriate pattern for size and shape of hip roll desired.
2. Cut pattern from heavy, densely woven cotton fabric. Canvas duck and pillow ticking are good fabrics to use for padded rolls. If the roll is to be seen, more decorative fabrics may be used. Since there is little strain on hip rolls, it is usually not necessary to flat line the decorative outer fabric unless it is very sheer or loosely woven.
3. Sew roll together along seam lines, leaving a 3″ opening for turning and to insert the padding material.

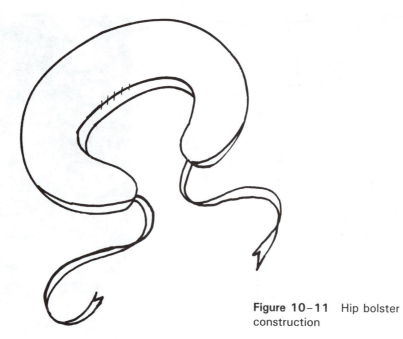

Figure 10–11 Hip bolster construction

4. Fill the roll with shredded foam or synthetic fiberfill until the roll is firm and evenly padded.
5. Stitch the opening closed by hand.
6. Attach ribbon or cord ties to both ends of the roll.

Making a Hoop Skirt

Hoop skirts have reappeared throughout history and achieve variation by the shape of the fabric, petticoat structure, or the length and placement of the tapes which control the hoops, and of course by the size of the hoops themselves. Cotton fabric is the best material from which to construct the body of the hoop, as it is for structural undergarments. Boning materials may be selected from plastic tubing or steel strapping materials.

1. Develop a pattern for the hoop skirt structure.
2. Cut pattern pieces from sturdy cotton fabric and stitch the pieces together.
3. Sew bias or twill tape casings as indicated on the pattern.
4. Insert boning through casing, adjusting length of boning to the amount indicated on the pattern or to achieve appropriate shape.
5. Fit hoop skirt to the waist by gathers, darts, or pleats, and add a waistband.

Making Bustles and Paniers

Bustles and paniers create extensions to the back and to the sides of a skirt. Bustles and paniers differ from hoops in that they require partial rather than full hoops. These hooped sections are held in place by fabric tapes or a fabric backing. The materials used in creating hoop skirts are appropriate for making bustles and paniers. Not all bustles are created with a boned framework. Stiffened fabric ruffles may be used to recreate smaller bustles.

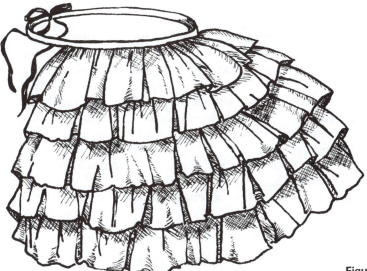

Figure 10–12 Ruffle bustle

Boned Bustle Construction

1. Develop a pattern for the specific bustle or panier.
2. Cut pattern pieces from a heavy cotton fabric.
3. Sew casings of twill tape or bias tape as indicated on the pattern.
4. Insert boning into casings and stitch the ends of the casings shut.
5. Sew together all fabric and boned pattern pieces, taking care to avoid hitting the bones while stitching.
6. Add waistband or tape for tying at the waist.

Boned undergarments may be washed and dry-cleaned if the fabrics used are washable or dry cleanable and the boning selected will not rust. Use a delicate cycle on the washing machine to reduce agitation, which can cause the boning to put stress on the casings, or wash them by hand.

Figure 10–13 Boned bustle

PADDING

Padding is used in two different ways in costuming. The first is to extend the body to create the fashionable silhouette of a given period. The second is to change the shape of the actor to correspond to that of the character he or she will play.

Hip bolsters are discussed in the previous section. Other fashionable padding devices are frequently stitched directly into the costume. The Elizabethan peascod belly and shoulder padding from the Italian Renaissance fall into the fashionable padding category.

Fat suits, pregnancy padding, and various deformities are usually created as separate units rather than built into a costume. In this way, the padding will behave as part of the body, not as part of the costume, and it can be reused.

Making Body Padding

Because body padding is intended to appear as a natural part of the actor's body, it is important that it be created to move naturally with the actor. Usually this requires that it be built on a garment that fits the actor snugly. This can be a constructed sloper, a leotard, a bodysuit, or a t-shirt, depending on how extensive the padding is to be and what is being worn over it.

Small pads used for minor enlargements of specific areas, such as small tummy pads, may be created separately and tied to the body. Although these are less bulky and easier to construct than full suit padding, they also tend to shift and ride as the actor moves and may look exactly like what they are: small pillows tied to the body.

Figure 10–14 Padding used in production of *Alice in Wonder*
Eastern Michigan University

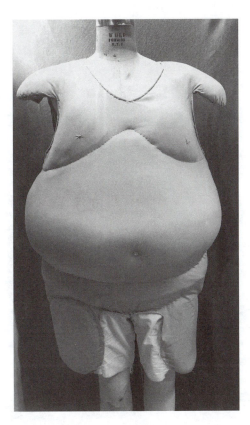

Figure 10–15 Body padding built for FALSTAFF, Krannert Center for the Performing Arts, University of Illinois

1. Construct a fitted garment covering the portion of the actor's body to be padded, or use a preconstructed t-shirt, leotard, or unitard. If stomach padding is required, a long vest will do. If padding will include legs and arms, a full fitted suit will be necessary.

2. Place the fitted suit on a dress form or, if the actor can spare the time, on the actual body. Build up the padding in desired areas, being careful to refer to anatomical drawings and photographs for natural placement of the bulk. Fiberfill and polyurethane foam make good lightweight padding materials. The padding may be pinned with safety pins or large T-pins at this point to be securely stitched by hand later on.

3. Cover padding with a fabric that has a smooth, slippery surface. Hand stitch the fabric onto the undergarment. Fabric with a silky finish is ideal for this purpose because the costume over the padding will be able to slide over the padding as it would over skin.

4. If padding is rather general, and not too expensive, a second t-shirt, unitard, or leotard, rather than individual fabric pieces, may be stitched on top of the first. In either case, make sure the transitions from padding to fabric are gradual and that definition is not lost in the process.

EXERCISES

1. Make a corset from a pattern in any historical pattern book.
2. Make a hoop skirt or panier using a pattern in any historical pattern book.
3. Design and create a piece of padding.

Hats

11

Because an audience is likely to be looking at an actor's face, anything around the face will receive a lot of attention. This is why hats and headdresses are so important to a theatre costume and why they must be carefully considered. While they may greatly enhance the effect of the total costume, they pose certain problems that must be dealt with initially.

One of the first problems is the fact that actors generally are unused to wearing hats. Although hats and headdresses have been an essential part of fashionable dress in most historical periods, they are not so today, and most people are unused to balancing and moving with something perched on their heads. Another problem has to do with the fact that hat brims often shade the actor's face. Directors frequently don't want to deal with hats either. An actor's movements may have to be modified with the addition of a hat. Will the hat be left on or taken off? If it is taken off, where does it go? Will it be held, placed on the set, or handed to the butler?

A hat must be striking and appropriate. It is an accessory where you do not want to compromise style or detail if possible. Hats can do much to complete the effect of a costume, and they likewise can detract if they are poorly made, inappropriately styled, difficult to wear, or if they obscure the actor's face in some way.

If these problems can be overcome, the costumer has the freedom to create one of the most essential and dramatic elements of an actor's costume. The next problems to be addressed are researching and developing the hat or headdress desired.

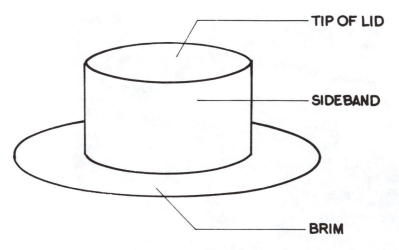

Figure 11–1 Parts of a hat

PARTS OF HATS

Typical hats consist of two major parts: the crown, the part that covers the head, and the brim, which finishes and extends outward from the crown. The crown may be broken down into the tip (or lid) and the sideband. Some hats have only a crown, but most have both a crown and brim. The manipulation of shape in these two areas provides infinite variety in the hat styles that have been developed throughout history.

Theatre hats may be made or adapted from existing structures. The materials used in hat construction are available in large fabric stores, and the techniques used to build the hats are not difficult to learn. Millinery, however, is a very time-consuming job. Many of the procedures require careful handwork and a great deal of patience.

MEASUREMENTS FOR HATS

Hat size refers to the average diameter of the head. This size may be determined for anyone by first measuring the circumference of the head and dividing that number by pi (3.14). Rather than converting each head circumference

Figure 11–2 Hat size conversion chart

Measurement around head	Hat size
19 inches	6
19 ½ inches	6 ¼
20 inches	6 ⅜
20 ½ inches	6 ½
21 inches	6 ⅝
21 ½ inches	6 ⅞
22 inches	7
22 ½ inches	7 ⅛
23 inches	7 ⅜
23 ½ inches	7 ½
24 inches	7 ⅝
24 ½ inches	7 ⅞
25 inches	8

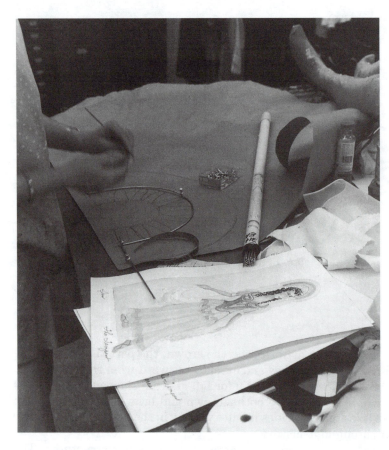

Figure 11–3 Headdress being constructed for THE TEMPEST, Krannert Center for the Performing Arts, University of Illinois

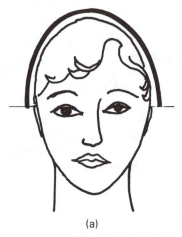

(a)

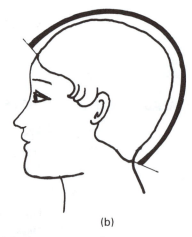

(b)

Figure 11–4 (a–b) Measuring the head for hat construction

to a hat size, you may wish to use Figure 11.2, which has the arithmetic done and rounded off to standard hat sizes.

The circumference of the head is not the only measurement needed in hat construction. The ear-to-ear measurement is used for tiaras, and a variety of headband-style headdresses. This measurement is taken from the place where eyeglasses would rest on one ear, over the top of the head to the same position on the other ear. Forehead to nape of neck is a useful measurement in the construction of snug-fitting hats and headdresses which cover the hair. This measurement is taken from the hairline at the forehead over the head to the nape of the neck.

USING OLD HATS

Old hats are useful in a number of ways. They can be used as they are, covered, painted, retrimmed, or taken apart and restructured. Basically any hat can be used, but especially useful are men's felt hats, which are easy to preserve and reshape and tricky to make, straw hats for men and women, and hats with veiling and trims, which can be revitalized. Top hats, whenever you can find them, are frequently needed as parts of a total costume. They are expensive to buy and rent, and difficult though not impossible to make. Be sure to keep these hats locked away when they are not being used, since they seem to be a popular souvenir as well as costume item.

Perking Up Old Hats

Brushing, sponging, and steaming can bring new life to crushed and dusty old hats. Steam is directed both inside and outside the hat to soften the material. The hat may then be shaped on a head block and allowed to dry.

Trimmings on old hats, such as veils, flowers, and feathers, may be freshened by steaming. A veil may be removed from the hat and carefully washed, starched, and pressed if it is not too delicate. Especially limp and dusty feathers may be carefully washed in a mild soap and water solution, then dried and fluffed with a hair dryer.

A felt hat may be reshaped by wetting and carefully and systematically pulling and stretching it over a head block or hat form.

If the hat lacks body after it has been reblocked, it may be sized with millinery sizing or clear varnish. It is essential that you use these materials carefully and in a well-ventilated area.

MAKING NEW HATS

Hatmaking is a skill that is not learned overnight. Professional milliners create miracles with buckram, wire, sizing, and trim. Theatrical costume hats may be made a bit more simply, but it is essential that the elements of fine millinery be known and applied so that the final hat enhances rather than detracts from the total costume.

Hatmaking is a skill which will improve with practice, but even beginners may achieve satisfactory results with a few lessons in the basics.

Materials Used in Hat Construction

Hat blocks.   Wooden hat blocks are used to stretch buckram, straw, and felt into different shapes. Hat blocks come in sizes and shapes that reflect the style of the hat to be stretched. Balsa wood wig blocks, which may be used to stretch the crowns of hats and to style and support wigs, are useful to have in a number of sizes. Additional shaped crown and brim blocks make hatmaking and hat restoration much easier for the milliner.

Hat stretchers.   A very useful tool for any costume shop is a hat stretcher. These stretchers enable the costumer to dampen and stretch a hat to fit an actor with a bigger head than the original hat. Electric hat stretchers work with heat in the stretching process. Hat stretching must be done slowly so as not to destroy the hat, and a hat stretcher will not be effective if the hat has an inner headsize wire.

Figure 11-5 Crown and brim block

Figure 11-6 Hat stretcher

Buckram. Buckram is a stiff, loosely woven fabric that contains a glue sizing. When exposed to steam or water, buckram becomes extremely pliable and easy to form. Buckram comes in black and white and in several weights. It is a primary support material for many structured hats, but is used in garment construction as a stiffener and in mask making.

Millinery wire. Millinery wire, a black or white fabric-covered wire available in different gauges, is used to structure the outer brims of hats. It is also used in millinery to create an inner headsize opening and to build and support hat decorations.

Wool felt. Like buckram, wool felt may be dampened and stretched into any hat form desired. 100% wool felt works best for this purpose, but felt with at least 50% wool will also work. For wool stretched hats it is necessary to stiffen the final form with millinery sizing.

Pushpins. Long, heavy pushpins are used to secure stretched buckram or felt to a head block. T-pins or thumb tacks will also work for this purpose.

Flexible foam. A number of materials may be used to pad and extend a headpiece. Flexible polyurethane foam is especially useful because of its light weight and ability to be cut and molded.

Steamer. A table steamer or hand-held steamer is useful in revitalizing old hats and stretching new ones. By directing steam inside or outside a hat, that portion of the hat will become flexible and able to be remolded.

Rubber cement. Rubber cement is used to glue fabric to buckram when needed. It is especially useful for inside curved areas of a hat.

Millinery sizing. This sizing gives body to felt hats. It may be brushed or sprayed on. Because it is toxic, it must be used in a well-ventilated area.

Trimmings. Old flowers, ribbons, veiling, and feathers may be collected to decorate new hats. Even when an old hat is worn out, the trimmings can often be saved and added to other hats.

Hand and machine sewing materials. Much millinery is performed by hand. Needles, thimbles, tapes, and threads are all used in millinery processes.

MAKING SOFT HATS

Soft hats are hats with no inner structure. They are pliable and manipulable and change shape depending on how the wearer wishes to use them. Hoods, mob caps, stocking caps, bag hats, veils and scarves, and turbans are all soft hats. Success with these hats often depends on the shape of the hat material, the way it is sewn, or the way it is wrapped. For this type of hat a paper pattern is not always useful. Sometimes a fabric pattern will work better and sometimes, as in the case of the turban, the costumer might just as well begin directly with the fabric. It is useful to understand the nature and shape of the flat pattern for these hats, however, in order to achieve a successful replica.

Hoods

The hood has been a useful, functional hat throughout the history of dress in the western world. It is used in ceremonial and symbolic dress as well as practical and everyday wear.

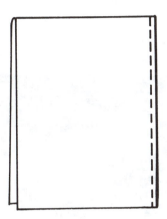 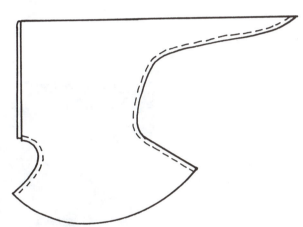

Figure 11–7 Two hoods

Initially the hood was created as a protection from the weather. The basic shape was a rectangle folded and stitched along one side.

This basic shape evolved into more complex and decorative forms. The basic premise was the same, but cutting and stitching became more complex. The hood sometimes was worn as a separate garment and sometimes was built into a cape or tunic, but the function of protection from the elements remained. When the hood was adapted for clerical and academic wear this function was lost, and these decorative hoods could only be worn as decoration down the back of a robe.

Bag Hats

Bag hats may be constructed of woven or knitted fabrics. They may even be made of leather. Bag hats, like hoods, started from a very basic flat pattern. Variation in bag hats comes from the hat material and the specific way in which it is cut, sewn, bunched, or gathered. A wide range of different hats is possible from a simple bag pattern.

Mob Cap

The mob cap is slightly more complex than the bag hat. Like other soft hats, the pattern for the mob cap is simple: in this case it's a circle. The technique

(a)   (b)

Figure 11-8 Mob cap variation

Figure 11-9 Measuring the head for a mob cap

for construction, while a bit more time consuming, is easy to understand. The point is to simply gather the edge of the circle into the appropriate headsize.

The gathering may be done with casing and cording or elastic. The line of gathering may be on the outer edge of the circle, to create a gathered bag hat, or a fixed distance within the outer perimeter, to create a cap with a ruffled brim.

The size of the initial circle, the stiffness of the fabric, and the placement of the gathering line allow the hatmaker quite a bit of flexibility within this relatively simple hat form.

Determine the size of the cap by measuring from the center of the head to the headband area, allowing as much fullness in the tape measure as you will want in the cap itself. Continue from the head out to determine the size of the brim ruffle if necessary. This measurement will be the radius of the circle for your pattern.

Cut the circle from the desired fabric and finish the outer edge with a hem or lace or other edging. Stitch a casing of bias tape at the appropriate distance in from the edge of the cap, leaving an opening for elastic. Cut the elastic to the head-around measurement and, with a large safety pin secured to the end of the elastic, thread the elastic into the casing. Fit and stitch the elastic in place.

Turban

Turbans may be made on a base, or they may be wrapped on the head each time they are worn. For security, the turban may be wrapped and tacked to a buckram frame. This will facilitate quick changes.

Fabrics used in turbans should drape and fold well, since the beauty and interest in a turban is in the folds themselves. The fabric for a turban should be cut on the bias with as much width as to allow for the number and depth of the folds desired.

A standard turban is wrapped from the center back or the center front around the head and back to the starting point. The length and width of the fabric being wrapped, as well as the tightness or looseness of the wrapping, will change the effect from one turban to the next. The ends of the fabric may be tucked under the wrapping or tucked through and left to hang decoratively at the side or back.

Veils, Scarves, Bands, and Neck Drapery

A milliner may be quite creative with scarves and veils. Like the hood, this is an ancient form of headwear. Studying the basic shape of the flat pattern for veils is important in the creation of headdresses that follow the same draping lines as those seen in historical research. Once again, early veils and scarves are based on simple geometric flat shapes: the rectangle and circle, primarily.

(a)   (b)

Figure 11-10   Headdress with circlet and veil

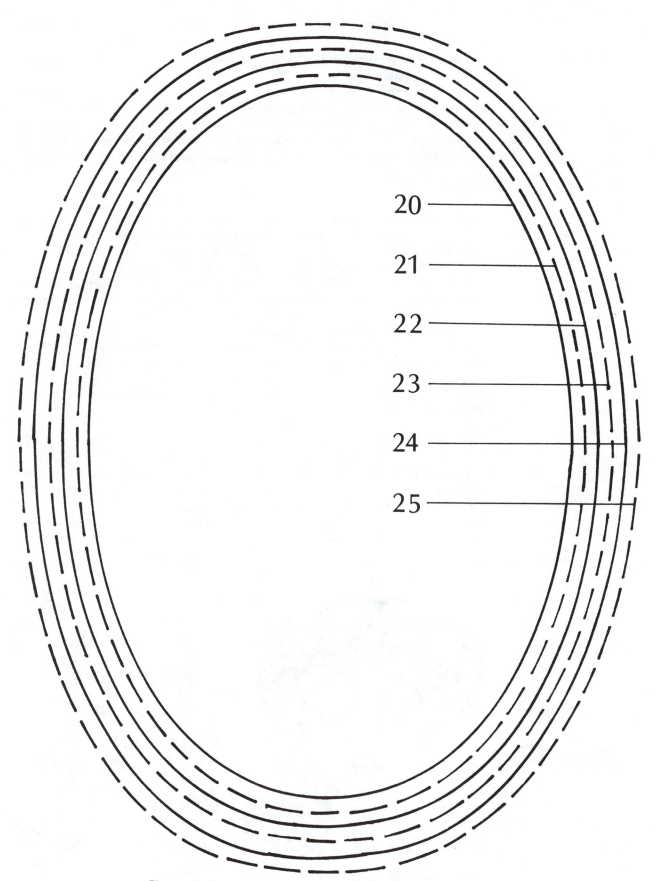

20

21

22

23

24

25

Figure 11-11 Pattern for a variety of head-size ovals in inches

Early Neck Draping. The wimple, the gorget, and the barbette were as simple in form as the veil. The secret to successful neck drapery is the bias cut, which allows the fabric to hug the neck and create beautiful folds around the face.

Circlets, bands, and padded rolls are often incorporated into headdresses to hold styles in place. These bands may be simple rectangles of fabric, braided fabric or leather, or metallic structures. Effective braiding and twisting of cords and fabrics may greatly enhance a simple headdress.

MAKING A BUCKRAM HAT WITH CROWN AND BRIM

Structured crown and brim hats are frequently created from buckram and wire and then covered in the final fabric. The crown of a structured hat may be stretched over a form or constructed with a separate sideband and tip. The following is a description of the process for making a hat with separately constructed two-piece crown and brim. This procedure may be followed regardless of the individual shapes the patterns may take.

Creating the Pattern

It is possible to find patterns for hats in books of costumes, most notably Denise Dreher's *From the Neck Up.* These patterns are good starting points for understanding the basic shapes in millinery patterning. With these patterns and your knowledge of pattern manipulation, you will have a world of possibilities open to you in the types of hats you can make for the theatre.

1. Create a pattern for the brim in heavy paper.
2. Because heads are oval (longer from front to back than from side to side), you must find a pattern to represent the head opening for the brim. Patterns which approximate the head oval sizes are included in Figure 11–11. Find the head oval that is 1/2″ larger than the head opening and transfer it to the brim.
3. Adjust the paper pattern by trying it on a headform or the actor.
4. The crown will be cut in one of three ways: tapered, flared, or straight up and down. In any case, the lower edge measurement should be the same as the oval opening.

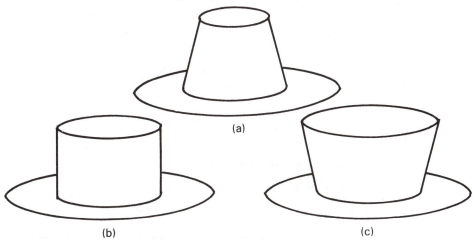

Figure 11–12 (a–c)   Tapered; straight; and flared crown styles

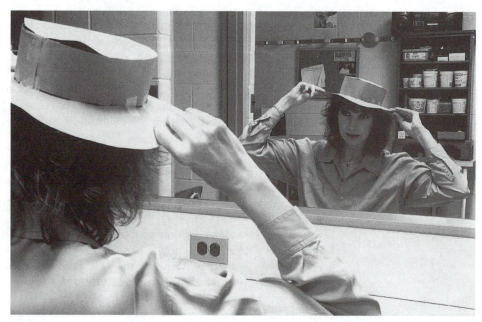

Figure 11–13 Fitting the pattern in paper

5. The tip or lid will likely be an oval or circle cut with the circumference equal to the length of the upper measurement of the sideband.

6. Tape the crown pattern together and attach it to the brim pattern to make final adjustments in fit and style.

Making the Buckram Structure

1. Place the brim and crown pattern pieces on the bias of medium or heavyweight buckram.

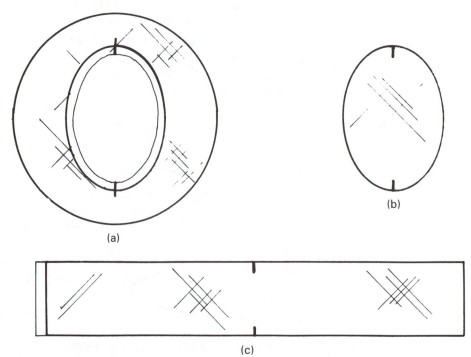

Figure 11–14 Seam allowance and marking on the buckram

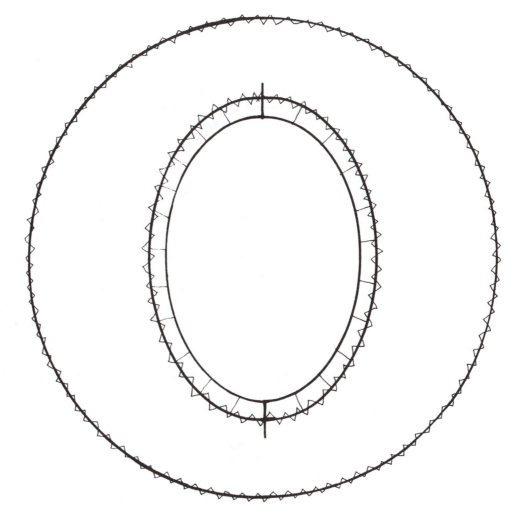

Figure 11–15   Millinery wire added to the brim

2. Mark all pieces for center front and center back. Cut the side crown piece with seam allowance in the center back, cut the tip without seam allowance, and cut the brim with seam allowance on the inner oval.

3. Hand-stitch or machine zig-zag millinery wire around the outer edge of the brim, the inner oval of the brim, and the outer edge of the tip. Clip the seam allowance in the head opening of the brim.

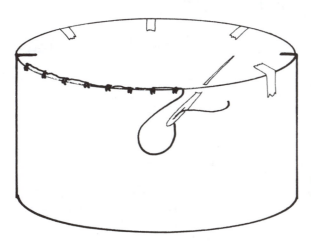

Figure 11–16   Hand-stitching the tip to the sideband

4. Hand-stitch the tip to the sideband of the hat, but do not join the sideband to the brim.

5. Try the pieces of the hat on the actor or headform at this time to get a better feeling for the final hat shape. Make final changes if necessary.

6. It is possible to paint the buckram structure with sizing at this point for greater durability. As always, make sure you use hat sizing or clear varnish in a well-ventilated room.

Covering the Buckram Structure

1. Cut all fabric on the bias. Add seam allowance to all edges of each pattern piece. You will need to cut two brim pieces for the upper and under brim. The under-brim piece should be cut without the head-size oval at this time.

2. Lining for the crown may be cut from the side and tip pattern pieces.

3. Mark center front and center back on all fabric pieces.

4. Cover the tip with hat fabric by hand-stitching close to the upper edge of the side piece. Trim away excess fabric.

5. Stitch the center back seam of the sideband fabric and slip it over the buckram frame, matching the center front and center back markings.

6. Fold the upper seam allowance in to the buckram frame and hand-stitch the fabric of the lid to the fabric of the sideband.

7. Turn the lower sideband seam allowance to encase the raw edge of the buckram and stitch it in place.

8. If the brim is to have a shape other than flat, bend the wire into position before covering it.

9. Beginning with the top of the brim, pin the fabric to the buckram form, then glue the fabric with rubber cement to the brim. Stitch around the head opening.

10. Turn outer seam allowance of the brim to encase the wired buckram edge and glue or stitch in place.

11. Clip seam allowances in the headsize oval and fold up.

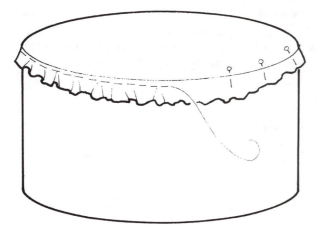

Figure 11–17 Covering the tip with fabric

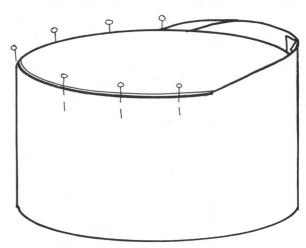

Figure 11–18 Stitching the sideband fabric to the tip

Figure 11–19   Creating a curved brim

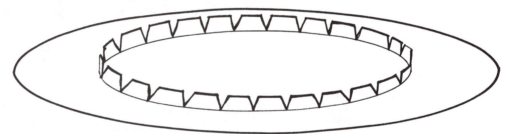

Figure 11–20   Fold up seam allowances on brim

12. Pin the under-brim fabric in place, then glue it to the brim. Fold outer edge of seam allowance under and stitch fabric of upper and under brim together. Stitch under-brim fabric to buckram around the inside of the head opening.

13. Cut the center oval from under-brim fabric and clip and fold seam allowances as with the upper-brim buckram and fabric.

14. Hand-stitch the crown and brim together after carefully lining up center front and center back markings.

15. A decorative ribbon hat band is often used to cover the hand-stitching that connects the crown to the brim.

Lining the Hat

1. Stitch the tip lining to the sideband lining and insert the lining into the crown of the hat.

2. Glue the wrong side of the tip of the lining to the wrong side of the tip of the buckram frame.

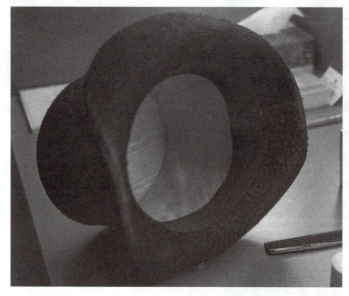

Figure 11–21 Lining and sweatband inside the hat

3. Stitch the lining to the brim seam allowance tabs.
4. Add a sweat band of leather or ribbon to finish the inside of the hat.

Finishing the Hat

1. Tack a hat band in place to decorate the hat and cover the hand-stitching attaching the crown to the brim.
2. Tack veils, ribbons, flowers, plumes, jewels, or other decorative items to the hat.
3. Stitch combs or ties in place, if necessary, to keep the hat in the proper place on the head. Or use hat pins if appropriate.

Figure 11–22 Decorative lining

STRETCHING HATS AND HEAD FORMS

Headdresses that are not strictly hats include such a variety of styles that we cannot possibly deal with them except in very general terms. Headdresses that cover the entire head might benefit from being built on a stretched buckram frame. Stretching buckram over a head block is useful for creating stretched covered hats as well as wig bases.

Procedure for Stretching a Buckram Form (Pulling a Skull)

1. Select a head block of the same size or larger than the head of the actor.
2. Cover the block with plastic wrap or aluminum foil to protect the form.
3. Cut a piece of medium-weight or heavyweight buckram large enough to cover the wig block.
4. Place the buckram in warm water for a minute until it starts to get soft. Then put it in a plastic bag for about three minutes to thoroughly soften.
5. Place the buckram on the head block so that the bias of the fabric lies front to back and side to side.
6. Pull on the bias in opposite directions to remove as many folds as possible from the buckram.
7. Hold the buckram in place by wrapping an elastic band low on the head block and pinning into it.
8. Continue to work the wrinkles out of the skull by removing individual pins and pulling the buckram beneath the elastic.
9. Allow the buckram form to dry overnight; then remove it from the form.

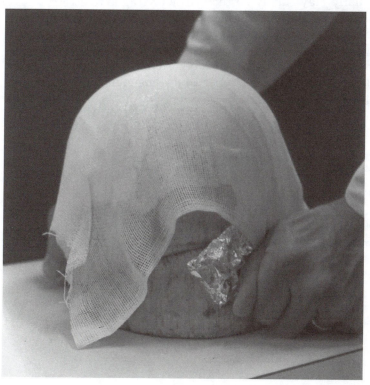

Figure 11-23 Stretching a buckram crown

10. Trim the outer edge of the skull to the desired shape with a scissors or utility knife.

11. If the form is too small for the actor, a section of the back edge may be removed, then replaced with elastic for a snug fit.

12. Finish the rough edges of the buckram with felt or bias tape. For extra strength you may add a piece of millinery wire to the outer edge.

You now have a form that can work as a frame for elaborate headdresses or wigs. This buckram skull may be built up with padding, then covered with fabric or artificial hair. If you are using the stretched skull for the crown of a hat, you may wish to stretch the dampened hat fabric over the skull before the buckram is thoroughly dry. This way the glue from the buckram will help to hold the fabric in place while they dry together.

A skull may be protected from perspiration by applying shellac to the inside.

Stretching Straw and Felt

Woven straw and wool felt may be stretched in much the same way as buckram. A major difference is that neither straw nor felt contain the glue sizing that buckram does, so when dry they usually need to have millinery sizing or clear varnish applied to strengthen and hold the shape. In addition, both straw and felt are somewhat more delicate and require a bit more care in the handling so as not to tear.

Felt and straw are sometimes stretched into crown and brim hats in one piece with an interlocking crown and brim block.

Old felt and straw hats may frequently be reblocked by dampening and restretching over forms. Again, care must be taken in handling the materials. Old straw particularly may simply be too brittle or fragile to stretch.

Other forms besides hat and wig blocks may be used for shaping hats. Flower pots, waste baskets, and vases have all been used to create hat forms. You may also build up a form to create new shapes; for example, placing a spool of thread on a wig block will result in a totally different block for stretching. This is another opportunity for a costumer to use ingenuity in the development of hat shapes.

EXERCISES

1. Refurbish an old hat by steaming, washing, pressing, stretching, or retrimming.
2. Create a stretched hat or crown with buckram, felt, or straw. Stretch a crown over a modified block.
3. Design and make a crown and brim hat.

Shoes and Footwear

12

It is sometimes difficult for a costumer to acquire the appropriate shoes and boots for a production. Occasionally they may be built from scratch, but more likely stock items or modifications of existing footwear are used. Whether the shoe is being modified from a stock item or built from the sole up, it is essential that the shoe fit well, provide support, and be comfortable for the actor. It is a good idea to complete work on the structural portion of footwear early so that the actor will have a chance to wear and get used to the shoes or boots during rehearsals.

The major difference between one shoe and another is the shape of the heel and the shape of the toe. If one could accurately reproduce a period shoe, it would probably be neither comfortable nor durable. It is important only that it look appropriate to the period or style it complements. Because you want the audience to be looking at the face of the actor and not the feet, shoe design is usually subtle, and extremes of style, even though they may be historically accurate, are usually avoided, unless of course it is the point of the costume to be ridiculous or extreme.

PARTS OF A SHOE

A shoe is made up of three basic parts: the upper, which is the leather or fabric body of the shoe; the sole, which is the section between the foot and the ground; and the heel, which elevates the back part of the shoe and the foot off the

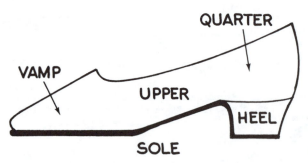

Figure 12-1 Parts of a shoe

ground. Inside the shoe itself is an insole, which finishes the interior of the shoe and protects the foot from the shoe construction, and sometimes a shank, which is a metal support between the sole and insole. The upper consists of two parts, the vamp, which covers the front of the foot, and the quarter, which covers the back.

USING EXISTING SHOES

Finding exactly the right shoe can be difficult for a couple of reasons. The typical costume shop is not equipped with materials, equipment, and knowledge for making shoes that fit properly and can provide good footing for the actor. Consequently, modern shoes are frequently adapted into adequate substitutes for those of other periods. Certain soft-soled boots, sandals, and slippers can be made by costumers from easily obtained materials, but intricately heeled, tongued, and soled shoes are often created from stock shoes, which may be resoled, reheeled, retongued, recut, repainted, or covered. Difficult shoe adaptations may sometimes be made by shoe repair shops or shoemakers. Dance shoes, including ballet, jazz, rhythm, and character shoes, can be easily adapted to a variety of situations and are especially useful, as are men's modern tie shoes, women's heels in a variety of 20th century heel and toe styles, and Chinese slippers for both men and women. Men's and women's slippers are inexpensive and may serve well alone or with modifications. Canvas tennis shoes are good bases for heelless footwear.

MATERIALS USED IN SHOE MODIFICATION AND CONSTRUCTION

Historically the uppers of shoes have been made primarily from fabric, leather, and, in this century, plastic. The soles of shoes have been made of wood, leather, cork, plastic, and rubber. It may be important to create the effect of authenticity with the shoes you are building, but sometimes it is better to imitate rather than use the authentic materials. Delicate brocade slippers, for example, might not last for the run of a show, but leather covered with brocade, or painted to look like brocade, will.

The following is a list and description of some of the materials and tools used in creating costume shoes and boots:

Leather. Large leather pieces as well as small scraps of leather and suede are useful in creating and modifying shoes. Heavy leather requires an industrial sewing machine and leather needles, but lightweight leather may be sewn on modern domestic machines and cut with regular scissors. Leather pieces may be made into extended tongues, flaps, boot tops, and spur covers to effectively change a modern pair of shoes into period footwear.

Figure 12-2 Soft leather boot

Vinyl. Vinyl, as well as a number of synthetic leather imitations, may be used as leather is used. Some vinyls look and move very much like leather. Vinyl does not breathe and may not be easily painted or dyed, however.

Decorative fabrics. Just about any fabric may be used to cover shoes. Delicate or loosely woven fabrics are likely to get scuffed or pulled apart after awhile. Upholstery fabrics have a nice weight and finish for footwear.

Glues. Shoemaker's glue, which may be found in shoe repair shops, is most useful for repairs on existing shoes. Contact cement, rubber cement, and hot-melt glue are fine for gluing fabric and trim to shoes.

Dyes and paints. Leather dye, commercial shoe coloring, and acrylic paint all work on leather and fabric. Vinyl is not as easy to color. Enamel spray paint will soften vinyl, and acrylic paints usually peel off eventually.

Leather punch. This useful tool will easily punch through shoes and leather pieces to create lacing openings or holes for easier stitching.

Wood. It is possible to create your own wooden heels to attach to existing shoes. To keep the heels from wearing down, they should be finished with rubber or leather where they touch the floor.

Trimmings. Buckles, bows, and braids are among the materials used to decorate and give a pair of shoes a distinctively accurate historical feeling.

Laces. Laces of leather and fabric in a variety of lengths, colors, and thicknesses are used to tie ancient and modern shoes and sandals.

Leather punch. For stitching into leather it is often necessary to use a needle and thimble just to pierce the material.

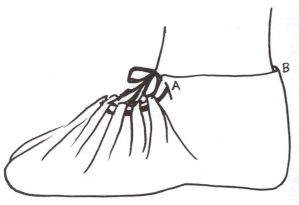

Figure 12-3 Soft-soled shoe

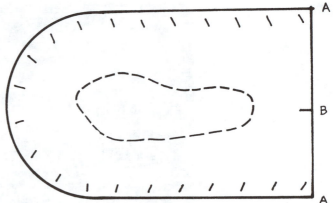

Figure 12-4 Pattern for soft-soled shoe

SOFT SHOES

Ancient footwear was often soft-soled sandals or sack-like shoes. These shoes were made from pieces of leather sewn or laced and tied together. The costumer today can certainly speed up this process and create reasonably soft-soled sandals and shoes. As with all shoes, it is important for the actor to rehearse in soft-soled shoes ahead of time. These shoes provide little support and may have a tendency to slip a bit on stage. Spraying the soles with a contact adhesive may provide a bit more traction if necessary.

SHOES WITH RIGID SOLES

Although it is possible for costume shops to create wooden, leather, rubber, plastic, or cork soles, it is often easier and more desirable to work with existing soles. These may be purchased from shoe repair shops.

Old shoes whose uppers have been hopelessly worn may be converted into useful costume shoes by attaching new uppers to them.

Although it is possible to modify or replace heels in the costume shop, it is often desirable to have a shoe repair shop do the work. Good footing is

Figure 12-5 17th century shoe created by adding a new heel, tongue, and decoration

essential for performers, and the materials and techniques possible for a shoe-maker will undoubtedly be better than those available to the average costume shop.

Sometimes, however, the specific heel or shoe treatment needed will not be available at a shoe repair shop. Fantasy shoes and 17th century high heels may not be successfully imitated by the modern heels and soles and uppers available to a standard repair shop. In these cases it is possible to create new heels out of wood to match a specific design. This procedure must be approached carefully. Breaking a heel or slipping on stage are disasters a costumer will not want to be responsible for. It is always a good idea to have a qualified shoe-maker check and attach new heels whether you make them yourself or have them made elsewhere.

BOOT TOPS AND SPATS

One of the easiest methods of creating a new effect with existing shoes is to create a boot top or a spat to cover all but the heel of the existing shoe. In this case the upper is not attached to the sole or heel except by an elastic band slipped under the instep. With this method the existing shoe is not destroyed in the process.

Procedure for Building Boot Tops

1. Select the desired boot pattern and enlarge to the appropriate size, or drape a pattern directly on the person who will be wearing the boot.

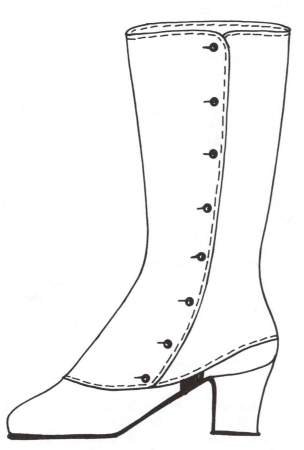

Figure 12-6 Spat

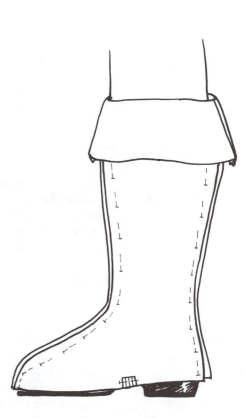

Figure 12-7 Creating a boot top

2. Cut the boot top out of a sturdy trial fabric similar in weight to the material of the final boot top.

3. Fit the boot top to the actor wearing the selected shoes. Mark the trim lines as well as where the boot will be taken in or let out.

4. Mark the position and length of the strap that will fit under the instep.

5. Fit boot tops to both legs and make sure the actor can slip in and out of them without splitting the seams. (If the final boot top is to be made out of a material that stretches, it may be fitted a bit more snugly to the leg.)

6. Cut the boot tops out of the selected fabric. If the final fabric is thin, the boot tops may be lined or boned to keep them in position on the leg.

7. Fit the final boot tops over the selected shoes and make final adjustments. Finish the edges of the boot tops and decorate according to the design.

Building Boots onto Existing Soles

1. Find a sole that imitates the sole of the boot you wish to build. For flat-soled boots old tennis shoes work well. The older the better, since the characteristic tread will be worn down and will not be a distraction to the audience should they catch a glimpse of it.

2. If you are working with a tie shoe, first trim away the tongue and eyelets with a sturdy pair of scissors or a craft knife. Slip-on shoes (slippers and loafers) may be used as is to provide more support for the upper boot.

3. Construct the upper boot according to the desired pattern. Use patterns from books or drape the desired shape on the leg and foot of the actor wearing the sole to be used.

4. After the upper boot has been sewn to size, fit it to the sole. Make adjustments in the stitching as necessary to fit the sole accurately.

5. Glue the upper to the sole and fabric of the existing shoe with hot glue or shoemaker's cement. If you are working with a shoe that has a leather sole, carefully pry the sole from the upper and tuck the fabric of the boot between the upper shoe and the sole.

PAINTING AND DYEING SHOES

Shoe dyes are available commercially in a wide variety of colors, which can be mixed for an even greater range. Leather stains may also be used to change shoe color. Flexible acrylic may also be used quite successfully to paint shoes you don't care too much about. Although the color will eventually crack or peel, the durability is really quite good. Enamel spray paint will work for emergency touch-ups on leather but tends to turn vinyl gummy. Solid colors as well as pattern and stencils may be applied to shoes to imitate different fabrics and finishes.

LEGWEAR

Leg wrappings, hose, socks, and tights have been worn for warmth and style, most likely since prehistoric times. It is sometimes difficult to tell whether the leg covering in a particular style is an extension up from footwear, an extension down from trousers, or a separate piece altogether. For the purposes of the costume designer, the legwear to be dealt with is footed legwear (hose, tights, socks, and the bands, laces, and devices used to keep those items in place).

Before the 4th century all socks and hose were made from non-knitted materials. Leather, linen, and silk were used for the construction of the leg pieces. The hose were often cut on the bias in order to better conform to the shape of the leg. Knitted legwear was not commonly worn until the late 16th century.

From illustrations of the Middle Ages we can see that leg wrapping was sometimes an intricate process. Historically leg wraps were worn over breeches, stockings, or all by themselves. Leg wraps may be made from fabric, leather, and knitted materials. Fabrics with some stretch are more likely to stay in place on stage.

A costumer's compromise for most period hose is dance tights, which are easily washed and dyed. Bias-cut cloth hose will give a more rustic appearance. Particolored hose (Figure 12–9) may be made by taking tights apart and dye-

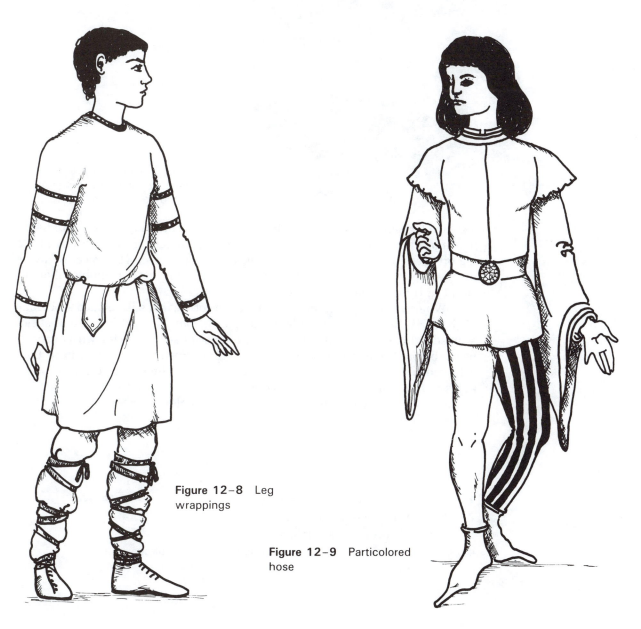

Figure 12–8 Leg wrappings

Figure 12–9 Particolored hose

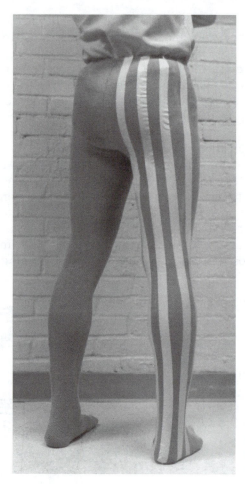

Figure 12–10 Creating striped particolored hose by masking portions of a leg with tape before painting

ing each leg separately, then restitching them. Tights may be decorated with felt-tipped markers or fabric paints. Bold striping effects are achieved by masking off areas of the tights and painting with an airbrush. It is nice to have a mannequin to use for decorating tights, though some actors will be willing to stand in tights while you paint them.

Women's tights adequately imitate the cotton and silk seamed stockings of the early 20th century. Modern panty hose may be used in place of sheer, seamed nylon stockings if a line is drawn up the back of the leg with eyebrow pencil before the panty hose are put on. Another way to create seamed hose is to fold and press stockings to find the center back line, then to carefully zigzag stitch a seam into the hose. To make sure you do not cause the hose to run it is a good idea to use a new ballpoint needle.

EXERCISES

1. Drape a boot pattern on yourself or someone else.
2. Make a boot top or a pair of spats.
3. Design and construct a soft shoe.
4. Using an old shoe as a base, design and build a pair of shoes or boots.

Masks and Armor

There is very little sewing involved in the construction of masks and armor. These important costume accessories are frequently molded rather than stitched to create form. You will note a similarity in construction materials and processes in the following discussion of these items. Once you have learned how to use a specific material, its applications will continue to become apparent to you in other areas.

MATERIALS NEEDED

Alginate. This is a cold water casting material used by dentists and theatre artists to make small area casts. The material is quick setting, very accurate, and nonreusable.

Moulage. Moulage is a reusable casting material, which is heated in a double boiler, then applied with a brush to the area to be cast. Moulage produces a very accurate cast but is somewhat trickier to use than alginate because the temperature of the material must be carefully regulated to prevent discomfort to the actor.

Plaster bandages. Plaster bandages, which are used by doctors to create leg and arm casts, are also used by costumers to create fast, easy, and effective

Figure 13–1 Donkey mask made from ethafoam rod

face casts upon which masks will be built. Alginate and moulage will produce a more detailed likeness.

Petroleum jelly. In order to release the mask from the mask form, petroleum jelly is rubbed onto the mold. It is also used to protect the actor's face while the casting material is being applied.

Plaster of Paris. Actually any type of plaster may be used to create positive face and body molds. I would not recommend it for creating casts directly on a human subject. Plaster of Paris is available at hardware and art supply stores.

Modeling clay. Nondrying modeling clay is ideal for sculpting and building up features on masks and armor before the final material is applied.

Celastic. Celastic is used for making both masks and armor. It is a woven fabric that has been impregnated with a plastic. It is softened with acetone and when dry makes a very rigid structure. It is frequently used for molded prop construction as well.

Acetone. Acetone is the solvent for softening celastic. It must be used in well-ventilated areas. Hands should be protected with rubber gloves when using acetone.

Buckram. This flexible material has its primary application in millinery. It is an excellent mask-making material as well. It produces a very lightweight and ventilated mask.

Cheesecloth. Draped cheesecloth is used with flexible white glue in mask construction. Like buckram it produces a lightweight, well-ventilated mask.

Wool felt. Felt with over 50% wool content may be used as a material for both mask and armor construction. Industrial felt is a particularly useful, heavyweight, and durable material. Wool felt may be sized with glue and set with varnish.

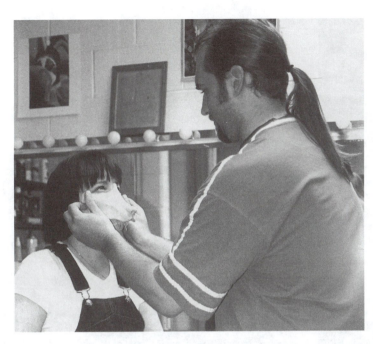

Figure 13-2 Flexible foam mask applied directly to actor's face

Plaster molds. Molds of the face and body are used to build masks and armor pieces. Wig blocks may be used for helmet molds.

Sandpaper, white glue, paint. These materials are used in the finishing stages of both armor and masks.

CREATING A PLASTER FACE MOLD

The first step in mask construction is to create a mold of the actor's face. It is possible to create a mask directly on the actor's face or on a facial mold of someone else, but the best and most comfortable masks are usually built on plaster casts of the actor's face. The following is a description of face-casting using plaster bandages. Moulage and alginate casting are described on the containers of these products.

Making a Negative Cast of the Face

1. Explain to the actor that this process is not painful, nor will it be time consuming. Assure the actor that he or she will be able to breathe at all times and that the plaster bandages can easily be removed at any time. Explain that it is essential that the actor remain still for the process if the cast is to be successful.
2. Cover the actor's clothing with a smock. Pin back the hair, then cover the entire face with a thin layer of petroleum jelly. Pay special attention to protecting facial hair. You may wish to cover eyebrows, eyelashes, moustaches, etc. with facial tissue as well as the petroleum jelly.
3. Tear plaster bandages into 4″ segments. Working with one patch at a time, dip each piece into tepid water, wring out immediately, and smooth onto the face starting at the forehead.
4. Work your way down the face, overlapping the plaster bandage patches as you go. Use the bias feature of the fabric when trying to

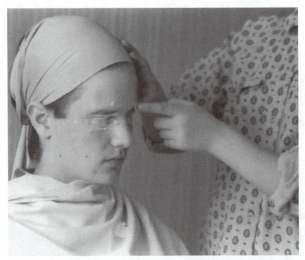

Figure 13-3 Protecting the actor's face with petroleum jelly

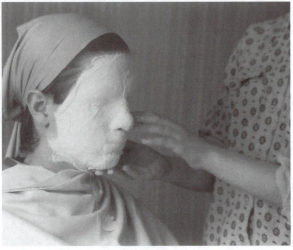

Figure 13-4 Applying plaster bandages to the face

Figure 13-5 Removing the negative cast

smooth the patch around the curved areas of the eyes, nose, and mouth. Make sure you leave the nostril openings clear for breathing.

5. Complete the first layer by going under the chin with the bandages.

6. Cover the face with a second layer of plaster bandages.

7. Wait for the plaster to set. Setting time varies with the type of bandage used; some are quick setting. The temperature of the water will affect the setting time as well. Warmer water will cause the plaster to set more quickly. Tell the actor that the plaster will begin to feel slightly warm at first, and then cool. After it cools, the actor will begin to feel the plaster pulling away from certain areas of the face. This usually happens in about five or ten minutes. When this happens, you may carefully assist in removing the mold. This is the negative mold of the face.

8. Before the plaster dries thoroughly, cover the nostril openings with a plaster patch to prevent plaster of Paris from running out these openings when the positive cast is made.

9. Set the negative cast of the face aside to thoroughly dry.

Making a Positive Cast from a Negative Cast

1. Grease the inside of the negative face cast with a light layer of petroleum jelly.
2. Mix enough plaster of Paris to fill the face mold according to package directions.
3. When the plaster begins to thicken, pour immediately into the face cast.
4. Allow the plaster to dry for several hours or overnight. Like the bandages, it will first become warm, then cool, then it will dry.
5. When the plaster is dry, carefully pop it out of the mold by lifting gently along the sides of the negative face cast.
6. This is the positive face cast. If it seems damp to the touch, you may wish to give it more time to dry before using it.

Figure 13-7   Pouring the plaster

Figure 13-6   Mixing the plaster

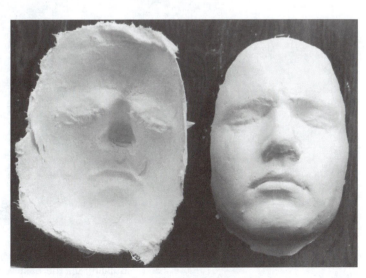

Figure 13-8   Negative and positive casts

MAKING A MASK

Both the positive and negative face casts may be used and reused in the creation of masks. Mask materials may be placed on top of the positive form or molded into the negative. In either case, the structure of the resulting face will be very much like that of the actor whose face was cast.

When you want the face to have a different structure or character, you may decide to build up the positive cast first before applying the mask material. It is still valuable to use the actor's own face cast, since you will be building away from that point.

1. Create the new facial features on the positive form with nondrying modeling clay. Leave the eye socket area free from buildup, since that is a crucial fitting point for a mask.
2. Cover the entire positive cast and clay with petroleum jelly.
3. Lay the mask material on the mold as follows:
   a. With buckram, soak the piece first in water, allow it to sit in a plastic bag for three minutes, then lay it on the form, pushing it into position.
   b. With cheesecloth, lay the fabric on the mold first, then paint it with a 50/50 solution of white glue and water. Build up several layers of the cheesecloth in this way.

Figure 13–10 Buckram mask

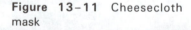

Figure 13–11 Cheesecloth mask

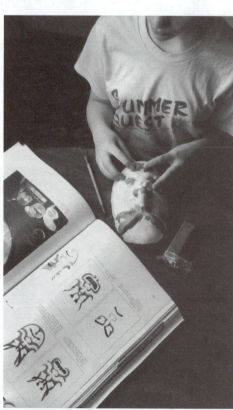

Figure 13–9 Building up the cast with clay

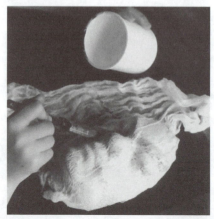

Figure 13-12   Felt mask

Figure 13-13   Dip 'n' Drape mask

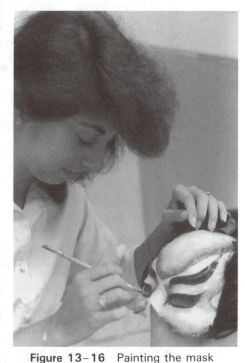

Figure 13-16   Painting the mask

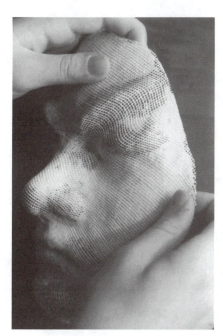

Figure 13-14   Mask removal

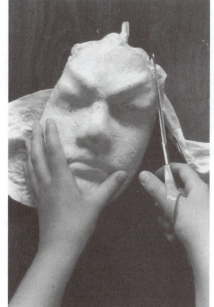

Figure 13-15   Trimming the felt mask

    c. With felt, soak the felt in glue and water, then place it on the form, and stretch and pull it into place.

    d. With "Dip 'n' Drape," tear the fabric into small sections, dip each in water until softened (from one to three minutes), then smooth the pieces onto the form, overlapping one another as you proceed.

4. Allow the mask to dry thoroughly. Then remove it and trim the edges with a utility knife or scissors.

5. Cut out eye and nostril openings if desired.

6. "Dip 'n' Drape" masks may be smoothed by rubbing flexible white glue, polymer, or varnish into the surface.

7. Paint or decorate the mask according to the design.

Figure 13–17 Final mask (Dick Schwarze)

The material used in each mask will produce a different quality mask in each case. The "Dip 'n' Drape" mask is the most delicate. Cheesecloth and buckram both produce a very light, porous, and heavily textured mask. Buckram is a bit more durable than cheesecloth, though more detail may be achieved with the finer cheesecloth. Felt will produce a smooth, rather heavy mask. Pick the material which will enhance the specific design and accommodate the necessary wear and tear.

ARMOR

Armor may be classified as hard or soft. Imitating hard or rigid armor for the stage involves processes similar to those used in mask making. Soft armor includes leather and chain mail protection. These are created without molds.

Finding Armor Molds

Armor molds are not as accessible as face molds. Although armor may be built directly on a body or on molds made from body casting, often the style of the armor dictates a distortion from normal body shape. This distortion or decora-

Figure 13-18 Armor molds

tion may be built onto a body cast the way facial features may be built onto a face cast with modeling clay.

Old armor pieces may be used as armor molds themselves. As long as they are rigid and protected, many sets of armor may be created from a single mold.

Vacuform armor is a lightweight plastic substitute for more rigid armor. It may be created in your shop if you have a large vacuform machine. Otherwise it may be purchased in a wide range of styles. Vacuform armor is very lightweight and not very protective. Vacuform armor will not make a good mold for celastic, since the solvent for the celastic will deteriorate the vacuform plastic. It is an acceptable mold for sized felt armor, however.

Armor molds may be made of cast or sculpted plaster or wood. They should be quite strong for celastic armor to resist the stretching of the fabric on top of them.

Creating Celastic Armor

Celastic dissolves in acetone and consequently must be used in a well-ventilated area with hands protected by rubber gloves. The process used in creating celastic armor is much like that described in creating masks with "Dip 'n' Drape" or felt. The major difference is that you use acetone rather than water or a glue-and-water solution as a solvent.

Once the celastic is dry, trim the edges with a utility knife. To create the impression of a polished metal surface you may sand the rough surface, then rub flexible white glue or gloss polymer medium into the surface. Paint the armor with enamel spray paint. A dusting of a dark paint in the crevices of the armor will enhance the shape and structure of the armor design. A metal color aimed at the prominent areas of the armor will create a very realistic metal look to the final armor.

Add grommets or leather straps for fastenings. Pad the inside of the armor with felt, foam, or leather as needed for comfort.

Figure 13–19 Metallic armor

Other Materials Used in Creating Hard or Rigid Armor

As mentioned above, vacuform armor will produce a very detailed and light-weight armor. Fiberglass also may be used to mold armor, but it is usually created from a negative cast rather than a positive cast. Like celastic, fiberglass must be used in well-ventilated areas with hands protected. Sized industrial felt may be used for armor in much the same way as celastic is used. The final piece may be finished with varnish to seal it before paint is added.

Soft Armor

Leather armor was worn in ancient Greece and Rome. These pieces were made of overlapping strips and pieces of leather. Armor like this may be easily reproduced by stitching, gluing, and lacing actual leather pieces together. Leather substitutes may include various suede and vinyl fabrics and sized and painted felt.

Chain mail was created from interlocking rings of metal. It would be quite tedious to reproduce this type of armor in this way. The most common method of creating theatre chain mail armor is to knit or crochet the chain mail from heavy gray or metallic yarn with very large needles. This is quite time consuming, though proficient needle artists seem willing to turn these suits out in their spare time. Loosely woven or heavily textured cloth may also be dyed or painted to represent chain mail from a distance.

EXERCISES

1. Make a cast of someone's face.
2. Design and build a mask using one of the materials described in this chapter.
3. Create a piece of leather, felt, or celastic armor.

Jewelry

14

Jewelry is probably the oldest decorative art form. It is an important element of a costume for its symbolic value and its beauty. It is created to be seen against the body or clothing and to become a focal point for the eye.

Theatre jewelry must have the essence of real jewelry in beauty and detail but must also be effective at a distance.

The category of jewelry embraces a range of accoutrements including crowns, tiaras, headbands, wreaths, hair fastenings, veil holdings, jeweled badges on hats, spectacles, eye patches, earrings, necklaces, armbands, bracelets, cuff links, rings, brooches, tie pins, medals, and ankle bracelets.

Sources of jewelry styles are costume books and museums that display actual jewelry. Sculpture where jewelry is incorporated, paintings, textiles, and architectural detail may provide inspiration for shape and structure of jewelry.

There are several things to consider before selecting or creating a piece of jewelry for a production. One must remember that jewelry is worn against the body or a piece of clothing. Any jewelry must enhance and complement the color and pattern of the fabric of a costume, the hairstyle, or the cut of a neckline. Because of the reflective nature of metal and gems, jewelry may be a distracting element on stage. Whether the item will be attached to a garment, used in a quick change, or worn by more than one person help determine how durable the piece must be and what type of fastener, if any, will be used.

Theatre jewelry has been made from inexpensive materials that look like costly gems and metals at a distance. Cardboard, wire, glass, glue, and paint are easily transformed into effective jewelry pieces.

Other materials that can be incorporated into theatre jewelry are hardware, old jewelry, fabric braids, cords and tapes, chain, cardboard, beads, leather, felt, and buttons. Jewelry clasps, rings, backings, and mountings are useful. They may be purchased from craft shops or removed and reused from old jewelry pieces.

Frequently real jewelry is too small or delicate to use on stage. Valuable jewelry certainly ought not to be used because it is simply too easy to break or lose.

MATERIALS NEEDED

Complete equipment for jewelry making involves a variety of hand tools and materials. Much may be done, however, with just a few basic materials.

Pliers. It is useful to have at least two pairs of pliers. If you can locate round-nose jewelry pliers, these are particularly useful for shaping wire. Otherwise needle-nosed pliers will do.

Wire cutters. You must have wire cutters to cut millinery wire and jewelry wire. If you use piano wire in jewelry construction, the wire cutters must be quite strong.

Utility knife. A utility knife, X-acto knife, or surgical knife is useful for cutting cardboard, wood, and plastic into exact forms.

Scissors. Small, sharp scissors are used for cutting paper and trim for jewelry.

Rhinestone setter. Although this is not a necessity, it is a useful tool for creating jeweled or studded collars, cuffs, belts, and accessories. Rhinestones may be set by hand, but a rhinestone setter saves time.

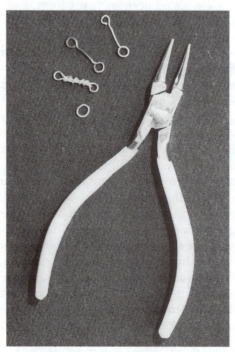

Figure 14-1 Jewelry pliers

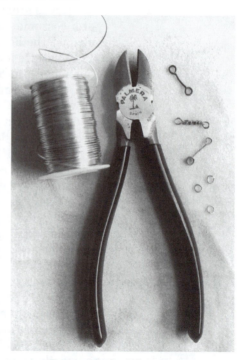

Figure 14-2 Wire cutters

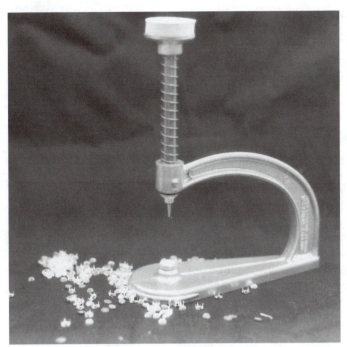

Figure 14-3 Rhinestone seller

Figure 14-4 Useful broken costume jewelry pieces

Ruler. A metal ruler with a cork back to hold it away from the surface being measured and marked is most useful.

Compass, protractor, set square. Various drafting tools are used to develop curved and geometric patterns for jewelry pieces.

Clamps, clothespins. Clamps and clothespins are used to hold jewelry pieces in place while they dry. Rubber bands can also be used for this purpose.

Paint brushes. Brushes in a range of sizes are useful for applying glue, paint, and bronzing powders. Inexpensive brushes may be used to brush away sandings from delicate pieces that are being worked on.

Sandpaper, steel wool, files. Sandpaper, steel wool, and files are used to refine and polish jewelry pieces.

Applicator sticks and tongue depressors. These sticks are used for stirring, applying glue, and as a material from which jewelry pieces may be made.

Wire. Millinery wire, piano wire, and jewelry wire are used for structural reasons as well as for linking jewelry pieces together.

Metal foil. Thin sheets of copper, bronze, and aluminum foil may be used to make tubular beads and to be worked into metallic pieces themselves.

Old costume jewelry. Old jewelry may be taken apart and used in other pieces. Fasteners, medallions, and chains may all be incorporated into new forms.

Glues. Flexible white glue, hot-melt glue, contact cement, shoemaker's cement, and airplane glue are all useful to the jewelry maker.

Trimmings. Small pieces of braid, ribbon, lace, and other decorative trims may serve as foundation, edging, and focal points in constructed jewelry.

CREATING JEWELRY PATTERNS

Patterns for large pieces of jewelry such as jeweled collars, tiaras, and girdles are best shaped first through draping. Shape and scale may be most accurately determined in this way. By using a dressmaker form or a head block, the appropriate size and shape may be adjusted in paper or muslin until correct. It is also a good idea to mock up smaller items such as brooches, medallions, and necklaces and pin them to a fitting form that has been dressed in the appropriate costume to study the scale and shape of the item in relationship to elements of the costume, such as the neckline or collar. Naturally, one may not always have the luxury of time to wait until the costume is complete before beginning the jewelry. But it is important to consider scale very carefully in jewelry. These items must be large enough to be seen from the audience without seeming unwieldy, garish, or comic (unless, of course, the intent is to be unwieldy, garish, or comic).

Once the shape is determined, it is always a good idea to place the pattern piece on the actor who will be wearing it. Scale and shape for such pieces may need to be adjusted if the actor is much larger or smaller than the fitting form or head block.

Figure 14–5 Draping jeweled collar pattern on fitting form

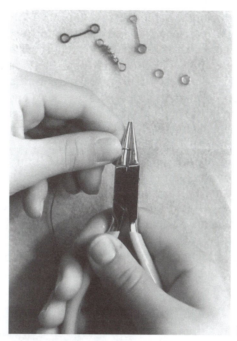

Figure 14-6 Creating wire loops

JEWELRY MAKING TECHNIQUES

Working With Wire

Wire is used to connect jewelry pieces and to hold beads. It may be used as stems for flowers and leaves. Piano wire may be used to shape very structural units such as collars and headdresses. Beading wire is used to hold small pieces together. Millinery wire, which is heavier than beading wire but not as rigid as piano wire, may be used to create smaller wired structures. Millinery wire is covered with black or white thread. The white wire may be dyed if the wire is not to be covered.

Creating Loops.   Jump rings may be made with either beading wire or snare wire, which is available in hardware stores.

1. Using round-nose pliers, grasp the end of the wire.
2. Wrap the wire around the one of the plier grips with your thumb to form a loop.
3. Remove the loop from the pliers; then clip the end where the wires come together.

Making Gems

Artificial gems may be purchased from specialty stores but are rather expensive. It is possible to recreate convincing gems and cabochons (polished stones) in a number of ways, using inexpensive processes.

One of the easiest ways of producing a polished stone is to drip blobs of white glue or hot glue onto foil. When the blobs are dried they will be ready to accept paint. Glass paint will color the transparent white glue without affecting the clarity and reflective quality. Depending on the original color of the hot-glue sticks, the resulting "stones" may be painted with acrylic paint, glass paint, or enamel to resemble a variety of opaque or translucent gems.

Pearls may be made in similar fashion with blobs of hot-melt glue painted with pearlized nail polish or acrylic paint. Baroque pearls may be fashioned over wooden beads with hot-melt glue and pearlized nail polish.

Commercial gems and pearls and those found in costume jewelry may be too brilliant for the particular need in your production. Dulling sprays will reduce reflection on gems, and pearls may be dyed in commercial household dyes to kill some of the typical whiteness of the artificial pearl. Black netting placed over gems will effectively reduce the brilliance of gems used on the stage without destroying their effect.

Sequins and plastic markers may reflect light and color for an inexpensive solution to overall gem application that will not be studied at close range.

Polymer resins may be used as well. Dyes may be added to the liquid form. In this way an entire tray of gems may be made at once. After the polymer has set, it may be cut with a knife or sawed into individual shapes. Facets may be added by sanding. If you pour the polymer resin into a tray lined with crinkled aluminum foil, the resulting gem will be more reflective when finished. Specific shapes may be created by pouring the resins directly into rubber molds.

Figure 14-7 Black netting over gem to reduce brilliance

Figure 14-8 Sequins, bingo markers, and furniture hardware

Figure 14-9 Polymer resin used to create gems

Creating Metal Jewelry and Medallions

Metal medallions may be found or created in a number of ways. Old jewelry is certainly a source for medallions. In addition, furniture hardware and lamp parts may often be used as metal parts of jewelry and medallions.

One method for creating repeated metal parts for large neck pieces and belts is to pour white glue into molds that have been greased with petroleum jelly, then dusted with bronzing powder. When the glue dries it may be popped out of the mold and the excess powder brushed away. Candy molds work particularly well for this purpose since they are flexible and come in shapes which are like period medallion and jewelry forms.

Hot-melt glue may also be used in molds to create repeated forms for jewelry. Plastic molds will melt with the heat of the hot glue, but metal hardware and furniture parts will accept the hot glue without damage. When the glue is dry in a few minutes, the piece may be peeled off, painted, and trimmed as desired. Hot-melt glue medallions are much faster to create because of the drying time involved. The piece resulting from this process will be flexible and lightweight.

Figure 14-10   Candy molds

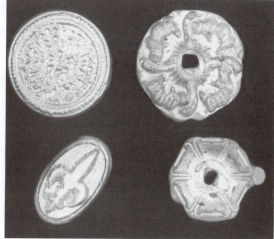

Figure 14-11   White glue and hot glue molded medallions

Figure 14–12 Painted lace medallion

Figure 14–13 Hot glue on fabric medallion

Lace fabric and trim may also be used to create metal jewelry backings and medallions. Dip the trimmed lace piece into a 50/50 solution of flexible white glue and water, then leave it on a piece of plastic wrap or aluminum foil to dry. The stiffened piece of lace will now accept enamel spray paint. When painted the lace produces a good imitation of filigree, and if glued to a solid metal covered surface it will look like hammered or molded metal.

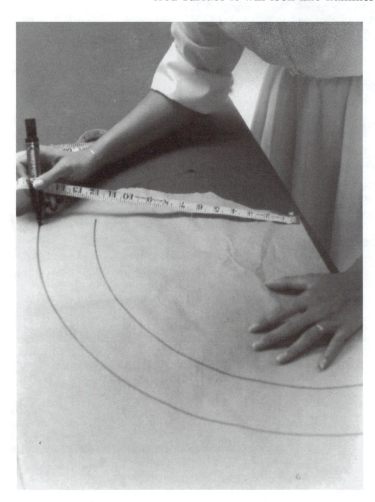

Figure 14–14 Creating the proper flare for a crown

CROWNS

If crowns are to be used in a production, they are likely to be a significant symbol. Like hats, which draw attention to the actor's head, crowns by their symbolic nature and their typically reflective substance will be items an audience will focus on. Care must be taken, therefore, in the creation of a pattern and the execution of the crown.

If the production is trying to realistically recreate a certain era and requires a specific historical crown, as in the Shakespearean historical plays, it is useful to find pictures of that particular crown and develop your pattern from the pictures. The same principles of flat pattern and draping that apply to garments and hats apply to crowns, in spite of the fact that the material you will be dealing with is more rigid.

Developing a Crown Pattern

1. Establish the proper flare for the crown. As mentioned in the discussion of crowns for hats, the flare of the crown will depend on the curve of the flat pattern.
2. Fit the crown flare pattern to the actor's head. Check the fit around the head and the flare. Make adjustments in the flare by darting or slashing the pattern at regular intervals, then taping it back together until the desired angle is achieved.
3. Even up the pattern. Cut the top of the pattern into the desired shape. Folding the pattern into quarters or sixths will help you evenly space the decorative treatment of the edge.

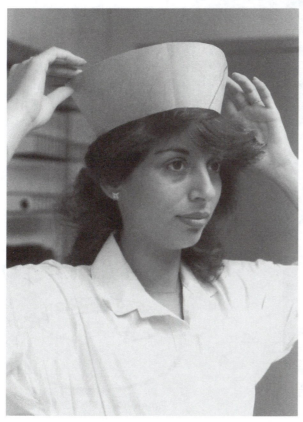

Figure 14-15 Trying on the crown

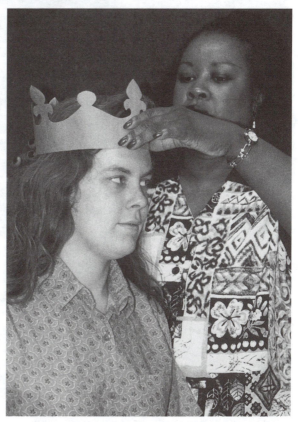

Figure 14-16 Checking the final pattern

Making a Celastic Crown

1. Cut the pattern from heavy celastic, leaving seam allowance only on the back edge.

2. Find a plastic bucket, or create a cardboard structure that represents the same flare as the crown. This will hold the structure of the crown in place while it dries.

3. Protect the bucket or cardboard form with aluminum foil. Establish a horizontal line on the bucket to match the circumference of the crown. This line should be parallel to the top and bottom of the bucket in order to establish proper alignment of the crown. Place the celastic crown in acetone, then wrap it around the bucket so that the bottom edge of the crown lines up with the line on the bucket. Overlap the back edge and work the celastic smoothly together.

4. When the crown is dry, slip it off the form and trim or sand the edges. Sand the outer surface of the celastic to give it a smooth finish.

5. You may decorate the crown in any number of ways. If you want the crown to appear to be made of worked or molded metal, you may add braid or cording around the edges. Cording may be used to create mountings for gems as well. Pieces of trim or lace may be glued onto the crown for texture and interest.

Figure 14-18 Place celastic on bucket

Figure 14-17 Fitting crown pattern to a bucket

Figure 14-19 Cording on edge of crown

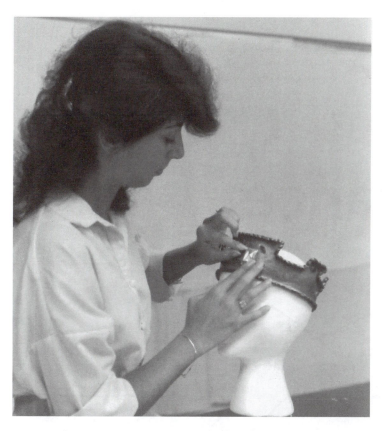

Figure 14-20 Adding gems to celastic crown

6. When you have completed the metal portion of the crown, paint it with a thick white-glue-and-water solution and let it dry.

7. Paint the crown with enamel spray paint. First direct black spray to the underside of the crown to create shadows. Then select a metal color and direct the spray from the top side of the crown to create highlights.

8. Add gems, fabric, or whatever else is necessary to complete the design of the crown.

These instructions apply to felt and buckram crowns as well. The materials and solvents are different, but the procedure is basically the same. With felt you may paint the glue sizing on after the felt is on the form. With buckram it is not necessary to soak the buckram in water before placing it on the form. Spraying it with water after it is on the form, then placing the entire form under plastic for a few minutes before allowing it to dry will work. For small crowns you may not even have to wet the buckram at all; the head opening should be wired, however. The texture of buckram and felt will differ from that of the finished celastic crown. Celastic seems to imitate polished metal most successfully.

EXERCISES

1. Practice making wire loops in a variety of sizes.
2. Make a pearl with hot glue. Make a gem using hot glue or white glue.
3. Create a medallion from lace. Create a medallion from a mold.
4. Design a crown, create the pattern, and construct it from celastic or buckram.

Appendix: Costume Maintenance

Many costume shops are the recipients of authentic historical garments. Though these frequently are too small and fragile to be useful as theatrical costumes, they are valuable in the understanding of historical pattern and construction methods. It is a task, then, to preserve these garments as well as the stock costumes that may be used again and again for the theatre.

TEXTILE DETERIORATION

Because natural fibers are dead products of plants or animals, they begin to decay from the moment they are picked or cut. Processing, spinning, weaving, bleaching, and dyeing all continue to destroy the natural fibers. Man-made fibers, most of which come from mineral products, are far less destructible. Deterioration of natural-fiber fabrics may be slowed, but not stopped. Light, dust, dirt, dampness, dryness, and insects all accelerate the process. Once made into a garment, the fabric is further weakened by perspiration and cleaning processes. The best place to store historical costumes is in a dark, protected storage area controlled for heat and dampness.

STORING HISTORICAL GARMENTS

Old costumes should not be handled any more than is necessary. They should be viewed by laying them on a flat table, or carefully supported when held.

Beaded dresses of the 1930s are particularly vulnerable to handling, since the weight of the beads is often too heavy for the delicate fabric on which they were sewn.

It is usually a better idea to store historical costumes flat and in drawers or boxes. Folding weakens the fibers, so, if possible, these garments should be placed in areas large enough to accommodate the entire length of the garment. Whenever folds are necessary, it is a good idea to pad the folds with tissue paper. It is best to line boxes or drawers with acid-free tissue paper or unbleached muslin to further protect delicate garments.

Hanging garments has advantages and disadvantages over flat storage. Costumes that are strong and not too heavy may be hung. Hanging eliminates the problem of fold strain, but adds strain at the point of support (shoulder or waist). Hanging cupboards should be protected from dust, and garments should be hung on padded hangers.

Some garments may be rolled in tissue around cardboard tubes. This is a good system for non-structured items such as shawls and pieces of lace.

Dry-cleaner bags may be used to cover items being stored. It is best not to seal the bags completely, but to allow some air flow to the fabric. This will discourage the growth of mold and mildew, but the bags will protect against most insects, dirt, and dust.

CLEANING

Most modern garments as well as fabrics purchased in a store indicate the method of cleaning. Hand-wash or machine-wash, water temperature, dry-cleaning, and dryer requirements are carefully listed to minimize confusion. The optimal cleaning process for historical garments is much more difficult to assess. Many white cottons and linens may be hand-washed. Colored fabrics are risky because the colorfastness of their dyes is uncertain.

Hand-washing historical garments is best done in a flat tray in order to allow the item to lie as flat as possible during the process. Water should be lukewarm, and a very mild detergent should be used. The garment to be washed should be placed in a net bag and then lowered into the water. The garment should not be rubbed or squeezed; instead, it can be pressed gently to release the dirt. A sponge can be used in this process so that the hands never actually touch the wet fabric.

Rinse the garment with lukewarm water until the soapy solution disappears and the rinse water is clear. It is wise to do the final rinse in distilled water in order to eliminate the danger of impurities left in the garment which will shorten the life of the fabric.

Roll or blot the garment with a towel and lay it flat, away from artificial heat or sunlight, to dry.

Old costumes should never be bleached to remove difficult stains, since the damage done in this process is likely to be worse than the stains themselves.

Pressing should be avoided or, if necessary, done with care, a muslin press cloth, and a low-temperature iron.

Dry-cleaning is a much harsher process than washing. Wool items usually dry-clean well, as does silk. Indicating the age and delicate nature of the piece to the dry-cleaning establishment may reduce the possibility of damage, or they may simply refuse to clean the items you are worried about. Delicate garments may be encased in loosely woven bags before cleaning to protect the fabric from abrasion caused by the agitation of the dry-cleaning machine.

Boning should be removed, if possible, before a garment is washed or cleaned.

MAINTENANCE OF COSTUMES DURING A PRODUCTION

Costumers have very little control over what a director may ask an actor to do in your beautiful costume. Crawling, climbing, and even "rending" the costume may be required for the dramatic action of the play. It is best not to be too attached to the costumes you create. Long trains will invariably become filthy and perhaps torn on stage. An actor has much to contend with during a performance, including the effective and natural wearing of his or her costume. It should, after all, look like something he or she chose to wear for one reason or another. Some actors seem to have an instinct and instant adaptability to a period costume. However, there are others who, in spite of careful guidance and direction by costume designers and costume crews, seem unable to manage the kind of care due that carefully constructed costume. Although it is not unreasonable to expect perfect attention to costume, it is sometimes unrealistic. For those who do not and cannot learn, we have sewing machines for mending and patching, washing machines, dry cleaners, and spot removers for eliminating dirt, and attendants to maintain the costumes during the run of a production. Because most audiences view costumes from a distance, many repairs and spots that would not be acceptable for street wear will not be visible in costumes.

In the case of long-running plays it is often necessary to replace total costumes from time to time because of undue wear and tear. Many items, such as tights and shirts, may be laundered after each performance or two to remove makeup and make the actors more comfortable.

Because of budgets or fabric modification treatments of costumes, it is often unrealistic to expect costumes to be cleaned during a short run. It is therefore a good idea to stress to the actors the importance of cleanliness for their own sake as well as for the comfort of everyone else.

A running costume crew is basically responsible for the maintenance of the costumes from dress rehearsal through the strike of the production. Laundering, pressing, dry-cleaning (if necessary), repairs, and checking all costumes in and out all are responsibilities of this important crew. In addition, assisting actors into difficult costumes and accessories (corsets, wigs, etc.) and helping with fast changes also are assumed by the costume running crew.

CLEANING MODERN COSTUMES

Costumes created from modern fabrics are not as delicate as historical garments, but they should be maintained and cleaned if they are to be used again. The same elements that destroy the fibers of historical costumes are at work on modern ones.

All costumes should be cleaned before they are returned to storage. If the garment may be machine-washed, this should be done immediately after use. Other costumes may be sent to the dry-cleaner, but it is important to inform the cleaner of any special techniques that were used in modifying the fabric for the costume. Hot glue, for example, does not dry-clean well, but it may be machine-washed on a cool temperature. Acrylic paints and textile paints if properly set will withstand both dry-cleaning and washing. Enamel spray paint usually disappears in the dry-cleaning process. To some extent you are taking a risk in any cleaning process whenever you attempt to clean a costume, especially one that has been complexly altered. The alternative is to air and store a costume without cleaning. It is up to you to make the decision as to whether more damage may be done in the cleaning process or by the dirt and perspiration left in it. You may wish to test-clean samples of the fabrics before making your final decision.

COSTUME STORAGE

Although it would be better for all natural-fiber fabrics to be stored as carefully as I have described the storage of historical garments, this amount of care is very impractical with theatre costumes. Certain elements of care can be observed, however, to prolong the life of the costume collection. Storage in a dark room with a controlled temperature and humidity is important. Padded hangers for heavy garments are a good idea. Naturally, all garments will last longer if they are neither handled nor worn, but in the case of theatre costumes this would defeat the purpose of their existence.

Many costumes may be altered and reused many times if they are carefully treated between performances.

Bibliography

ARMSTRONG, HELEN JOSEPH. PATTERNMAKING. New York: Harper & Row, 1987.

ARNOLD, JANET. PATTERNS OF FASHION (three volumes). London: Wace and Co., 1964–1985.

_____. A HANDBOOK OF COSTUME. New York: S. G. Phillips, 1974.

BOUCHER, FRANCOIS, 20,000 YEARS OF FASHION. New York: Harry N. Abrams, 1968.

BRADFIELD, NANCY. COSTUME IN DETAIL. Boston: Plays, Inc., 1968.

BRUHN, WOLFGANG AND MAX TILKE. A PICTORIAL HISTORY OF COSTUME. New York: Hastings House, 1955.

BUCKNELL, PETER A. AND MARGARET HAMILTON HILL. THE EVOLUTION OF FASHION. London: Batsford, 1967.

CHRISTIE, ARCHIBALD H. PATTERN DESIGN. Mineola, New York: Dover, 1969.

COLTON, VIRGINIA, ed. COMPLETE GUIDE TO SEWING. Pleasantville, N.Y.: The Reader's Digest, 1976.

COULDRIDGE, ALAN. THE HAT BOOK. Englewood Cliffs, N.J.: Prentice Hall, 1980.

COVEY, LIZ AND ROSEMARY INGHAM. THE COSTUMER'S HANDBOOK. Englewood Cliffs, N.J.: Prentice Hall, 1980.

_____. THE COSTUME DESIGNER'S HANDBOOK. Englewood Cliffs, N.J.: Prentice Hall, 1983.

DAVENPORT, MILLIA. THE BOOK OF COSTUME. New York: Crown, 1948.

DAVIS, MARIAN L. VISUAL DESIGN IN DRESS. Englewood Cliffs, N.J.: Prentice Hall, 1980.

DRYDEN, DEBORAH M. FABRIC PAINTING AND DYEING FOR THE THEATRE. New York: Drama Book Specialists, 1981.

DREHER, DENISE. FROM THE NECK UP. Minneapolis: Madhatter Press, 1981.

EDSON, DORIS WITH LUCY BARTON. PERIOD PATTERNS. Boston: Walter H. Baker, 1942.

EMERY, JOY SPANABEL. STAGE COSTUME TECHNIQUES. Englewood Cliffs, N.J.: Prentice Hall, 1981.

EWING, ELIZABETH. DRESS AND UNDRESS: A HISTORY OF WOMEN'S UNDERWEAR. New York: Drama Book Specialists, 1978.

FERNALD, MARY AND EILEEN SHENTON. COSTUME DESIGN AND MAKING, 2d ed. New York: Theatre Arts Books, 1967.

FINCH, KAREN AND GRETA PUTNAM. CARING FOR TEXTILES. New York: Watson-Guptil, 1977.

GOSTELOW, MARY. THE COMPLETE INTERNATIONAL BOOK OF EMBROIDERY. New York: Simon & Schuster, 1977.

GRIESBACH, C. B. HISTORIC ORNAMENT: A PICTORIAL ARCHIVE. New York: Dover, 1975.

HANSEN, HENNY HARALD. COSTUMES AND STYLES. New York: Dutton, 1956.

HILL, MARGOT HAMILTON AND PETER BUCKNELL. THE EVOLUTION OF FASHION. New York: Drama Book Specialists, 1967.

JACKSON, SHEILA. COSTUMES FOR THE STAGE. New York: Dutton, 1978.

KOHLER, CARL. A HISTORY OF COSTUME. Mineola, New York: Dover, reprint 1964; orig. 1928.

LAVER, JAMES. A CONCISE HISTORY OF COSTUME AND FASHION. New York: Scribner's, 1969.

MOTLEY. DESIGNING AND MAKING STAGE COSTUMES. New York: Watson-Guptil, 1974.

NORRIS, HERBERT. COSTUME AND FASHION, Vols. I–III,VI (vol. VI with Oswald Curtis). London: J. M. Dent, 1924–1933.

PAYNE, BLANCHE. HISTORY OF COSTUME. New York: Harper & Row Pub., 1965.

PICKEN, MARY BROOKS. THE FASHION DICTIONARY. New York: Funk & Wagnalls, 1973.

PRISK, BERNEICE. STAGE COSTUME HANDBOOK. New York: Harper & Row, 1966.

RUSSELL, DOUGLAS. STAGE COSTUME DESIGN. Englewood Cliffs, N.J.: Prentice Hall, 1973.

SHAW, WILLIAM HARLAN. BASIC PATTERN DRAFTING FOR THE THEATRICAL COSTUME DESIGNER. New York: Drama Book Specialists, 1974.

TARRANT, NAOMI. COLLECTING COSTUMES: THE CARE AND DISPLAY OF CLOTHES AND ACCESSORIES. London: Allen & Unwin, 1983.

TILKE, MAX. COSTUME PATTERNS AND DESIGNS. New York: Hastings House, 1974.

TOMPKINS, JULIA. MORE STAGE COSTUMES AND HOW TO MAKE THEM. Bath, England: Pitman Press, 1975.

TOZER, JANE AND SARAH LEVITT. FABRIC OF SOCIETY. New York: Laura Ashley, Ltd., 1983.

WAUGH, NORAH. CORSETS AND CRINOLINES. New York: Theatre Arts Books, 1954.

_____. THE CUT OF MEN'S CLOTHES. London: Faber and Faber, 1964.

_____. THE CUT OF WOMEN'S CLOTHES. London: Faber and Faber, 1968.

WHIFE, A.A. A FIRST COURSE IN GENTLEMEN'S GARMENT CUTTING. London: Tailor and Cutter, Ltd., 1960.

WILCOX, R. TURNER. THE DICTIONARY OF COSTUME. New York: Scribner's, 1969.

_____. THE MODE IN COSTUME. New York: Scribner's, 1948.

WILSON, EUNICE. A HISTORY OF SHOE FASHION. New York: Theatre Arts Books, 1974.

YARWOOD, DOREEN. THE ENCYCLOPEDIA OF WORLD COSTUME. New York: Scribner's, 1978.

Index

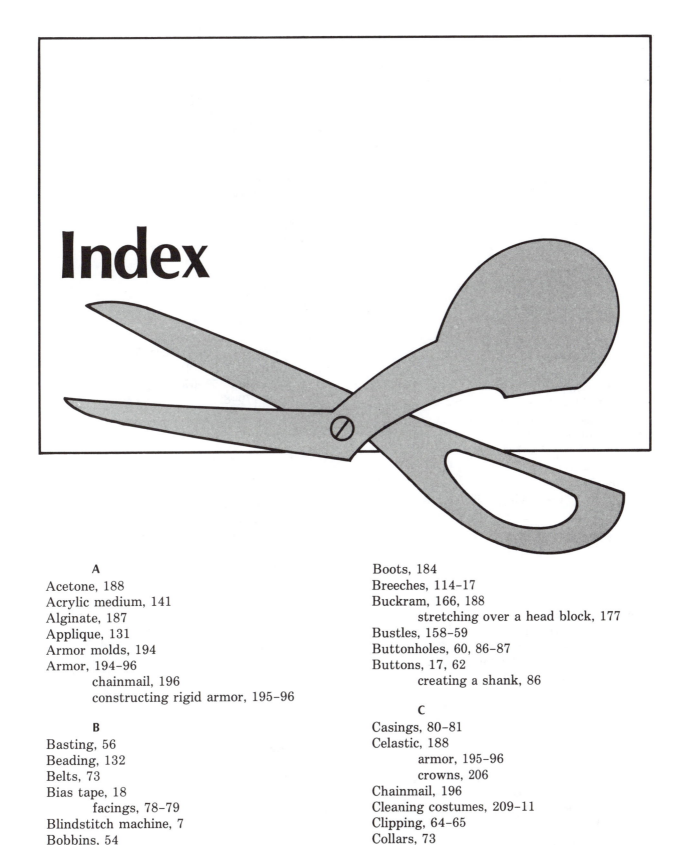